The New Nature Writing

Environmental Cultures Series

Series Editors:

Greg Garrard, *University of British Columbia, Canada*
Richard Kerridge, *Bath Spa University, UK*

Editorial Board:

Franca Bellarsi, *Université Libre de Bruxelles, Belgium*
Mandy Bloomfield, *Plymouth University, UK*
Lily Chen, *Shanghai Normal University, China*
Christa Grewe-Volpp, *University of Mannheim, Germany*
Stephanie LeMenager, *University of Oregon, USA*
Timothy Morton, *Rice University, USA*
Pablo Mukherjee, *University of Warwick, UK*

Bloomsbury's *Environmental Cultures* series makes available to students and scholars at all levels the latest cutting-edge research on the diverse ways in which culture has responded to the age of environmental crisis. Publishing ambitious and innovative literary ecocriticism that crosses disciplines, national boundaries, and media, books in the series explore and test the challenges of ecocriticism to conventional forms of cultural study.

Titles available:

Bodies of Water, Astrida Neimanis
Cities and Wetlands, Rod Giblett
Ecocriticism and Italy, Serenella Iovino
Literature as Cultural Ecology, Hubert Zapf
Nerd Ecology, Anthony Lioi

Forthcoming titles:

Civil Rights and the Environment in African-American Literature, 1895-1941, John Claborn
Climate Crisis and the 21st-Century British Novel, Astrid Bracke
'This Contentious Storm': An Ecocritical and Performance History of King Lear, Jennifer Mae Hamilton
The New Poetics of Climate Change, Matthew Griffiths

The New Nature Writing

Rethinking the Literature of Place

Jos Smith

BLOOMSBURY ACADEMIC
LONDON • NEW YORK • OXFORD • NEW DELHI • SYDNEY

BLOOMSBURY ACADEMIC
Bloomsbury Publishing Plc
50 Bedford Square, London, WC1B 3DP, UK
1385 Broadway, New York, NY 10018, USA

BLOOMSBURY, BLOOMSBURY ACADEMIC and the Diana logo
are trademarks of Bloomsbury Publishing Plc

First published in Great Britain 2017
Paperback edition first published 2018

© Jos Smith, 2017

Jos Smith has asserted his right under the Copyright, Designs and
Patents Act, 1988, to be identified as Author of this work.

Cover design: Paul Burgess (Burge Agency)
Cover image © Shutterstock

All rights reserved. No part of this publication may be reproduced or
transmitted in any form or by any means, electronic or mechanical,
including photocopying, recording, or any information storage or
retrieval system, without prior permission in writing from the publishers.

Bloomsbury Publishing Inc does not have any control over, or responsibility for,
any third-party websites referred to or in this book. All internet addresses given
in this book were correct at the time of going to press. The author and publisher
regret any inconvenience caused if addresses have changed or sites have
ceased to exist, but can accept no responsibility for any such changes.

A catalogue record for this book is available from the British Library.

ISBN: HB: 978-1-4742-7501-9
PB: 978-1-3500-9218-1
ePDF: 978-1-4742-7503-3
ePub: 978-1-4742-7502-6

Names: Nemeth, Charles P., 1951- author.
Title: A comparative analysis of Cicero and Aquinas : nature and the natural law /
Charles P. Nemeth.
Description: New York : Bloomsbury Academic, 2017. | Includes bibliographical
references and index.
Identifiers: LCCN 2016051165| ISBN 9781350009462 (hb) | ISBN 9781350009486
(epdf)
Subjects: LCSH: Cicero, Marcus Tullius. | Thomas, Aquinas, Saint, 1225?-1274.
| Natural law. | Philosophy of nature.
Classification: LCC B553 .N46 2017 | DDC 186–dc23 LC record available at https://
lccn.loc.gov/2016051165

Typeset by Deanta Global Publishing Services, Chennai, India

To find out more about our authors and books visit
www.bloomsbury.com and sign up for our newsletters.

For my parents, Maggie Yaxley Smith and Chris Smith

Contents

Illustrations	viii
Acknowledgements	ix
Introduction	1
1 The Local	35
2 The Wild	71
3 Edgelands	103
4 The Periphery	127
5 Archipelago	157
6 Geologies	179
Afterword: Lyric Place	203
Bibliography	209
Index	225

Illustrations

Figure 4.1 Timothy Drever. 'Four-Colour Theorum', Kenwood House, 1969 — 136

Figure 4.2 Tim Robinson. Detail, 'Map of Aran', 1996 [1980] — 146

Acknowledgements

I am indebted to a great many people for their support, encouragement and advice over the last few years as this book has developed, among them Nick Groom, John Brannigan and Andy Brown for responding to drafts of chapters. I would like to thank Andrew McNeillie for his continual support, and for introducing me to Tim Robinson's work. I would like to thank Tim Robinson for answering my stream of questions, and Sue Clifford and Angela King for the long and lively conversations over coffee in Shaftesbury, and Robert Macfarlane and Kathleen Jamie for their thoughtful responses to my inquiries. I am particularly indebted to my fellow editors on *The Clearing*, Isabel Galleymore, Ben Smith and Luke Thompson, with whom I have discussed at length many of the issues raised in this book. I would also like to thank members of the board of the Atlantic Archipelagos Research Consortium, in particular Nicholas Allen and Fiona Stafford for their encouragement. I am grateful to the editors Neal Alexander of *Literary Geographies*, Terry Gifford and Anna Stenning of *Green Letters* and Les Roberts of *Humanities*, each of whom has cast very keen eyes over aspects of this book's argument. I am also grateful to staff at the Bodleian Library and the University of Exeter Special Collections for their help and support. Finally, I am particularly indebted to the 'Environmental Cultures' series editor Richard Kerridge for his wise guidance and advice in preparing this book for publication.

Introduction

One figure, like no other, looms large in setting the ground for the contemporary form that has come to be called the New Nature Writing. Richard Mabey is an author whose work has consistently pioneered new ways of thinking about landscape, nature, place, culture and the range of interconnections that all of these share. Often this has meant reminding us of *old* ways of thinking about these things but he has always had a sharp eye for the new meanings that our modern context provokes. His monumental *Flora Britannica* (1996) is a book that embodies some of the best qualities that have become characteristic of the New Nature Writing as a form, so much so that it has inspired an array of like-minded volumes on different topics.[1] It is knowledgeable, innovative and inclusive; it relates to a long tradition of similar books while at the same time expanding what that tradition might be capable of; it looks at the plants, flowers and trees that are its subject with a sharp eye for local distinctiveness; and it meets the changed and changing conditions of the modern world around it with unflinching resourcefulness. Like many of his other books, it looks at the relationship between humans and wildlife as it has played out in the most diverse and distinctive ways. Some of the plants he writes about – like the lewdly nicknamed cuckoo-pint, or lords-and-ladies (*Arum maculatum*) – have collected over ninety different names over the years, each recording a different way of thinking about and relating to that particular plant (8). What better metaphor for the rich and fluid contours of culture itself, intricately plural even across the one small archipelago of nations that the book examines? It reminds us, as he has himself, that 'culture isn't the opposite or contrary of nature. It's the interface between us and the non-human world, our species' semi-permeable membrane' (2006: 23).

---

[1] Mark Cocker's *Birds Britannica* (2005) and Peter Marren's *Bugs Britannica* (2010), both of which he has also contributed to, but also more recently Mark Cocker's *Birds and People* (2013) and Robert Macfarlane's *Landmarks* (2015).

One of the things that make *Flora Britannica* so remarkable is the democratic method Mabey adopted in researching and writing it. He began the book with the characteristically forthright and down-to-earth intention of simply 'asking British people whether nature had now dwindled to no more than an object of nostalgia in their lives, or whether it was still entwined in their everyday habits and beliefs' (qtd. in Derwent 1996: 50). The book was an attempt at a 'true social history, an up-to-date ecology of plants and human beings' (50). At the time, he was well positioned with a morning spot on the BBC's *Countryfile* where he was able to appeal to the public for contributions and the appeal was picked up by subsequent features on radio and in various magazines. The project took four years and received many thousands of responses in a variety of forms: 'postcards, tapes of discussions, snapshots and family reminiscences, as well as long and detailed essays on the botanical folklore of individual parishes and individual species' (Mabey 1996: 9–10). Unlike traditional scientific texts on plants and animals that name and describe the species and its likely environment, it collected and published a body of work from the variety of local cultures, ordinary memories and vernacular knowledges that flooded in from the public. The plants became bright focal points around which people felt encouraged to 'articulate their feelings about place and nature in general' (10). The outcome is an historic addition to the canon of British nature writing that, as much as it presents a remarkable image of British flora, also presents a remarkable image of Britain itself, broken down into microcosms of tightly packed cultural history.

Far from showing nature as 'dwindled to no more than an object of nostalgia' as he had feared, people's accounts of plants, flowers and trees seemed interwoven with modernity in the most surprising ways. One community in Sheffield described fighting to save some quite unlikely rows of Mediterranean fig trees growing on the banks of the River Don. As it turned out, at the height of steel production in the 1920s the river water was used as a coolant in the factories and ran at 'a fairly constant 20°C – warm enough for fig seeds washed into the river from sewage outfalls to germinate and thrive'. As such, the local people felt these trees were a part of the 'industrial heritage of the area' and worth fighting for (1996: 66–7). It is a story that shows how trees continue to embody forms of cultural memory and can express and articulate history in the most surprising ways. The proliferation of bright pink rosebay willowherb across areas of London that were badly bombed after the Second World War is another poignant example (1973: 35).

The story of Oxford ragwort describes the spread of the species nationally from a single specimen 'reputedly gathered from the volcanic rocks of Mount Etna' (1996: 376). Escaping the University Botanical Garden in Oxford, seeds made their way, no doubt by gusts of wind or carried in folds of clothing, to the local railway station and are thought to have proliferated along the granite-chipped arteries of the Great Western Railway to become the most abundant ragwort in most British cities. It is a story that suggests some of the adaptability and mobility of the modern plant life that we pass every day without a thought. There is the story of a 250-year-old sweet chestnut tree on George Green in Wanstead. This tree became a powerful symbol of the battle to resist the building of the M11 link road in 1993 when conflicts between police and road protestors were at their height. The tree itself was occupied by protestors from June until it was felled in December that same year. Those inhabiting the tree received some four hundred letters of support (9). *Flora Britannica* is a book that has helped to set a bewilderingly original benchmark for British nature writing, keeping it at once firmly rooted in the popular cultures of everyday life *and* reaching for innovative new literary forms, challenging the long tradition to adapt with a keen eye on the challenges of a changing modern world.

In thinking about books like this, and others like *The Unofficial Countryside* (published as early as 1973), it is hard to hear talk of 'the *New* Nature Writing' in the twenty-first century without wondering if, in fact, much of the best of what is 'New' today might not have already been going on for some time. When Jason Cowley identified and named 'the New Nature Writing' in 2008, it was on the back of a wave of reviews in the national presses of books such as Robert Macfarlane's *The Wild Places* (2007), Kathleen Jamie's *Findings* (2005) and Mark Cocker's *Crow Country* (2007) (as well as Richard Mabey's own *Nature Cure* (2005)). Some reviewers had identified what they were calling a 'resurgent interest' (Moran 2008: n.p.) in a well-established form while some believed they could detect the arrival of a 'new genre of writing' (Bunting 2007: n.p.). A degree of uncertainty, then, hovers over the relationship of the New Nature Writing to the past here and has even led to quite an angry challenge from the mountaineering author Jim Perrin who admonished Cowley, arguing that there was nothing in this new form to suggest 'a radical departure from the practice and preoccupations of its antecedents' (2010: n.p.).

With this uncertainty in mind, throughout *The New Nature Writing: Rethinking the Literature of Place*, I do, surprisingly, adopt Cowley's uncertain title to describe this contemporary form. However, I do so critically and, perhaps more importantly, I do so with an important qualification that attempts to expand the length of the period that the title describes. In this book I make a case for dating the emergence of the New Nature Writing to the early 1970s when, following the founding of Friends of the Earth UK in 1971, a new popular environmental movement began to spread via a fresh counterculture of activism and campaigning hitherto unheard of among the traditional conservation bodies. More precisely, I date the origins of this form to 1973 when, in the same year, both Raymond Williams's *The Country and the City* and Richard Mabey's *The Unofficial Countryside* were published, two books that would fundamentally change the way people thought and wrote about landscape in Britain. Williams drew attention to the political and economic realities embedded within, and structuring, a tradition of countryside writing, challenging a particular form of wealthy, metropolitan nostalgia that idealized rural life in ways that disavowed the reality of struggle for ordinary people. Mabey, in his book of the same year, used the conventions of countryside writing to, themselves, challenge the tidy border between country and city and turned a self-reflexive eye on the ambiguous terrain between the two that has come to be called the 'edgelands' since (more on this in Chapter 3). Chapter 1 in particular will show a cultural context that directly connects these developments in the early 1970s to some of the key works that began to be published in the early 2000s. It will do so with reference to an influential arts and environmental charity called Common Ground, with whom Richard Mabey has worked over the years. It will show, for example, how the work of this charity helped to shape the thinking of two key works that would have a powerful influence on the more recent wave of New Nature Writing, Roger Deakin's *Waterlog* (1999) and Alice Oswald's *Dart* (2002). Understanding the New Nature Writing within this earlier context helps to ground it in a culture of environmentalism and conservation practice. This is instructive for two reasons. First, doing so encourages us to understand the form in ways that connect the literature to real-world changes in British cultures of grassroots conservation and heritage as they have developed over the last thirty to forty years. Second, such a holistic view draws attention to the opportunity that the New Nature Writing presents as a form through which to read and reappraise contemporary attitudes to place in Britain and Ireland today.

I do not claim this to be a comprehensive study of the form. The New Nature Writing is too vast and abundant and, perhaps more importantly, still evolving for any such comprehensive study at the present moment and there are aspects that are not fully explored here. What this book offers is something a little more particular and partial in its view of the form, as the subtitle 'Rethinking the Literature of Place' suggests. I aim to explore the New Nature Writing with a particular theme in mind here, of contemporary British and Irish attitudes to place and its meanings in the context of global environmental crisis and cultural and economic globalization. The themes of the New Nature Writing are not limited to place and, inevitably, there will be aspects of the form that fall outside of the discussion here. One such theme is animals, and human/animal relationships, which has been a huge part of the New Nature Writing, especially in the very fine work of Mark Cocker, Helen MacDonald, Patrick Barkham and Miriam Darlington, among many others. But in many ways that theme would have taken a different direction and no doubt formed its own book eventually and I felt it important to keep the discussion as focused as possible on the given theme of place.

The proliferation of curious and inventive literary works such as *The Unofficial Countryside* and *Flora Britannica* has unearthed an intricate labyrinth of horizons to the contemporary place-world, inspiring broad public and academic interest.[2] As I will go on to show, the creative and self-reflexive attitudes to place that we can see at work in the New Nature Writing are themselves intertwined with a wider creative and self-reflexive attitude to place in real-world contemporary contexts. The chapters that follow will show salient connections to projects of globally inspired eco-localization, among

---

[2] For overviews, see: *Green Letters*, Special Issue, 'Twentieth-Century Nature Writing in Britain and Ireland', 17:1 (2013); Daniels and Lorimer (2012): 3–9; Dee (2011): 21–30; Hunt (2008): 70–7; Macfarlane (2007): 13. Matless (2009): 178–88; and Tonkin (2008). Examples of UK academic conferences with direct interest in this subject: 'Affective Landscapes', University of Derby, 2012; 'The New Nature Writing', Bath Spa University, 2012; 'Landscape, Wilderness and the Wild', Newcastle University, 2015.

them: the work of the arts and environmental charity Common Ground or the Transition Towns network; experimental, small-scale conservation initiatives such as the Trees for Life 'rewilding' project in northern Scotland; or battles against large-scale developments such as that fought on the Isle of Harris against Redland Aggregates at the turn of the century. All of these are demonstrating a shift in the contemporary meanings of place and the ways in which people identify with locality (the collaboration between the architecture collective Assemble and the Granby Four Streets Community Land Trust, awarded the Turner Prize for Art in 2015, might be added to this list).

Edward Casey has aptly described place as 'an ongoing cultural process with an experimental edge' (1993: 31). I aim to show that literature plays an important role in projecting and steering that 'experimental edge'. In doing so I follow a method of literary geographical criticism developed by Damian Walford Davies in his *Cartographies of Culture*, a book which explores the relationship between literature and forms of counter-mapping. Urging forward debates about the relationship between literature and maps (as two separate epistemological forms) that have surrounded distant reading projects such as Franco Moretti's, Davies has argued instead that cartography ought better be understood as a modality 'immanent in the literary work itself' (2012: 14): 'Whatever the contours of its own imaginative worlds, the literary text has always functioned as a mapper of alternative space and as a prompt to go beyond mere "formal geometries" to challenge the various "substantive geographies" that condition the limits of our social lives on the ground' (12).

The New Nature Writing, as a form emerging from the early 1970s, has questioned and stretched the genres and traditions of landscape writing and has developed alongside a culture of conservation practice that has done likewise with the ordinary cultures of place. In doing so there has been a sustained interest in the more ambiguous *styles* of place that have inspired the chapter titles of this book. Locality, wildness, edgelands, the periphery, archipelago and geology have all served as subtly ambiguous lenses through which place itself has been rethought. With close attention to such ambiguous styles of place and their representations in literature, this book explores a resourceful and imaginative counter-mapping of the contemporary place-imaginary through a range of different, tightly focused perspectives. Localized as such counter-maps might be, I share the belief articulated by Mabey himself that 'microcosmic views' like this might be 'not just powerful metaphors, but actually the nano-bricks for rebuilding things' (Mabey qtd. in Douglas 2005: n.p.). Through six key studies *The New Nature Writing: Rethinking the Literature of Place* presents a clear critical overview ten years after the term 'the New Nature Writing' was first coined, relating it to the long traditions of topographical writing, landscape aesthetics, naturalists' fieldwork and environmental thought and practice. It presents a detailed appraisal of the key works with carefully contextualized close readings that bring together research in literary criticism and cultural geography to their mutual benefit. It leads the reader through the key debates and discussions that have aired throughout the last decade, drawing in wider critical and theoretical material to build an argument about the re-energized cultures of place in the period 1973–present.

Nature writing

Compared to the American tradition, which has gathered its own plentiful body of literary criticism, if we focus strictly upon the form named 'nature writing', the British tradition has been much less well mapped and much less consistently reflected upon. There were only two self-titled anthologies of nature writing in Britain in the twentieth century, one edited by Henry Williamson in 1936 and one edited by Richard Mabey in 1997. This may be in part a question of terminology. There have been no end of anthologies of 'countryside writing' in Britain but these might suggest something slightly different, and something of which the literary critic has grown wary in the wake of Stella Gibbons's *Cold Comfort Farm* (1932) and Raymond Williams's *The Country and the City*. As Jeremy Burchardt has suggested, such writing has, at times, risked alignment with a conservative view focused on the chalk downland of south-east England and 'progressively eliminated conflict, modernity and tension from the field of vision' (2002: 75). However, W. J. Keith's *The Rural Tradition* (1974) maps out a canon of authors that serves as an exception to this, critically appraising what might be closest to a British tradition of nature writing as we understand it today. He reflects on a body of authors, from Gilbert White through Richard Jefferies and Edward Thomas to H. J. Massingham, who published non-fiction prose accounts that struggled to see things differently and that wrestled with new ways of writing what they saw. However, the authors Keith considers are not concerned with nature alone but with the cultures and traditions of rural life as well, making the description purely as 'nature writing' problematic.

There is an issue here about the *nature* of the title 'nature writing' itself. Are we to understand it as a straightforward and *natural* process merely of transcribing experiences and observations of one's surroundings? Eric Lupfer has dated the use of the term to the end of the nineteenth century in the United States, to the tradition of essays descending from Henry David Thoreau and John Burroughs, and has drawn attention to the debt it owes as a genre to certain 'elite literary institutions whose influence strongly determined its form, its audience, and the cultural capital it represented' (2003: vii). Dana Phillips has also challenged the idea that the nature writing essay is merely a 'natural' account of an excursion and has likewise drawn attention to the conventions emerging from transcendentalism and this same late-nineteenth-century tradition in the work of more recent American authors such as Annie Dillard (Phillips 2003: 186). To an extent, this rings true of the British tradition as well since, in some of the earliest examples of the term's use in Britain, there also appears to be a trace of a tradition defined in opposition to its American counterpart, if not an American influence. Alfred Richard Orage's *Readers and Writers: 1917–1921* (1922) has a very brief chapter titled 'Nature in English Literature' in which he begins to set out a distinctively English tradition of 'Nature-writing' including Richard Jefferies and W. H. Hudson (88–90). But in doing so he adopts the American hyphen to the term ('Nature-writing') that descends from the school of 'Nature-observation' and 'Nature-study' practised by the author and horticulturalist Liberty Hyde Bailey who promoted the study of nature in the tradition of Thoreau and Burroughs with an almost religious zeal (1911: 2–49). At heart, what Orage is doing is making an argument that suggests that English authors have been 'Nature-writers' for some time, though they have called it something else and that, in fact, the form might really be authentically rooted in England.

Similarly, in Henry Williamson's *An Anthology of Modern Nature Writing* (1936), despite the absence of any reference to nationality in the title, there are no American authors included. Williamson begins his introduction suggesting that 'most people leave such books ["nature writing"] alone, and suspect with a tendency to derision, the idea of "nature loving"' which is 'bad, inefficient, amateurish, imitative, pretentious writing', that is, showy and ostentatious, clinging to literary convention rather than based on experience (ix). Cleansing the work he collects in this anthology of such loose affections, Williamson promises writings that are 'the observations of intelligent human beings; and that none of them arouse feelings of fear, lust, anger, or injustice' (ix). Such feelings, he later confesses, he believes to have been what caused the Great War twenty years past, in which he served on the front line. Williamson does not give very much more away than this and it is not entirely clear who or what his comments are aimed at, though 'Nature-loving' was a phrase itself associated with the American 'Nature-study' movement (see Scott 1900: 115). Perhaps this 'anger, or injustice' might be related to Thoreau's 'civil disobedience', fuelled as it was by the philosophy of German Romanticism, or perhaps it is only a broader and more general sense of Romanticism, in either the American or British tradition of nature, concerned with the powerful feelings that natural scenery might inspire. Either way, Williamson distances his book from the self-conscious and affectionate rhetoric of a different form of 'nature writing' ('imitative, pretentious writing'), just as it emphasizes the authenticity of its own approach ('the observations of intelligent human beings').

When Jason Cowley offered up the title of the 'New Nature Writing' in 2008, he too seemed aware of the dangers of naturalizing the form and, like Williamson, set out some quite bold coordinates. Cowley distanced the contemporary form from what he called the 'old nature writing', by which he meant 'the lyrical pastoral tradition of the romantic wanderer' (2008: 10). However, rather than emphasizing, as Williamson did, 'observation' as the countermeasure to Romanticism (there is an odd confusion of 'Romantic' and 'romantic' in Cowley's phrase), this time he aligned the New Nature Writing with something that would sound more modernist in form, with writers 'who approached their subject in heterodox and experimental ways' (10). Unfortunately, the claim suggests rather erroneously that 'old nature writing' was not heterodox or experimental. Keith's *The Rural Tradition* shows non-fiction prose concerned with nature and rural life to have been just this, in fact, from as early as Gilbert White onwards. For example, he shows George Sturt – who published as George Bourne for fear that he would lose business at his wheelwright's shop if his fellow townsfolk found out he was a writer – agonizing over how to write about rural life. Critical of Hardy's use of fiction,

Sturt wonders: 'Sometimes, even, I think that a new art must be invented, proper to unrecorded and intangible beauties of the commonplace' (qtd. in Keith 1974: 154). What is curious about this tradition is that it is precisely a wariness of literary artifice which turns these writers to experiment with new forms. In Sturt's case this involved publishing transcriptions of conversations with his gardener 'Bettesworth' (Frederick Grover), an idea that immediately throws up curious editorial questions for him as an author.

The way Cowley positions this edition of *Granta* in 2008 might misunderstand the tradition then, but it does express an interesting – and distinctively British – anxiety about the relationship of nature writing to Romantic and modernist traditions. More recently, a wave of publications have begun to flesh out this idea of a modernist tradition associated with landscape and place. Alexandra Harris's *Romantic Moderns* (2010) is a book that works at this same fault line in relation to the aesthetics of a 'modern English renaissance' in the 1930s, challenging our assumptions about the alignment of the modernist tradition with the global city (10). Harris explores an interface between the experimental abstraction of the period and a carefully located landscape tradition in the work of Virginia Woolf, John Piper, John Betjeman, Paul Nash and others. The authors and artists that she examines are unusually interested in a sense of national identity at a time when such attachments were being disavowed by modernists in favour of international and transnational metropolitan forms. 'What can read as a sign of retreat', Harris argues, 'can also, perhaps, be read as an expression of responsibility – towards places, people and histories too valuable and too vulnerable to go missing from art' (14).

Jed Esty has also drawn attention to what he calls 'the anthropological turn' of late modernism in which the interests of key figures such as Virginia Woolf and T. S. Eliot saw a geographical 'contraction' in the 1930s and 1940s (2004: 2). Esty draws attention to the declining British Empire as a context for this contraction but rather than reading it as a terminus for the modernist project shows a complex attempt at 'social and aesthetic renewal' (3). In this view English modernism 'trades lost civilizational reach for restored cultural integrity' in such a way as to carry the modernist tendency to experiment and innovate into a preoccupation with national culture (16). He shows this at work, in its most progressive form, in Eliot's *Four Quartets* (1941–3) and Woolf's *Between the Acts* (1941) but also gestures to instances when such insularity took on more conservative and reactionary forms of nationalism as well. We might see the New Nature Writing as extending this tradition of 'social and aesthetic renewal' and its associations with a 'Romantic Modern' tradition, especially its revival of place as a subject in its own right. Perhaps the most vocal champion of nature writing today, and one of its most ambitious practitioners, Robert Macfarlane, returns to the late Eliot of the *Four Quartets* at the end of *The Wild Places*, for example, and the late Virginia Woolf haunts Olivia Laing's *To the River* (2011).

However, as Richard Kerridge has pointed out, recent nature writing has also had to contend with certain individuals 'who brought nature writing into disrepute', authors such as H. V. Morton, H. J. Massingham and even Henry Williamson himself, for each of whom, in his own way, 'authentic rural life, free from encroachment, was the antidote to the modernity that had produced the [First World] War' (2001: 138). In fact, it is in this same essay that Kerridge first uses the term 'new nature writing', several years before Cowley, when he argues that 'environmentalism calls for a new nature writing, clearly differentiated from the conservative tradition and aware of its appeal and dangers' (138). I shall argue here that one of the ways in which it has heeded this warning is by tightening the focus of its geographical scale, wary of what Macfarlane has described with suspicion as 'the sourer and sharper versions of old patriotisms' onto a 'progressive parochialism' (2016: xix). As Chapter 1 will show, the influence of the environmental movement on the tradition of nature writing would decouple its alignment with a conservative and nationalistic landscape aesthetic and ground it in a more tangible localism that was the scale at which environmental concerns were being confronted. Writing and artwork that explores this local register tend to emerge at an argumentative tilt to nationalist conventions, influencing a more intricate and heterogeneous picture of pluriform locality. And it is, in part, for this reason that I date the emergence of this *New* Nature Writing form to the 1970s. I argue that the very shift that Kerridge calls for in 2001 had, in fact, already begun to take place, but that it was after 2000 that it really found its popular audience. Key figures explored here, such as Richard Mabey, Sue Clifford, Angela King and Tim Robinson, all began work in the 1970s on projects that would have – and are still having – a lasting effect on the contemporary form.

It is interesting to note that sixty years after Henry Williamson's anthology, in 1997, we see a very different way of framing 'nature writing' in Richard Mabey's *The Oxford Book of Nature Writing*. Mabey's approach is far more expansive, historically and geographically, slipping the former bounds of the national imagination. It begins with Aesop's fables and Aristotle and includes poets, women, scientists, ecologists, anarchists, travel writers, diarists and all from a variety of different countries. Though the writing is clearly full of that acute and intelligent observation that Williamson describes, Mabey goes a little further in defining what binds his own broader selections showing the effects of the more recently aroused moral questions of ecology and environmentalism: 'What characterises the most convincing nature writing is a willingness to admit both the kindredness and the otherness of the natural world' (1997: vii); and 'the inextricable links between all parts of the natural world mean that its importance is an ethical as well as a scientific matter' (ix). This sense of 'kindredness' and ethical concern for wildlife has been amplified since the popularization of environmental thought by groups like Friends of the Earth from the 1970s onwards and the often local *and* global register of such feelings is one of the driving factors that has made the affiliation between nature and nation, even landscape and nation, highly problematic. However, critical thought from across a range of disciplines has more recently brought about deeper changes that affect the way we understand the 'nature' of nature writing, suggesting ways in which the 'New' of 'New Nature Writing' ought to qualify a new understanding of 'Nature' itself as well as a new form of writing.

After nature

We are told now that we have entered 'the Anthropocene', a new geological epoch characterized by our impacts on the land, the oceans and the atmosphere (see Crutzen and Stoermer 2000 for the earliest mention and Steffen et al. 2015 for the most recent and convincing). It is a recognition that has vast implications and might be compared to other historic reorientations prompted by Copernicus and Darwin. One of the big changes this provokes is the destabilization of a very particular enlightenment sense of 'Nature' as the separate and mechanistic universe in which humans live. The beginning of the

Anthropocene is still being debated but since what is now known as 'The Great Acceleration' in human development, beginning around 1945, a measure may be taken in a range of disciplines showing that the planet has begun to operate outside the traceable parameters of the Holocene (the last 11,500 years) as a result of our species' way of life (though it should be added that the responsibility lies heavily weighted towards the wealthy nations). Between the years 1945 and 2000, figures show that atmospheric concentrations of CO_2, acidification of the oceans, consumption of fertilizers and fuel, usage of water, and human population have all risen, on the planet as a whole, dramatically above Holocene levels. During the same period, figures also show that stratospheric ozone levels, biodiversity, tropical rainforest and woodland, coral reefs and areas of unexploited fisheries have likewise all seen a level of decline outside the parameters of the Holocene (Steffen et al. 2015: 4–7). We have come to recognize that the planet is now in a volatile state of change on a trajectory that will be disastrous for the sustainability of ecosystems and the future of biological life if it continues.

What does this do to our cultural understanding of 'Nature'? First perhaps, it puts the word in inverted commas or gives it a capital letter: that is to say, it estranges us from what we have, for a long time, taken for granted. Attention has been drawn to the way the naming of 'Nature' as an object establishes a distance between us and it, a distance characteristic of, and symptomatic of, the continuous exploitation that has led to such vast anthropogenic disruption. Clearly, to continue to behave now as if 'Nature' were as 'eternal and separate' as we once believed it to be would be fatal (McKibben 1990: 7). For some, the word itself comes so loaded with just such an implication that they believe the very idea of 'Nature' risks preventing a truly 'ecological thought' that ought to be instead concerned with exposing and opening up such categories (Morton, *Ecology Without Nature*). Part of the problem is that, for many, the view of 'Nature' as out there, as always out there, enchantingly reposed for our pleasure is very appealing. This idea of 'Nature' is bound up in complex ways with recreation activities, picturesque aesthetics, national heritage and even forms of conservation and environmentalism. Timothy Morton (2007) has suggested that 'putting something called Nature on a pedestal and admiring it from afar does for the environment what patriarchy does for the figure of Woman. It is a paradoxical act of sadistic admiration' (5). The recognition of the Anthropocene forces us to look very carefully at our cultures of 'Nature' and ask if they too, however well intentioned, are part of the problem. Is there, enshrined within them, a belief that 'Nature' is 'eternal and separate'?

The challenge of Morton's work is to think beyond this 'Nature' that is admired 'from afar'. In fact, the challenge of Morton's work is to ask whether the very breadth of ideas suggested by 'Nature' (upper case, lower case, in inverted commas or not) are not all underpinned by this sense of 'sadistic admiration', by the very need to delimit and name, to *produce* 'Nature' by fixing it apart from the human. Part of the problem with this argument is that for many people in perfectly ordinary contexts 'nature' does not equate to 'Nature' as an Enlightenment ideal, separate and mechanistic, but refers simply to the stuff of which we, and everything, is made. Just as men and women have continued to successfully struggle for relations beyond the 'sadistic admiration' of the male gaze, so in perfectly ordinary contexts we might imagine that people have found ways to adapt their lives to relate to wildlife in the places they inhabit in equitable and non-violent ways. However, at an institutional level and in the large-scale manner that our day-to-day lives are implicated in systems of what Ulrich Beck has called 'organized irresponsibility', the deconstruction of such a loaded and complex term can lead to a political position worth exploring (1999: 149). Geographers too have, for some time, been suspiciously unpicking the alignment of 'Nature' with 'a transcendent archetype' to reveal what Jamie Lorimer has called 'a power-laden process of purification' (2015: 25).

In fact, this anxiety about the separation of 'Nature' is one that has preoccupied British nature writers themselves. 'I can remember being called a "nature writer" for the first time,' Richard Mabey writes, 'and flinching at the implication that this was different from simply being a writer' (1984: xi). Mabey feels uncomfortable about the way the term seems to suggest a limitation of scope, that being a 'nature writer' might imply a decision to, for example, turn away from the *cultural* life of Britain, something he has repeatedly checked as counter-intuitive. When cordoned off in this way, 'nature' tends to convey an evacuation of politics and ethics. Robert Macfarlane has also argued that 'nature writing is an unsatisfactory term for this diverse, passionate, pluriform, essential, reviving tradition,' though he concedes that, nonetheless, 'it is the best there is, and it serves as a banner to march beneath' (2003: n.p.). Kathleen Jamie too has been troubled by the fact that 'our best "nature writers" are equally concerned with culture, and the fact that we live immured in both' (2013: n.p.). British nature writing wears its title with some anxiety and discomfort then, aware of the danger of seeming to endorse a separation of the affairs of 'Nature' from the affairs of the country, even the world, at large.

Beyond the aesthetic production of 'Nature' as a particular style of distant and enshrined object then, how might those self-consciously involved with and engaged with the world do things differently? Stephen Daniels and Hayden Lorimer have suggested of the current enthusiasm for landscape writing that some of 'the newest examples … bear witness to landscapes and environments that exist, *after* nature', often foregrounding those in which historical, industrial, technological and commercial developments are most marked (2012: 4). But recognizing the living process of historical and human development in the landscape also draws attention to the living process of changes in flora, fauna and the elements at large and the way in which these processes evolve and change together. Elizabeth Ellsworth and Jamie Kruse, writing more broadly of the way artists and authors have responded to the challenge of the Anthropocene, have described a 'turn away from static, mechanical models of "nature" to dynamic models that see the world as a field of continuous emergence' (2013: 16). This sense of post-natural volatility and the disorientated concern it provokes connects to the agenda of many of the writers considered in this book as they revisit familiar geographies with an open mind, to bear witness, reconnect, rethink and rewrite. However, the post-natural view of landscape is not reconfigured by mapping a change in 'Nature-as-object' alone. It is not about changing the definition of 'Nature' but rather about changing our understanding of the whole relationship between 'Nature' and the 'Human' that constitutes 'Nature-as-object' in the first place. 'Putting something called Nature on a pedestal' involves occupying a very particular version of what it means to be 'Human' as well. Concomitant to this challenge to the idea of 'Nature' as a stable and separate object is a challenge to the idea of the 'Human' as objective, homogeneous, coherent, authoritative and in control, itself distant from that objectified 'Nature'.

A thoughtful response to this comes from a recent book on the conservation of *Wildlife in the Anthropocene* (2015). Geographer Jamie Lorimer argues that, in this new epoch 'there is no single Nature or mode of Natural knowledge to which environmentalists can make recourse' but that rather 'multiple natures are possible' (7). For Lorimer, 'the Anthropocene is multinatural' (7). This is part of a wider recognition that human knowledge itself is multiple, heterogeneous, located, contingent and therefore political; that 'there are multiple forms of natural knowledge – not all of which are scientific or even human – informing a myriad of discordant ways of living with the world' (7). 'Nature' gives way to 'multiple natures' for Lorimer, and each of these 'natures' is inflected differently by its distinctive location: *materially* inflected in the day-to-day processes which produce and affect it in different situations; and *epistemologically* inflected in the way that ordinary cultural processes describe and understand it differently in different locations. So at points of lively interconnection 'Nature' and the 'Human' both multiply in locally distinctive ways. We might recall Richard Mabey's claim that 'Culture isn't the opposite or contrary of nature. It's the interface between us and the non-human world, our species' semi-permeable membrane' (2006: 23). In Lorimer's 'multiple forms of natural knowledge – not all of which are scientific or even human' and in Mabey's 'semi-permeable membrane' there is an acknowledgement that agency and even expertise might come from the non-human as much as from the human, and therefore that we are involved in a more collaborative process than we often acknowledge. Ignoring this can lead to attempts to dominate and control in ways that stifle what might be a richer experience. This is something that Chapter 2 explores in greater depth in relation to the wild. For Lorimer, the idea of 'wildlife' comes to explain this vibrant site of interconnection between the human and non-human in which the human relinquishes some of his or her detached superiority: 'We can think of the wild as the commons, the everyday affective site of human-nonhuman entanglement. Politics in the wild involves democratizing science, relinquishing the authority that comes with speaking for a singular Nature' (2015: 11). This democratization of science that Lorimer's work on conservation promotes is the flip side of its proliferation, and localization, of multiple 'natures'. Both of these foreground wildlife and place as always already intertwined in the most ordinary of ways that are too often invisible in the shadow of the isolated spheres of 'Nature' and the 'Human'. This is an idea that will be central to the reading of place throughout this book.

In Lorimer then, there is a curious response to the epistemological challenge of the Anthropocene that shifts down the scale towards the local, towards more intricate and proliferate forms of space and place. This largely runs counter to other theorizations of the Anthropocene that have shifted up in scale towards the planetary. However, one of the central arguments behind this book's rethinking of place in contemporary literature is that the books it explores reveal ways in which environmental uncertainty has produced a shift in *both* of these directions at once, to the intensely local and to the globally interconnected; and that, crucially, these shifts are part of the same response. In Lorimer's version of wildlife conservation there is a sense of optimism and possibility via its reading of a democratized agency that even extends collaboratively to the non-human. However, in criticism that shifts up in scale towards the global, the question of agency presents a much more challenging problem. Concerned not simply with the recalibration of human/non-human relations '*after* nature', but with what impedes a sustainable future at a planetary scale, criticism concerned with the Anthropocene has asked what the emergence of this challenge does to our sense of history and our sense of agency as historical peoples. For Dipesh Chakrabarty, the Anthropocene has seen a 'collapse in the age-old humanist distinction between natural history and history' (2009: 201) out of which the human emerges as a 'geological agent' with the power to change the planet (206). But as a geological agent, the human does not enjoy the same individual freedoms that it is used to as a 'biological agent'; the human can only be a geological agent 'historically and collectively, that is when we have reached numbers and invented technologies that are on a scale large enough to have an impact on the planet itself' (206–207). It may well be within our power to slow down various anthropogenic disruptions but this will require facing the challenge of acting 'as a species', something which we have not faced previously, and something which also begins to question what, or who, is meant by the 'we' that must engage with this change (219; see also Yusoff 2016).

Timothy Clark has described such a species agency as a 'tragic environmental Leviathan', 'a power that barely recognises itself as such and which is not really capable of voluntary action or planning, as it arises from the often unforeseen consequences of the plans and acts of its constituents' (2015: 14–15). Nonetheless, drawing on work by Ursula Heise, he suggests that the goal of humanities work concerned with the Anthropocene might be to 'aid a sort of species-consciousness' that helps to articulate a shift towards 'a new kind of eco-cosmopolitanism capable of uniting people across the world without erasing important cultural and political differences' (17). Considered in this way, we can perhaps better understand the localization and democratization of Lorimer's 'multinatural' Anthropocene as enriching precisely those cultural and political differences. Locality and place, for all their fineness of grain, might be productively rethought as a plausible foundation for just such eco-cosmopolitanism. They offer those 'microcosmic views' that Richard Mabey suggests might be 'not just powerful metaphors, but actually the nano-bricks for rebuilding things' (Douglas: n.p.). The networked projects of eco-localization looked at in Chapters 1 and 2, the devolved, archipelagic mobility looked at in Chapters 4 and 5 and the trans-local alliances such as the one explored at the end of the book in Chapter 6 all begin to show how the New Nature Writing offers a window on to the alternative spatial structures that are emerging in contemporary British and Irish cultures of place.

However, both place and the local have come under fire from recent environmental criticism responding to the Anthropocene, suggesting that it might be necessary to rethink their contemporary meanings. The body of New Nature Writing that this book examines affords a very singular opportunity to consider just this. Emerging from the early days of the environmental movement's arrival in the UK in the early 1970s, this unusual literary form revives and reworks its own British and Irish tradition of nature writing to produce a sustained, self-reflexive examination of attitudes to place that confound the usual expectations. Ursula Heise's pioneering work in this area has offered a critical examination of 'place-based rhetoric' among authors and ecocritics of the American tradition and has urged a greater recognition of the 'deterritorialized' and 'cosmopolitan' realities that are explored in work that engages with a wider 'sense of planet' (2008: 51). Although Heise is not, herself, in any strict sense, a constructionist, her concerns about 'place-based rhetoric' stem from the way it has developed in a reactionary bubble isolated from a wider context of critical and theoretical thought that has, over the last twenty years, dismantled many of the key concepts that it holds on to (such as identity, place and of course, more recently, nature) and shown them to be culturally constructed. The American tradition is founded on what she calls, after Zygmunt Bauman, an 'ethic of proximity', one that is inherited from the Norwegian philosopher Arne Naes (for whom 'the nearer has priority over the more remote – in space, time, culture, species') (Naes qtd. in Heise 2008: 28). Emerging from this, Heise argues, there is an over-weighted moral emphasis put on place as a means by which to 'reconnect with the natural world' (2008: 28). Such reconnection helps us to 'overcome the alienation ... that modern societies generate' (29). In this sense place becomes a retreat into nature away from modernity. This leads to an outmoded and worrying essentialization of place that puts too much emphasis both on the bounded definition of place itself as a stable unit of meaning and on the ways in which 'identity, whether individual or communitarian, is constructed by the local' (42).

This critique has been further articulated by Morton's *The Ecological Thought* (2010), in which it is argued that 'fixation on place impedes a truly ecological view' (26) by not being progressive, spacious and global: 'Our slogan should be dislocation, dislocation, dislocation,' he argues, as it reaches towards an ecology that is more fluid and decentred (28). Less carefully argued than Heise's work, but equally important for the way it forces an enlargement of thinking in relation to environmental issues, Morton's own writings against place have been founded on an understanding of what he calls 'a powerful Western myth' in 'the idea of authentic place', one that owes much of its strength to the idea of nationalism (55). He destabilizes this myth and argues that 'the local isn't familiarity but the uncanny, the strangely familiar and the familiarly strange' (50). Both Morton and Heise, then, are arguing against a very specific formulation of place and the local that is concerned with essence, authenticity, identity and stability, with boundedness and definition. However, these movements of deterritorialization and destabilization draw attention to the socially constructed nature of place in a way that this book will show has been overtly embraced in the recent British and Irish tradition, not to fix place but to rethink it. One reason for this is that its emergence has been from precisely the traditions of theoretical thought that Heise shows the American tradition to have retreated from.

This book's argument begins by carefully re-tracing the origins of the New Nature Writing, not in 2008 as Cowley does, but some time earlier in the work of Richard Mabey (as explored further in Chapter 3) and in the work of the arts and environmental charity Common Ground. Chapter 1 explores Common Ground's influential development of a fresh place-based cultural practice founded on an ethos of 'local distinctiveness' which embodies the environmental slogan 'think globally, act locally'. Timothy Morton begins *The Ecological Thought* with a telling omission of this slogan revealing a certain prejudice that goes some way to explaining his dismissal of the possibility of an ecology that might consider scales of the local and global at once: 'Small is beautiful. Diet for a small planet. The local is better than the global. These are the slogans of the environmental movements since the late 1960s. I'll be proposing the exact opposite of the sentiments they express' (2010: 20). Had he included 'think globally, act locally' (perhaps the most famous of environmental slogans) the opening argument would have been complicated in an important way.

Common Ground's treatment of the local is a very particular one, in fact, already calved away from a stable and bounded version of the nation as a coherent whole and already connected to a global movement of environmental concern. It departs in important ways from the accusations that Heise and Morton have made of the American tradition in respect of its engagement with three key contexts. The first of these is its emergence from an informed global environmental movement. The founders of Common Ground were, for example, all a part of Friends of the Earth during the 1970s. By the time Agenda 21 was proposed at the Rio Earth Summit in 1992, arguing as it was for the stimulation of 'environmental citizenship' and 'local democracy' *from the ground* up as a way of making global environmental issues a household reality, Common Ground had already been developing projects across the UK that had done precisely this for nearly a decade. The second key context is the Marxist literary criticism of Raymond Williams and John Barrell concerning the rural landscape and the wider intellectual work on space, heritage and landscape that was emerging from authors whose work challenged the homogenizing powers of nationalism under the Thatcher government such as David Lowenthal, Patrick Wright, Stephen Daniels and Doreen Massey (many of whom worked with Common Ground over the years). The third and final context was the tradition of landscape history that has descended from the work of W. G. Hoskins and that revealed, in what some might mistake for a wild or a natural landscape, a palimpsest of intricate historical narratives in which human life and culture, geology, forests, climate and wildlife were deeply intertwined. These three important contexts meant that the emergent principle of 'local distinctiveness' and the place cultures that have since been informed and influenced by it were much more nuanced and critically aware than the representations of place that Heise and Morton read in the American tradition. Chapter 1 sets out some of this important context in more detail and provides evidence of the influence of Common Ground on key texts that served as progenitors to the more recent wave of New Nature Writing.

How, then, does the version of place and the local emerge distinctively in this British and Irish tradition? This book explores three important ways of reading place through the New Nature Writing that help to rethink and reappraise its contemporary meanings. First, it reads representations of place in the New Nature Writing for the way that they foreground its dynamic properties, in that the form puts emphasis on place being an open-ended and experimental process, an ongoing performance of social and cultural reality that is in often difficult dialogue with other scales of place such as national administration and global environmental challenges. In particular this is revealed through the emphasis of the artists and authors discussed on recognizing place as, in the words of Doreen Massey, 'the unavoidable challenge of negotiating a here-and-now' (2005: 140). In this sense the literature is read as itself an experiment in place with the potential to feed into the cultural life of that place, especially in light of the fact that so many of the authors are themselves also engaged with activities of grassroots environmentalism or heritage. Second, it reads representations of place in the New Nature Writing as relational, even at times as cosmopolitan, in the sense that they explore networks of subnational and regional spaces within and beyond Britain through the movements, allegiances and relationships *between* the places and the authors discussed. It does this under the influence of recent work in cultural geography, in literary criticism associated with place, and in archipelagic criticism. It explores place in the context of mutable configurations of space across these diverse islands and in light of a devolved geography of what Andrew McNeillie has called this 'unnameable archipelago' (2007a: n.p.). Third, and last, it reads representations of place in the New Nature Writing as self-reflexive in the sense that they are in a dialogue with the long traditions of topographical writing, nature writing and rural writing. This forces an often quite conflicted engagement with such inherited modes as chorography, travelogues, the picturesque, the pastoral and the wilderness excursion narrative. The book aims to show that a new vision of place is emerging, one struggling to articulate new meanings '*after* nature', revealing how popular attitudes towards geography today have come to be characterized by a tension between anxiety and uncertainty on the one hand and by a new-found sense of possibility and imagination on the other. It is such a tension that makes the New Nature Writing such an important body of work for understanding changing attitudes in Britain today, but it is also what makes it such a difficult and complicated body of work, one that has divided opinion and drawn debate after debate in the public sphere.

Debate

Criticism of the New Nature Writing tends to pull in two clear – and clearly opposite – directions. On the one hand, as we will see below, there are the naturalists who believe that the form should distance itself from aesthetics and stick to the facts, that there is no place for lyricism in a genre that has strayed from its origins in scientific writing. On the other hand there are the environmental critics who also feel that the form should let go of hackneyed rhetorical tropes such as the excursion narrative (and other forms that attempt to be faithful to real-world experience), but these critics argue that it should, instead, embrace more ambitious aesthetic forms. This polarization of opinion provokes some important questions about a dilemma between fidelity and artifice at the heart of the New Nature Writing and it repays some closer inspection.

At the Museum of Modern Art in Machynlleth in October 2010 the mountaineer and author Jim Perrin ended his William Condry Lecture with a volley of criticism launched at the New Nature Writing as it was being promoted and championed by *Granta*. For inspiration he turned to the Etonian naturalist and editor James Fisher who, in the 1940s, wrote the following against nature writers of his time who he felt had an 'excessive consciousness of the exquisite nature of their prose'. Perrin suggested that it equally well 'pins most of our so-called "new nature writers" firmly to the specimen-board' (in an image suggestive of his preferred perspective):

> Do these people really believe that the search for truth is less important than the search for poetry or art or aesthetic satisfaction or 'happiness'?

> Do they not understand that the purest source of these imponderables is in the realms of fact, and that the establishment of facts is most simply done by the ancient methods of logical science? Once facts are despised, fancies replace them; and fancies are poisonous companions to the enjoyment and appreciation of nature. (Fisher qtd. in Perrin 2010: n.p.)

It characterizes a familiar conflict that seems to arise from time to time in relation to nature writing, and one we saw an echo of in Henry Williamson's introduction to his 1936 anthology. Aesthetics and facts are opposed to each other, as are poetry and truth, in such a way that is hard to imagine in relation to another literary form such as the novel. A similar argument is made in a recent American collection of essays offering a new approach to the aesthetics of nature after environmentalism which recommends 'disinterestedness' and 'which demands that appreciators purge aesthetic experience of their own particular and personal interests and opinions' (Carlson and Litnott 2008: 12). Elsewhere, one of its editors, Allen Carlson, has suggested that 'concerning the art-based approaches, it is argued that they do not fully realize the serious, appropriate appreciation of nature, but distort the *true* character of natural environments' (2009: 9; emphasis added). Such a representation of 'nature' as an object that we can know the 'true' character of, in both cases here, has come to feel a little antiquated for reasons that this introduction has already made clear but also, oddly, it embodies an animosity towards human feeling and the aesthetics they produce, however modest.

The difficulty haunting this perspective can be traced back to a tension at the level of the 'facts' that Fisher describes. John Searle has distinguished between what he calls 'brute facts' and 'institutional facts' (1995: 2). 'Brute facts' are those that would be facts with or without our witnessing or describing or agreeing with them. 'A flower grows from the soil' is a brute fact for Searle, even before I write it down as such. 'Institutional facts', however, are more contingently based on human agreement. They are facts because we accept them and behave accordingly and because we talk about them as facts. That a certain tall-stemmed, small-headed yellow flower is known as a 'Common Ragwort', for example, is an institutional fact that he describes as 'language dependent' (64). The facts that Perrin and Fisher, Williamson or Carlson, are describing are 'brute' but there are important ways in which brute facts interact with institutional facts and can produce wildly different cultural perspectives.

To extend the given example, Common Ragwort is legislated against in Britain as a threatening weed because it is so poisonous to animals but on the Isle of Man, where it is known as 'Cushag', it is nonetheless admired as a national flower (Mabey 1996: 376). This is because the 'brute' fact of the flower's growth comes into contact with the variety of human responses to it that are based on values that differ according to particular cultural priorities and spark these different institutional facts as a result. I am not about to enter the rocky terrain of suggesting that brute facts are undermined by institutional facts, nor that the nature writer should be unconcerned by brute facts. However, it should be remembered that institutional facts might be understood as a very ordinary, basic and early layer of culture itself and that they, of course, soon give way to aesthetic forms. Aesthetics emerge as a refined and often individualized articulation of these institutional facts and we need to be very careful before dismissing them as 'fancies'. Simon Malpas, for example, describing what Carlson calls a 'distortion' of the natural environment, has argued: 'Art is what touches upon differences between us that form the basis of community, and remind us of the necessity of being in common. In the surprise fragmentation of sense elicited by the work there is the possibility of touching on the sense of plural community' (2003: 93). With this in mind, it is not so easy to oppose facts to aesthetics since aesthetics might be understood as a style of fact in themselves.

A more helpful way of thinking about this tension between fidelity and artifice was suggested by Raymond Williams in *The Country and the City*. Williams describes a form of country writing (and the same could be said of nature writing) running through the twentieth century which moves 'at times grossly, at times imperceptibly, from record to convention and back again, until these seem inextricable' (1973: 261). By 'record' Williams means those works that have tried to capture in all good faith the real lives of those living in rural areas, books such as William Cobbett's *Rural Rides* (1830) or George Bourne's *The Bettesworth Book* (1901). By 'convention' he means those works that 'scribbled over' the real lives of people in the country, possessed by a Georgian vision that used rural England as an image for 'its own internal feelings and ideas' (258). An image of a form pulled in both directions emerges then, wanting to be true to its subject but also wanting to fit with the popular expectations of the tradition. In the awkward debate between fact and aesthetics that haunts nature writers, we can perhaps see a shadow of this more helpful opposition of 'record' to 'convention'. It is more helpful because 'convention' here refers to one particular aspect of aesthetics; that is, its *reproduction* of tradition and its satisfaction of expectations. No doubt we would agree with Perrin if his argument had been with authors who ignore the facts of the world before them in favour of purely literary conventions. However, this cannot be said for the authors that this book explores. The way in which today's writers are engaged with convention is often quite argumentative, wrestling to resist it in favour of the new realities of a changing world. We might think of the edgelands literature considered in Chapter 3 which explodes an easy opposition of country to city in the rural tradition (think of the revisions suggested by the titles of these books alone: Richard Mabey's *The Unofficial Countryside*; Paul Farley and Michael Symmons Roberts's *Edgelands: Journeys into England's True Wilderness* (2011); Ken Worpole and Jason Orton's *The New English Landscape* (2013)). Or we might think of Chapter 4's exploration of Tim Robinson finding his way through a conflict in the mapping practices of the Ordnance Survey and the Irish tradition of *dinnseanchas*. Or Chapter 5's devolved account of the landscape vision that has emerged from the literary journal *Archipelago*, a vision at a consistently argumentative tilt to conventional orientations of 'the Isles'.

John Joughin and Simon Malpas tell us that 'it is impossible now to argue that aesthetics is anything other than thoroughly imbricated with politics and culture' (2003: 3). This is by no means to suggest that all forms of aesthetics are politically engaged in a self-aware manner. Historical formalism has shown that 'enmeshed in a web of institutional and cultural as well as social and political histories, literary forms are overdetermined by their historical circumstances and thus multiple and variable in their results, *neither consistently ideological nor inherently demystificatory*' (Cohen 2007: 3; emphasis added). There is, of course, a case to be made for certain forms prevalent in nature writing, just as could be said of so many forms in other genres, to have been determined by the literary marketplace. Timothy Clark has asked how far the celebration of 'the poetic as a kind of green psychic therapy' is bought and read as 'the wishful illusion of an industrial consumerist society rather than as a site of effective opposition to it' (2011: 23). Stephen Poole has even suggested rather rashly that the whole nature writing genre might be a 'solidly bourgeois form of escapism'

(2013: n.p.). There is, then, an uneasy relationship between environmental literature and the culture industry, but in Clark's more measured articulation this is a concern rather than a dismissal and it is a concern that speaks more broadly of the relationship between literature and the culture industry rather than of environmental literature alone. How something is read and absorbed by the public, what one might learn from the 'escapism' of art, what thoughts are incubated and what actions are provoked, are difficult things to measure.

However, as I aim to show in this book, the aesthetics of many of the authors associated with the New Nature Writing have emerged in a form of self-reflexive conflict with convention, struggling to see things differently and write things differently. But they have not done so by turning to brute facts alone. The British and Irish landscape is so overwritten with divergent cultural histories that it is often hard to tell the brute facts from the institutional facts. That much of the Highlands are a treeless wilderness appears to be a brute fact about nature but as Chapter 2 will show, this masks a contentious political reality. It is through fresh and innovative writing that the implications of this are explored, writing that is alert to the subtle, ongoing dialogues between layers of history, and layers of genre that have lodged themselves in our expectations and in our ways of looking. This is not a disavowal of truth in relation to place but a recognition that knowledge, that ways of looking at, and thinking about, and listening to place are political and that this tension between facts and aesthetics that appears to divide opinion over the New Nature Writing might in fact be the very point at which some its most interesting work emerges, books such as Richard Mabey's *Flora Britannica* and Robert Macfarlane's *Landmarks* which break completely new ground. As they trouble the boundary between brute and institutional facts they intervene in their own ways.

Perhaps the New Nature Writing could even afford to be *more* ambitious in its various aesthetics, as criticism from the polar opposite direction attests. Dana Phillips, writing of the contemporary American tradition, has called for artwork and literature that resists the dreary realist tendency of 'monocultural and monotone' 'landscape writing' which he feels reduces the complex to the simple (2003: 19). Timothy Morton has also argued for a much more dramatic break with tradition, caught as he feels American nature writing is in a habit of trying to 'escape the pull of the literary' (2007: 31). Morton challenges nature writers for, in a manner less than self-conscious, attempting to close the gap between language and the world, but in so doing making use of more and more complex forms of rhetoric that are mired in convention. One trope in particular Morton uses as an example goes something like: 'As I write this, I am sitting on the sea shore. ... No,' he scoffs, 'that was just pure fiction; just a tease. ... As I write this, a western scrub jay is chattering outside my window. ... That was also just a fiction,' he scoffs again. 'What's really happening as I write this is' and so on and so forth (29). In trying to close that gap, to somehow break down all the distancing effects of language and to communicate his or her experience as directly as possible in a '(non)aesthetic form' the nature writer unwittingly creates a complicated rhetorical maze that Morton dismisses as 'kitsch' (30). The way out of this maze for Morton is to stop resisting 'the pull of literary'. Dana Phillips also adds that the form 'has yet to develop tropes enabling it to come to terms with the fractured (and fractal) realities of nature', also spurring authors on to embrace the pull of the literary, to stretch their imaginations and techniques (2003: 20).

In its self-reflexive dialogue with the longer tradition, the better New Nature Writing that has been published in Britain and Ireland does not fall into this trap. It is too anxiously alert to its position in a long intertwining of traditions; and it is often too conscious of the contours of language as a medium as well. In fact, as we will see in Chapter 4, Tim Robinson has even taken precisely the fractal geometry of Benoît Mandelbrot 'as a source of metaphor and imagery' for exploring the multifocal linguistic depths of place (2011: 252). Nonetheless, there is a warning here that authors might take on board about a retreat from language or the literary. For Williams, the pull of a desire for 'convention' and the pull of a desire for an honest 'record' have meant that writing often exists precisely in their 'inextricable' mixture (1973: 261). Fresh aesthetic interventions lie in the careful and thoughtful mediation of the two rather than in the retreat from either one. The place-imaginary that this book looks at through the New Nature Writing is one that goes beyond the attempt to separate record from convention but that rather examines the political expression emerging from the ways in which their relationship is mediated.

A more alarming debate about the New Nature Writing arose recently when Mark Cocker drew attention to the contrast between the popularity of this form and the abject condition of much of the British landscape and its wildlife: 'How can we produce pastoral narratives when the realities underlying them are so sharply defined and their implications – social, political and cultural – so profound?' (2015: 45). He gives the example of William Atkins's *The Moor* (2014) which takes British moorland as its subject matter but that, with its wealth of discussion of the literary connections of English moors, manages to ignore completely the issue of grouse shooting in Scotland. This is despite the fact that, as Cocker points out, 'Most moorland exists today to deliver a cash crop of grouse to a super-rich elite who think little of paying between £3,000 and £12,000 per person for a day's shooting,' and the fact that the taxpayer is subsidizing the conservation practices that maintain such areas as moorland despite the damaging impact that they have had on species other than grouse (such as the almost extinguished hen harrier) (45). Cocker suggested that there has been a concerning shift lately in the preoccupations of the New Nature Writing from 'nature and culture' to 'landscape and literature' (by which he means the subject of the discussion has shifted from grounded conservation projects to purely literary representations) and that this has seen a disconnect from the uncertain, real-world political realities of our imperilled wildlife (44). He even goes so far as to align the 'New' of the New Nature Writing with that of New Labour, 'a project that has been uprooted from its original generative stock' (43).

Cocker's argument should serve as a profound warning and should be related to the wider debates about the politics of the New Nature Writing as it develops, but it should not inspire a nervous flight from aesthetics. On the contrary, what his argument provides is a prompt to consider the historical relationship between the aesthetics of the New Nature Writing and the shifting politics of contemporary Britain. In *The Country and City* Raymond Williams challenged the nostalgic idealization of rural life but the real project of that important book was to historicize the aesthetics of the countryside, to examine it as the expression of wider political and economic realities that existed in the relations between the country and the city. In the same way we ought to be conscious of the way the aesthetics of the New Nature Writing express and engage with the wider political and economic realities of the country at large in relation to its uncertain condition of social and cultural unity and in relation to a wider world navigating its way through environmental crisis. Robert Macfarlane responded to Cocker's article by considering some of the values being promoted through the aesthetics of what he called the recent 'cultures of nature' that have proliferated in the UK: 'community over commodity, modesty over mastery, connection over consumption, the deep over the shallow, and a version of what the American environmentalist Aldo Leopold called "the land ethic"' (2015: n.p.). An important warning about the relationship between literature and activism, from a literary critical point of view, Cocker's dismissal of so much of this body of work merely as 'pastoral' lacks the proper engagement with literary aesthetics.

The chapters that follow go to great lengths to examine works of the New Nature Writing as they have been shaped by, and as they have helped to shape, a wider culture of grassroots conservation, environmentalism, ecology and heritage in Britain and Ireland today. Chapter 1 lays the ground by reappraising the idea of the local in response to the recent dismissals of place (considered above) as reactionary, bounded and insular. This chapter looks back to the early work of Common Ground and their rooting of the big questions of the environmental movement in tangible and local realities. A new and more complex version of the local emerges as a result of this, one that is open, experimental and alert to contemporary conflict and change. I explore this through the charity's first publication, *Second Nature*, an anthology of specially commissioned nature writing that very carefully disentangles itself from a tradition of nationalist landscape aesthetics typical of the period 1930–60. I go on to trace the direct influence Common Ground had on two key literary works that have themselves exerted a strong influence on the later formation and popularization of the New Nature Writing: Roger Deakin's *Waterlog* and Alice Oswald's *Dart*. The chapter closes with a reading of Tim Dee's simultaneously local and global work *Four Fields* (2013). This reading is informed by Fiona Stafford's reconsideration of the local as an outward-looking literary phenomenon concerned with a search for what disparate locations and lives might have in common. The local emerges as a vital scale at which public engagement with global issues can find a meaningful purchase. A particular version of place comes to be conceptualized, in similar terms, as an ongoing, outward-looking and imaginative process of creative activity linking deep history with the present and the future.

Chapter 2 turns to a range of books that have recently shown an interest in the wild and its curious relationship to place in such densely populated and historically layered landscapes as Britain and Ireland. Unlike the American understanding of wilderness as remote and pristine, a modest sense of the wild as closely entangled with human affairs has grown up in a distinctive way on this side of the Atlantic. However, in part because of this close association of the wild with the human and historic landscape, the subject has divided opinion and has become a contentious issue, so the chapter explores three very different views on the wild through three key books: Robert Macfarlane's *The Wild Places*, Kathleen Jamie's *Findings* and George Monbiot's *Feral* (2013). Though in the end these three appear to arrive at a similar understanding of wildness as a lively process of interaction across the connective interface between the human and non-human, they each arrive at it by different means and these means themselves are culturally significant and are carefully explored. It concludes by considering the way projects of rewilding have been connected to diverse, pioneering community land initiatives, building on the previous chapter's re-evaluation of localism. Through other works by these same authors it examines what appears to be an emerging grassroots politics associated with the wild, one that connects in outward-looking ways to other projects across Europe and one that is beginning to make important demands for the reform of national policy on conservation and land ownership.

Chapter 3 looks at a much more ambiguous style of place as it turns to the edgelands. Edgelands, described as the 'interfacial rim' between country and city, have inspired a range of authors and artists recently because they offer an opportunity to trouble and question conventions of landscape aesthetics. This chapter explores three key works that have taken to these ambiguous spaces of 'terrain vague' and asks 'what might the future hold for them?' It begins by looking at perhaps the first work of the New Nature Writing as it is understood here – Richard Mabey's *The Unofficial Countryside*, a groundbreaking work that adapts a method of investigating such landscapes to playfully challenge both rural and urban traditions of writing with a very sharp eye for the resourcefulness of modern wildlife underneath. In so doing it presents a particular version of 'nature' (a term critically examined here) as inextricably entangled with modernity in these spaces and develops the previous chapter's engagement with the wild. Nearly forty years later, Paul Farley and Michael Symmons Roberts returned to similar territory in *Edgelands: Journeys into England's True Wilderness*, endeavouring to draw attention to landscapes overlooked by high, and even much popular, culture.

It examines their fascination with the architecture and ordinary cultures of these unlikely places, unpicking their playful prose forms as they parody and subvert picturesque and the pastoral modes from within. A vision of feral modernity emerges that complements Mabey's vision of modern nature. The chapter concludes, however, with a critique of Farley and Roberts' *Edgelands* for its attitude to history, arguing that a full account of edgelands ought to, at some point, confront the difficult question of an 'edgelands heritage'. In this final part, the chapter explores the complicated possibility of such a heritage through Ken Worpole and Jason Orton's *The New English Landscape*. In the end it argues for all of these authors as, in fact, engaged in a much needed and nuanced form of contemporary heritage work insofar as they are helping both to reveal and make cultural meanings in these underappreciated places.

Chapter 4 takes an in-depth look at the varied practice of Tim Robinson. There has been little academic research published on his work as yet despite an illustrious career, first as an artist of the London avant-garde in the late 1960s, then as a map-maker in the west of Ireland and finally as a now very highly regarded author of place. In part, this dearth is due to the difficulty of approaching these three diverse strands collectively, but in part it is due to his very deliberate move out to the extreme periphery of the British and Irish archipelago in 1972. This move came at a time when a whole generation of artists were beginning to think critically about the modernist alignment of culture with the city in the context of rising concerns about the environment and a contraction of British imperial power. Robinson's move to Aran brought him to consider the possibility of mapping and writing about an intangible heritage that had been misunderstood by nineteenth-century British colonial administration. The process raises the existential question of how the artist – in whatever medium – might do justice to a place that he or she takes as a subject. Aran's peripheral geography and the labyrinthine Connemara shoreline become physical metaphors for the intricate horizon of the contemporary place-imaginary. Writing about place reveals the fractal depth of the shared and interlocking spaces of history and community as they grow and change for Robinson. His work is thought to anticipate the field of 'deep mapping', a part creative, part academic, interdisciplinary form of cultural work interested in the transformative power of bringing to the fore marginalized experiences and forms of intangible heritage. With this in mind Chapter 4 builds on the previous chapter's argument about innovative and artistic forms of heritage work within the context of deep mapping to explore the rich spatial dynamics of all three aspects of Robinson's work. The significance of his initial dramatic move from centre to periphery is eventually complicated by the more intricate and archipelagic geographies of what he comes to call 'the view from the horizon'.

Chapter 5 echoes this shift in spatial register from 'centre/periphery' relations to the more complex and decentred relations of archipelagic thinking. The literary journal *Archipelago* has served as something of a masthead for a range of authors associated with the New Nature Writing but its vision of Britain is an unconventional one. Inspired by recent work in Four Nations History and archipelagic criticism, what emerges is a politically and culturally devolved view on 'the Isles' that gives preference to the northern and western periphery and the cultural geographies of the coast. This chapter offers an account of the prose (and some poetry) of the journal's editor, Andrew McNeillie, before looking carefully at some of *Archipelago*'s favourite authors and artists and how their work has been presented in the journal as a way of understanding the particular reconfiguration of space that the journal offers. What emerges is, on the surface, a turn to the periphery which, like Robinson's own turn in the last chapter, sees the literatures and cultures of micro-regions speak back to the centre, but the chapter looks more closely at this familiar dynamic to reveal a more complex and decentred archipelagic space underneath this, one with an emphasis on artists working (quite literally at times) in the cosmopolitan spaces '*between* and *among* islands' (Stratford et al. 2011). The chapter concludes with a reading of a collaborative work by Scottish poet Douglas Dunn and English artist Norman Ackroyd that emerges from boat trips taken by the two around the Scottish coast. The littoral vision that *Archipelago* publishes captures uncertainties about the future unity of Britain in the context of Ireland's own experience of independence, but it does so celebrating the dynamic possibilities of mobility and clustered relationships that archipelagic criticism argues has been so crucial yet under-acknowledged to British and Irish literary history. In the end, the editorial vision has come to nurture and stimulate the possibility of a deliberate, forward-looking movement of archipelagic literature to match the historic and cultural geographical work of archipelagic criticism.

The final chapter considers the accumulated new meanings of place as they have been developed throughout the book and asks what bearing they might have on the challenge faced by the Anthropocene. It does this by considering the relationship of place writing to geology. Geology has in fact come to hold a strong and significant fascination for authors concerned with writing about place. The austere presence of materials which have emerged from a scale of time difficult to relate to our own modest and limited scale has offered a humbling corrective to our modern experience. Such encounters have been resistant to a particular intersection of environmental and Romantic traditions of thought that searches for a 'reunion' with nature. In doing so they have spoken to some of the dilemmas emerging from the recognition of the Anthropocene as a geological epoch defined by destructive human development. As such, they present a useful way of concluding the book's rethinking of place in a modern context and suggest a response to the recent dismissal of place by environmental critics. Stone and geology are explored in the work of three authors here – Kenneth White, Tim Robinson and Alastair McIntosh. In texts by each of these we can read a consistent effort to reimagine the cultural geography of place by turning towards a deeper understanding of the stone beneath their feet. Far from regarding stone as a source of stability and reliability, these three find themselves accommodating unstable, vertiginous, precarious and plural truths that are drawn upon as a source for, what White calls, 'cultural renewal'. Realizing the impossibility of conciliation to such a non-human scale of presence also leads to the opening of what Heidegger calls a 'clearing' (*Lichtung*), both in terms of an aesthetic space in the poetics of landscape writing but also in terms of a lived place and the dynamic creativity at the heart of place culture. Heidegger's version of the clearing as an entanglement of earth and world is complicated here by recent developments in, on the one hand, new materialism's recognition of 'a geological affect' (Bennett) and, on the other, by the Anthropocene's recognition of humans as a 'geological agent' (Chakrabarty). However, his notion of the strife (*Streit*) produced by their entanglement only intensifies and its instantiation of an originary truth, that is the truth of the work of art, is read both in place writing and in place culture as a way of rethinking place in response to the challenges of the Anthropocene.

By broadening the focus of the period described by the New Nature Writing, this book shows how examples were set by an earlier generation of authors like

Richard Mabey, Sue Clifford, Angela King, Roger Deakin and Tim Robinson. Reconnecting the New Nature Writing with this earlier cultural context to which it is deeply indebted forces an acknowledgement of a generation whose commitments to real-world change have set a high benchmark. We need this benchmark today. If the New Nature Writing as a form is to grow and develop in a way not determined and dictated by the literary marketplace – and if it is to avoid the risk of becoming, as Clark warns 'the wishful illusion of an industrial consumerist society' – it is crucial to remember such a benchmark set by these important earlier authors (2011: 23). Not as something to aspire towards but as something to exceed, as an established foundation to build on in new and ambitious ways. This book endeavours to show that there are much more complex, experimental and self-reflexive processes going on in these works than just the 'pastoral' but it does so by connecting them to this tradition of socially engaged environmentalism that runs back to the 1970s. It encourages readers to look carefully and unpack the forms at work in the New Nature Writing since in them, in the questions that they provoke, there is a fresh understanding of the ways in which the cultures of place are changing in Britain and Ireland today.

1

The Local

In the autumn of 1984, three debates were held at the Institute of Contemporary Art (ICA) in London on successive Thursday evenings to launch the first publication of a new arts and environmental charity that went by the name of Common Ground. The book being launched – *Second Nature* – was an anthology of largely prose non-fiction essays and artworks by some forty authors and artists, all exploring landscape, nature and place in a contemporary context. Though it was not advertised as 'nature writing' per se, it nonetheless represents the first collection of British nature writing to have been published after the rise of the environmental movement in the UK throughout the 1970s. Central to the interests of the book was the charity's guiding principle, 'local distinctiveness', foregrounded in the first paragraph of the preface, a principle almost ubiquitous to British conservation and heritage organizations today[1] (Clifford and King 1984: vii). For Common Ground, the idea of 'local distinctiveness' held an intertwining of nature and culture, the personal and the political, the local and the global, and the past, the present and the future. 'We have all become well-informed about the world's ecological crises,' claimed Richard Mabey in the introduction (he had been invited by the charity to edit the anthology's written contributions),

> about the destruction of the tropical rain forests, the pollution of the oceans, the profligacy of agribusiness, and even about the economic connections between all these. Yet this knowledge has remained curiously remote, not connected in any obvious way with our ordinary everyday experience. [*Second Nature*'s] origins lie in the need – widely felt, and focussed as a theme for this book by Common Ground – to bring the argument in a very literal

---

[1] A study undertaken by Common Ground in 2005 showed over two hundred uses of the term 'local distinctiveness' in the official documents of government agencies and local authorities (Common Ground 2005: n.p.).

sense back home, to the local landscapes that are most people's firsthand experience of nature and to the variety of personal meanings which they hold for us. (1984: ix–x)

The emphasis on the local was intended to make the more general issues of environmentalism immediate and tangible.

The book, and the three public events at the ICA, were, as the charity claimed, an effort to 're-open the debate about our relationship with the land and with nature', not just as a discussion for professionals with a specialist interest but as a 'practical and philosophical concern for us all' (Common Ground 1983). Press releases and posters of the time had asked provokingly: 'Nature: "red in tooth and claw", polluted and exploited wasteland or pastoral haven, repository of a lost golden age?', 'Who Owns Nature?', 'Who should decide the future of the countryside? Is it a public or private responsibility?' (Common Ground 1983). The debates were free and encouraged anyone who wanted to join in while the editors of the book promised to 'freshen perception' and to help readers 'to see nature and landscapes in new and exciting ways' (Clifford and King 1984: vii). Together they endeavoured to balance the general and the particular, inviting people to look at their own relationship with nature wherever they might be from, rural or urban alike.

Far from promoting that 'ethic of proximity' that Ursula Heise has found to be so detrimental to certain place-based writing in the American tradition (that sense that 'the nearer has priority over the more remote – in space, time, culture, species'), Common Ground's principle of 'local distinctiveness' emerged precisely from a much wider global concern and a desire to put that concern to work in practical ways (Naes qtd. in Heise 2008: 28). It was promoting the idea that the local was something always already embroiled in cross-cutting struggles with national and international issues. Common Ground itself had been founded a year earlier in 1983 by Sue Clifford, Angela King and Roger Deakin in an attempt to address what they felt was an emerging blind spot in the conservation movement of the time. All three had been active members of Friends of Earth in the 1970s, King as their first wildlife campaigner, Clifford as a member of the board and Deakin later as a creative consultant. But all three had begun to feel that Friends of the Earth was putting undue emphasis on statistical and scientific evidence and a professionalized terminology (Smith 2012: n.p.).

The intention, for Friends of the Earth, was to productively engage with national bodies and political administration but these three felt that increasingly this risked alienating people at a time when environmentalism needed to work itself up from the grassroots in local and everyday situations as well. They also felt that emphasis on statistically endangered species of plants and animals, and on Sites of Special Scientific Interest and national parks, important as they all were, left more ordinary and commonplace landscapes exposed and unprotected. A bluebell wood or a primrose bank, a local common or a village green, might not show up on the list of priorities for national conservation and heritage but that did not mean that these places were any less valued by the people who lived locally and drew pleasure and meaning from them. And this was at a time when 'agribusiness' was working its way into both the British vocabulary and the landscape itself, making pervasive changes at an alarming rate. In fact, agricultural developments were exempt from the planning process brought in by the post-war Town and Country Planning Acts leaving people with little recourse to oppose these changes (Shoard 1981: 85).

The cover of *Second Nature* wore a ballpoint-pen sketch of sheep by Henry Moore and might have suggested to some that this would be a collection of essays on the sedentary virtues of the southern English countryside but this was far from the case. In fact, the essays brought together a wide variety of traditional, political and intellectually sharp perspectives on British landscapes, rural and urban, north and south, agricultural, industrial, post-industrial, even militarized, from rural historians such as Ronald Blythe to passionate defenders of nature such as John Fowles to Marxist literary critics such as John Barrell and Raymond Williams. The book offered diverse attempts to explore ways of writing about place, nature and even the rural that went beyond what Williams had called 'the sentimental and intellectualised accounts of an unlocalised "Old England"' but that were instead politically alive and engaged with a distinctly localized and changing, modern world (1973: 20). The book quite self-consciously emulated a nature writing tradition in its non-fiction prose form while at the very same time, in its engagement with the wider 'environmental crises', it refused to reproduce such nostalgic nationalism that nature writing had, at times throughout the middle of the twentieth century, become conflated with.

Jed Esty has shown a particular tendency in rural writing of the period 1930–60 to search out a romantic and insular nationalism during the period of declining imperial power. He describes this as a small and quite retrograde part of that wider 'anthropological turn' (which also included the attempt at 'social and aesthetic renewal' in the later work of Eliot and Woolf) (2004: 3). It was one in which, faced with the dramatic contraction of the British Empire, English artists and authors began to redeploy 'colonial tropes' such as exoticization and primitivism to, among other things, the English rural landscape itself (41). The result in this case was an introverted domestic tourism and something of a retreat into 'a preservationist national past' through which 'the island itself became one large museum' (42). It was the way in which just such preservationist nationalism had inveigled its way into the conventions of landscape aesthetics that *Second Nature* was resisting. It refused to engage with landscape and place as something to be consumed in a generalized form by a spectator or tourist, rooting its aesthetics, instead, in more local attachments. Esty singles out H. V. Morton's hugely popular *In Search of England* (1927) (which in ten years had seen twenty-three editions) as an example of the domestic tourism that would take new owners of automobiles out of the city in search of relics and traces of a timeless rural nation that is held aloft above an alien and daunting wider world.

Morton begins *In Search of England* with an image of the country revealing itself to him while suffering from what he fears might be meningitis in Palestine while it is still under British administration: 'Perhaps in instinctive contrast to the cold, unhappy mountains of Palestine, there rose up in my mind the picture of a village street at dusk with a smell of wood smoke lying in the still air and, here and there, little red blinds shining in the dusk under thatch' (1927: 2). He puzzles over why, being from London, he would return to such an image of the countryside as home in his mind rather than something more urban, concluding: 'I have learnt since that this vision of mine is a common one to exiles all over the world: we think of home, we long for home, but we see something greater – *we see England*. This village that symbolizes England sleeps in the subconsciousness of many a townsman' (2). A search for such a psychological, generalized national archetype, then, inflects the book's breathless travels with a sensual and emotional romanticism in which place names 'curl themselves around [the] heart' and places themselves are, again and again, 'felt' as soon as they are entered (77).

Patrick Wright gives an account of such bracing, sensual nationalism, full of 'mythicising vagueness' in his attack on an emphatically national heritage industry, *On Living in an Old Country*, written during the Thatcher years and published just a year after *Second Nature* (1985: 79). He describes it as 'a kind of sacrament encountered only in fleeting if well remembered experiences' (79). He quotes from H. A. L. Fisher's essay on 'The Beauty of England', published in a collection edited by the Campaign for the Protection of Rural England in 1932:

> The unique and incommunicable beauty of the English landscape constitutes for most Englishmen the strongest of all the ties which bind them to their country. However far they travel, they carry the English landscape in their hearts. As the scroll unwinds itself, scene after scene returns with its complex association of sight and hearing, the emerald green of an English May, the pellucid trout-stream, ... the church spire pointing upwards to the pale-blue sky, the lark rising from the plough in the March wind, the morning salutation of blackbird or thrush from garden laurels. These and many other notes blend in a harmony the elements of which we do not attempt to disentangle, for each part communicates its sweetness to the other. (Fisher quoted in Wright 1985: 79)

Here we have Williams's 'unlocalised "Old England"' in a sensual reel of garish ('emerald green') but vague ('blackbird or thrush') spectacle.

It is never to the same gushing extent but we can nonetheless find similar *moments* of mythification and insular retreat in Henry Williamson's *An Anthology of Modern Nature Writing* (1936). There is much to distinguish this collection from the sentimental work of Morton and Fisher as Williamson is a circumspect editor, endeavouring to bring to the public a selection of the best writing about nature, from authors of 'integrity' whose 'powers of observation' keep things 'fresh, interesting, living' (x). Nonetheless, there are notable moments that fall foul of this generalized rural imaginary as well, suggesting that it was part of a wider cultural and historical structure of feeling that began to shift later on. Williamson reproduces a section from Edward Thomas's *The South Country* and ends it on the image of a mythic, rural old woman sat symbolically between an historic stately home and the new modern road: 'Just beyond, a gnarled lime avenue leads to a grey many-windowed house of stone within a stately park. Opposite the gate an old woman sits on the grass, her feet in the dust at the edge of the road; motor-cars sprinkle her and turn her black to drab; she sits by the wayside *eternally*, expecting nothing' (103; emphasis added). Raymond Williams addressed a similar conceit in Thomas when the poet created the figure of 'Lob' in his poem of that name, a 'single legendary figure' and 'immemorial peasant', 'a version of history which succeeds in cancelling history' (1973: 256–7).

Likewise, later Williamson reproduces an introductory paragraph from George Bourne's *Memoirs of a Surrey Labourer* (1907) in which Bourne explains why the man whose lively tales he so carefully transcribes 'never knew that he had been made the subject of a book'. 'It would have been a mistake to tell him,' he suggests, since 'obscure and unsuspicious he continued his work, and his pleasant garrulity went on in its unaccustomed way'. It is as if the labourer's primitive state was something to be protected from the modern world of publishing (104). The anthology even opens with a series of extraordinarily vivid scenes of rural life and labour excerpted from Hardy's *Tess of the D'Urbevilles* (1891) but the effect is to feel you are reading a rather strangely abridged version of the novel in which all class consciousness and social relations have been censored, their particular tensions swallowed up by something much more diffuse and generalized (1–15).

Compare these to *Second Nature*'s opening essay which begins in Cumbria but not with the Cumbria of the Lakes so familiar to the Romantic explorer and the modern tourist, a region Andrew Gibson has described as 'that privileged repository of the national soul' (2017: n.p.). It begins further west near the coast, appropriately enough just outside the national park with an essay by the poet Norman Nicholson who describes his childhood home of Millom, a mining town on the Duddon Estuary. Millom was a centre for the mining of iron ore during the Industrial Revolution and the industry's mark still sits on the landscape confusing traditional notions of the rural with a more complicated accretion, 'a world of rock and bare fell-sides, slate walls and threadbare pasture, of half-bankrupt farms, deserted mine-shafts, short-time working and the dole' (9). Millom is a place on the periphery in a range of different ways. And yet Nicholson finds it interwoven with a tenderness and beauty as 'the rarest flowers were to be found among the old mines, [and] the best place to see wildfowl was the reservoir of the ironworks' (10). Even the geology of the place, the local slate in its full variety of texture and colour, is best examined in 'the walls of the back streets which were built with it' (10). Nicholson's town in all its 'local distinctiveness' is a place in which the earth and its flora and fauna are conspicuously intertwined with the human and historical landscape, its industrial and economic upheavals. By beginning *Second Nature* with Nicholson's intensely local essay about Millom, a town on the overlooked margins of one of the most symbolically *national* landscapes in the UK, and a town in which the pressures of modernity are overtly on show, something of an editorial bias shows through. Here the local seems a contested space at odds with a nationalist landscape aesthetic and a reading of *Second Nature* as an intervention in the very tradition to which it is contributing offers itself up. The local asserts its distinctiveness in all its difficulty and complexity as a tough survivor of the changeable global economy of commodities. The local is not, in this sense, a retreat from modernity here but its very currency, the material being composed and recomposed by it.

Second Nature's later and much tighter focus on 'local distinctiveness' had an urgent contemporaneity that set it apart from the broad-brushed generalizations of Morton and Fisher. Its authors were also rarely to be found 'looking in' on the local in the manner of Morton's pacey and impassioned blur but were more often than not personally invested in some way in the places they wrote about. In fact, what emerges through the book is a busy, heterogeneous vision of contrasting localities that question and break down the binary opposition of country to city and in its place show much more discrete, complex and individual values. Kim Taplin's essay and poems for *Second Nature* describe what she calls 'the new enclosures' of land imposed by the US and UK governments at new military sites, particularly those of Lakenheath in Suffolk, High Wycombe in Buckinghamshire, Falsane in Dumbartonshire and of course Greenham Common in Berkshire (119–31). There are vividly observed images of, for example, a warbler ('is it a marsh warbler or a reed warbler?' she wonders) on a river bank over a patch of sprouting water-mint ('I saw down its throat as it sang') but it is also framed 'under the roar of the F-11 bombers' (120). This particular desire to get the intensely local *right*, even down to the particular type of warbler, while the machinery of nuclear war passes overhead is, to an extent, quite eccentric but it also hammers home a point.

'Any natural thing truly seen and told conveys essence,' she argues in a phrase carrying echoes of John Ruskin (119). The military occupation of land misunderstands this 'essence', so her argument goes, but forces its misunderstanding into reality nonetheless, imposing it on the land. For Taplin the daunting scale of this international military intervention makes getting the local *right* all the more important. The struggle to convey that elusive 'essence' stands for a desire to do justice to a place that means something to her, and is, as she goes on, 'one reason why we need art as well as committees in defence of nature' (119). The difference between these unconventional, urgent and localized writings in *Second Nature* and either the fleeting domestic tourism of works by Morton, or the generalized nationalism of Fisher's essay for Campaign for the Protection of Rural England (CPRE) – elements of which at times crept into the kinds of nature writing being promoted in the 1930s – makes for a striking contrast. We can read in this contrast something of the shift in nature writing that emerged after the environmental movement. It is a shift characterized by a move towards the local, not as a retreat from modernity, but as a return to it from the generalizations of a national landscape aesthetic.

Second Nature would be set the difficult task of straddling two traditions, using each to intervene in the other. On the one hand it was an anthology of nature writing like Henry Williamson's; on the other it was a collection of environmental essays in the (more recent) tradition of Edward Goldsmith's *A Blueprint for Survival* (1972). As nature writing it was more politically and globally conscious; as an environmental call to arms it was more personal and localized. For Common Ground, the local was important because it was the scale at which 'the reference is reality, indifference is unusual, [and] detachment is difficult' (Clifford 1996: 6–7). Arising from the culture of protest and activism that had characterized the early years of Friends of the Earth, Common Ground put a premium on the global citizenship and participatory democracy embodied by the influential slogan 'think globally, act locally'. Landscape aesthetics were not something to be divorced from such a commitment to action and the emphasis on 'local distinctiveness' as the principle driving *Second Nature* was an attempt to provoke new ways of looking at and thinking about landscape, nature and place in the hope that they, in turn, might lead to an intensified identification with place and an accompanying surge in local cultural activity.

Following the particular version of the local that emerged in Britain out of the environmental movement, and more particularly out of Common Ground's rooting of environmental thought in a British tradition of nature writing, I will trace the idea of the local through three literary texts in this chapter: Roger Deakin's *Waterlog* (1999), Alice Oswald's *Dart* (2002) and Tim Dee's *Four Fields* (2013). The first two of these texts arose in close connection to a local community conservation and heritage project by Common Ground called 'Confluence' which ran for three years from 1997 to 2000 along the River Stour in Dorset. By examining the connections between this elemental and watery project and, in particular, Deakin's and Oswald's influential books, I will show the way some of the 'heterodox and experimental' leanings of the New Nature Writing can be traced to, and have taken inspiration from, a particular intersection of environmentalism and the arts rooted in this new localism (Cowley 2008: 10). All three of these books, though, offer experimental attempts to reframe the landscapes they are writing about, grounding them in the aesthetics of local distinctiveness, often at an argumentative tilt to the aesthetics of nationalism. Far from leading to a form of localism founded on an insular assertion of fixed identity, in these books this produces work that is eager to experiment, that is playful and alive to ambiguity, that attempts to include marginalized voices and problematic conflicts and that is vitally connected to the wider world. In the end, drawing on the work of Fiona Stafford, I argue that, far from being what divides us, the local is precisely what we have in common as a global community and that this is something that has come to find an important register in the work of contemporary nature writing.

The British tradition of nature writing, as it has been inflected by that generation of environmentalists and conservationists of which Mabey and Clifford, King and Deakin were a part, has foregrounded socially and politically contested sites, plural meanings and values of place heritage, and new ways of looking and writing that have helped to stimulate a fresh culture of localism. In this tradition the local is not a site of retreat but a vital scale at which we can apprehend the changing world in which we live. Among geographers studying the rise of what has become a very broad spectrum of activity covered by the term 'new localism' (which can include anything from grassroots anarchism to top-down government planning initiatives), the definitions of 'localism' and the ways in which it is framed and understood have become increasingly nuanced. Nick Clarke has recently surveyed these different definitions and suggested that among the most recent (and, I would argue, the most useful) is that given by post-structural geographers who view the local and localism 'as open, porous, permeable, heterogeneous, incoherent, dynamic and incomplete; a product of mixture, encounter, intermingling [and] characterised by juxtapositions and co-presences' (2013: 499). In this, Clarke is influenced by Doreen Massey's more progressive understanding of place which has, for some time now, argued that 'the identities of places are always unfixed, contested and multiple' (1994: 5).

In the 1990s, Massey interrogated what she called a 'reactionary' view of place (that emerged in relation to the rise of local studies) 'as bounded, as in various ways a site of an authenticity, as singular, fixed and unproblematic in its identity' (1994: 5). It is just such a critique of place and locality that has been extended by environmentally minded literary critics such as Timothy Morton and Ursula Heise in their respective moves towards a more fluid and decentred 'ecological thought' and an 'eco-cosmopolitan' sense of planet, both of which were addressed in the introduction. Building on the work of these important critics, I argue that Deakin, Oswald and Dee show that such fluid and cosmopolitan moves can come precisely *through* local work. However, it is worth gesturing here to a debate between Massey's view of places as open and unfixed and the work of Arif Dirlik who has argued for what he calls a 'critical localism' in which a place might be, if not bounded, nonetheless 'grounded'. The local, as he sees it, 'suggests groundedness from below, and a flexible and porous boundary around it, without closing out the extralocal, all the way to the global' (1996: 155). Though it might seem strange to begin an exploration of such watery and riverine localism with such an earthy metaphor, it is precisely through such a 'grounded' and 'critical localism' that place and the local begin to open up in intricate and relational ways. But Dirlik's point is that they can do so – they can be 'open and relational' – without simply becoming *space*. For the people that live in these places or are invested in them, these places can maintain something of their autonomy, their capacity to assert, contest and create identity and meaning for themselves, whether through community activism and conservation work, or through written and artistic representations, or even through those lively points of intersection between the two.

Confluence

In 1997, Common Ground began work on a three-year celebration of the River Stour in Dorset. Its project 'Confluence' was a celebration more broadly of water itself and the vital but often overlooked role it plays in our lives, but as ever it sought to explore the broader theme through a lens focused on the local. In this case though, the local implied a shift both up and down the scales of place, both down the scale to a fluvial register that drew attention to one particular aspect of the towns and villages it focused on but also up the scale insofar as it drew a number of these places into relation with one another and with wider, water-related issues. In an introduction to the project's anthology of poetry *The River's Voice* (2000), Clifford and King gestured towards some of the emerging concerns around global water security that were being aired in environmental debates at the time: 'Consider the melting of the ice caps, the damming of the Hwang Ho, the dramatic retreat of glaciers in the Himalayas and the Rocky Mountains,' they proposed; 'consider the drying up of the world's fourth largest inland sea, Lake Aral in Central Asia' (where 60,000 square kilometres of water had evaporated over three decades). 'Then look at the spring, stream or river which is the reason why your settlement is where it is' (14). It was also in 1997 that the social historian and contributor to *Second Nature* Colin Ward published his book *Reflected in Water*, a critique of the creeping privatization of water in Britain and a study of the wider displacements of millions globally through dam-building.

Clifford and King and Ward were concerned that water, something they believed to be a common good belonging to all, was being abused and mismanaged in private hands and undervalued as a fragile global resource. They felt that the long history of local communities' relationships with water was being lost and with it a body of knowledge and culture that might be of value in an increasingly unstable-looking future. This prompted an attempt to find imaginative ways of reacquainting people with the rivers, streams, wells and springs in their local areas; ways of opening the idea of a river up into a more expansive and interconnected view of the whole catchment, its geology, its histories, its people, its uses; the many different names and their meanings, the wildlife, flowers and trees; and all of these things as a part of what the charity described as an 'assemblage', one founded again on that principle of local distinctiveness (Clifford and King 1999: 8).

The fluid subject matter of the project also set out to draw attention to the living process of place itself and led to the form of the project being focused on music and performance. Not only this, but it was also choreographed carefully across space and time. Confluence saw Common Ground commission and organize around forty, mostly musical, participatory events running from source to sea along the River Stour over a period of three years. The project set out to unearth and celebrate local and oral histories of rivers, farming practices, folklore, names of even the smallest streams, architecture and archaeology, customs such as well dressings and baptisms, and the languages and cultures of the kinds of livelihood associated with rivers, all as a way of opening them up imaginatively. It also, however, opened the places themselves up as well, drawing attention to the fact that all of these disparate places in the catchment of the Stour were connected by the same water on which they depended. The emphasis on music encouraged the widest participation and soon new choirs were formed, and new ballads, carols, poems and drinking songs were written and performed by residents that drew on their memories, local knowledge and research of the river catchment.[2] From source to sea, it had people working together to produce one long living performance that, early on, looked ahead to the later events and, later on, reflected on the events gone by. The project was trans-local then, but more than that, it served as a living metonym for much wider interconnections around water itself. While the emphasis of the project seems to have been, at times, a little too emphatically celebratory, perhaps at the expense of the darker side of river stories – histories of drownings, for example, or contemporary battles against pollution – it did nonetheless encourage a dynamic and outward-looking view on the local, encouraging people to consider the influx and outflow of water through a town, a parish, a street, even a house.

Rivers have long been deployed in the traditional 'high culture' of Europe to demonstrate power and territory, and to support and establish national myths and their imagined communities. We might think of the classical statues of the Tiber and the Nile unearthed in Rome in the early sixteenth century and placed

---

[2] Detail about this project comes from two key sources: first, it comes from the booklet *Rivers, Rhynes and Running Brooks* (Clifford and King 2000a); and second from selected editions of the *Confluence Newsletter* editions 1–10 (Common Ground 1998–2000). These are to be found in the Special Collections Library at the University of Exeter.

next to one another in the Vatican by Pope Leo X. In an anthropomorphized display of power and prestige they proposed the association of one great civilization with another. From that moment on, as Claudio Lazarro has shown, rivers featured as speaking parts in civic and political theatre, symbols of their localities and public mouthpieces of territorial relations under the power of the state. This tradition found its way to England when, in 1545, John Leland wrote his long poem *Cygnea Cantio* praising Henry VIII in the voice of a swan swimming the River Thames from Oxford to Greenwich, a route that takes in Windsor, Hampton Court and the Tower of London on the way. By the nineteenth century, the same route had become a two-day excursion by boat for wealthy passengers providing what Simon Schama calls 'an entire course of gratifying instruction in the history of the British constitution' (1995: 363). It was John Leland, too, who had first ventured out in 1539 to travel England and write a topography of the country, gathering the nation into one comprehensive text in the hope that King Henry VIII would 'have ready knowledge at the fyrst sighte' of his domain, a project that would soon be continued by William Camden and Christopher Saxton (qtd. in Schwyzer 2009: 244).

We might also think of Michael Drayton's early-seventeenth-century poetic atlas of Britain *Poly-Olbion* (published in two parts in 1612 and 1622) in which the geography and a certain imaginative history of the country is spoken in the voices of the rivers themselves, gathering the country into a harmonious unity comparable to Saxton's first *Atlas* (1579). The River Dart in the West Country, for example, tells the tale (repeated from Geoffrey of Monmouth) of the founding of Britain by Brutus and his boat full of soldiers after the Trojan war. It is an originary myth intended to secure a classical lineage for the nation. They make landfall at Totnes a little upstream on the River Dart, kill the aboriginal giant Gogmagog and discover the race of Britons, so called after Brutus (we will return to this tale when we look at Alice Oswald shortly) (Drayton 1612: 11–12). Each of these allegorical representations of a river performs its own riverine aesthetic in order to lay claim to territory or to assert an identity, to gather in and govern the nation.

However, in such nationalist aesthetics, rivers become entities symbolically separated from their material reality. They seem fixed in a reified and idealized air at odds with their everyday treatment and use. In his *H_2O and the Waters of*

Forgetfulness (1986), the Austrian critic and philosopher Ivan Illich sets out to explore the 'dual nature' of water through what he calls a 'historicity of matter' (4). In understanding the history of water, rather than inquiring after its cultural representations, images and meanings that might offer an ideal and figurative account, he inquires after the material processes that *produce* water in its civic and social form. How do we treat it and change it from one thing into another? What does it become through us and how does that new thing relate to its earlier form running down from the moors or mountains? Thinking along these lines we might ask what it means, then, when a contradiction occurs between the symbolic representation of rivers as, in the words of Simon Schama again, 'the arterial bloodstream of the people [of a nation]' and the state of crisis that had emerged in the 1970s and 1980s in the UK over the pollution and degradation of its actual rivers (1995: 363). By the time of Confluence, great improvements had been made in water quality but it was nonetheless reported in 1995 that nearly a quarter of all drinking water in England and Wales was failing to meet the requirements of a new pesticide test (Ward 1997: 120). The government had also begun to bend and undermine European conservation laws. The EU had set environmental standards on how much pollution was permitted to be drained into rivers as opposed to the open sea so, as Colin Ward recounts, the Secretary of State for the Environment, John Gummer, in 1994 declared forty-eight inland kilometres of the River Humber in the north and a similar distance on the River Severn in the west to be open sea. It was a decision that was later to be found 'unlawful' in the High Court (119–20).

In opposition to such national manipulations of the cultural geography of rivers, Common Ground were keen to explore a riverine art grounded in the very localized ways in which ordinary life was connected to water. Confluence would not be a project *about* the River Stour so much as a project *on* and *with* the river, involving the people who lived on its banks or along its tributaries. The project began at the river's source, in the landscaped gardens of the Stourhead estate and the first event saw a storyteller take people on a walk around the appropriately mythic structures of the park telling creation myths from various different cultures in a tour focused on the idea of origins. Downstream at Fontmell Magna, at the crack of dawn on 1 May, people were invited to take a guided walk along the river to listen to the chorus of birds before settling down over breakfast to a performance of a new piece of music based on the song of the riverside birds they had been listening to as they walked. Collaborating with a local historian, the resident composer Karen Wimhurst wrote a new choral work for a ruined watermill in Sturminster Newton that resurrected an historic glossary of working terminology associated with the mill. It was performed one evening when the mill itself was floodlit and recordings of its working parts were amplified across the river to people on the far bank. A new eight-piece group called the Cutwater Band made a number of public appearances over the three years working their way downstream playing river-based folk songs on the many bridges to groups of picnickers sat in meadows on the banks. In the evenings there was a raucous 'Fish Cabaret' in Gillingham which was so popular it was followed a year later by a similar 'Rain Cabaret' in Winterborne Stickland. Musicians and a group of plumbers came together in one instance to develop a range of musical instruments made from household plumbing. Performances were led by the 'boghorn' which made use of the inflow and outflow of a toilet bowl and was accompanied by a calorifier adapted with a top-mounted trombone slide and various percussive instruments made from dolly tubs, steel pipes, a galvanized immersion heater and a set of ballcock maracas.[3]

Perhaps the largest and most surprising event of the project was in the summer of 2000, when the streets of Blandford Forum were taken over by a 'Water Market' where a diverse array of perspectives on the river found themselves exhibited together for the day. At the Water Market you could take to the river for canoe lessons, try your hand at water divining, seek advice from plumbers and hydro-energy engineers or learn about riverbank wildlife conservation; you could try organically grown local watercress, freshly caught trout and a range of different mineral waters from natural springs in neighbouring counties. Confluence was an intensely local project but by the end it had received coverage in a number of national newspapers, the idea of water markets had caught on in other counties and the sound of the boghorn had been heard across the country on BBC Radio 4. There was something captivating about its heterogeneous way of thinking about, and working with, landscape and water in imaginative but quite ordinary ways. Albeit rather

---

[3] Detail about these events comes from selected editions of the *Confluence Newsletter* editions 1–10 (Common Ground 1998–2000). These are to be found in the Special Collections Library at the University of Exeter.

celebratory, Confluence stimulated a dynamic creativity at the heart of the places in which it worked. It generated a revitalized exploration of how the people of the places identified with their locality that was simultaneously grounded in reflections on local history, culture and wildlife and outward-looking and global in its thematic concerns.

There are two books associated with this little-known project that have come to be much better known than the project itself and that themselves have served as important precursors to the wider New Nature Writing as it came to be identified later on after 2005. They are Roger Deakin's *Waterlog* and Alice Oswald's *Dart* both of which were pioneering in their own way. As has been mentioned, Deakin had worked with Clifford and King at Friends of the Earth and in 1983 had founded Common Ground with them, working on projects associated with trees especially. *Waterlog* was not a part of Confluence and Deakin, by that time, was not working particularly closely with Common Ground but it is a book that emerged from those early attempts to turn a fresh eye on landscape and revitalize a tradition of topographical writing, and Deakin would visit Dorset for a launch of the book at a Confluence event in 1999 (both Clifford and King are also thanked in the acknowledgements as well) (Common Ground (December 1998–August 2000) 4: 2).

Waterlog is a book of domestic British travel writing with a difference. Unlike the first topographical and chorographic works of Leland, Saxton and Camden, and unlike the much later works of domestic tourism by H. V. Morton and J. B. Priestly in the twentieth century, Deakin was not in search of the nation. *Waterlog* is not a book that views the land as dominion to be summed up and mapped, or as scenery to be consumed at arm's length. On the contrary, Deakin immersed himself completely and set out to swim a fairly ad hoc selection of the country's lakes, seas, channels, tarns, rivers and ponds. Though the book travels, it does not attempt to bring together a consistent national geography of Britain. Rather, it is an attempt to alter our perspective, to localize it in a distinctly corporeal way, looking for what he calls a 'frog's-eye view' (1999: 1). Deakin was, as his friend Robert Macfarlane has suggested (borrowing a phrase from John Hanson Mitchell), an 'explorer of the undiscovered country of the nearby' (2010b). Deakin describes swimming as 'a subversive activity' because it breaks out of the 'signposted, labelled, and officially "interpreted" … virtual reality of things' (1999: 4). Swimming appeals to him because it offers a more intimate perspective: 'You are *in* nature, part and parcel of it, in a far more complete and intense way than on dry land, and your sense of the present is overwhelming' (1999: 4). Wordsworth casts a long shadow over the book and the search for such intimate geographies stems from a fear that 'the world is too much with us' and that we might be better guided by something closer to the earth, or nature, that which subtends our human environments. The style of thinking that comes from swimming with its 'overwhelming' experience of the present is a loosening of the usual human, rational grasp. It too offers an intense localization of experience that opens out onto something much larger but, for Deakin, it is a form of personal, embodied experience opening out onto a lively and enchanted sense of wonder at elemental creation. The book flirts with the idea of retreat, escape, refuge but it is not so much the refuge that is of interest as the liminal edge between the world and the elemental immersion.

Escape gives way to trespass in Deakin's desire to get under the driven and purposeful geography of modern life and he is not afraid of the conflicts this throws up. After swimming in a river near Stockbridge he is chased off by two figures described in Dickensian caricature as 'a portly porter with a beard and Alsatian, and a gangling figure on a bike with binoculars, strawberry pink with ire' at whom he quotes Cobbett, defending his 'rights as a free swimmer' (1999: 31). Elsewhere he coins the verb 'to quive' ('I *quived* silently into the reeds and floated there up to my nose like a crocodile until they had gone') from the name of the relentless pursuer of the protagonist in Geoffrey Household's *Rogue Male*, Major Quive-Smith (1999: 60). Running through the book is a certain self-confessed 'boyish pleasure' (another phrase from Wordsworth) that is exuberant and playful and seems to wave its truant pages at the 'getting and spending' of the inland world (60). It is this exuberance perhaps that has made the book so influential on the wild swimming movement that seems to have flourished in the book's wake (see, e.g., Kate Rew's guidebook *Wild Swim* (2008) which acknowledges a debt to Deakin and *Waterlog*).

However, like the Confluence project that was contemporary to it, it does also make a powerful argument for becoming better acquainted with our waters in their modern form, at times with a level of pollution '240 times over the recommended safe limit' (Deakin 1999: 141), at times drastically 'over-abstracted' (175) or 'humiliated' in 'outsized concrete canyons' (67–8). The Romantic theme of 'getting back to nature' is complicated throughout by that dual identity of water again, reminding us of Jamie Lorimer's multiplication of 'natures' discussed in the introduction to this book (2015: 7). After swimming in the River Lark in Suffolk and discovering that it was once known locally as the Jordan for the baptisms that had been performed in it until 1972, Deakin phones the Environment Agency to enquire whether it might once again be safe to do so only to be told that his question is 'multifunctional and could not therefore be answered over the telephone' (1999: 66). After following up the inquiry with a letter he is warned of a whole list of diseases associated with sewage effluent and advised not to immerse his congregation (he is mistaken for a priest) (66).

One of the most striking passages in fact comes towards the end when he visits Camden Council's Oasis leisure centre in Covent Garden where, in the late 1990s, you could swim in an outdoor pool for only £1. As he looks up at the city, juxtaposed with such a built and developed environment, something of the ambiguous and liminal geography of water is amplified. Immersed in water he is at the interface of the human and elemental environments, looking in from a partial outside. If one of the achievements of the new form of nature writing to emerge from *Second Nature* was to overcome the binary opposition of country and city established by a metropolitan perspective on the rural, here it is turned on its head in an elemental and liminal 'frog's eye view' on the capital city itself. *Waterlog* is a book about our capacity to feel enchanted by that most local of all apprehensions, personal immersion, 'full of mysteries, doubts and uncertainties' (86).

> All around, London was breathing, clicking and buzzing under an orange sky. Floating on my back in the pool and looking up, I saw the balconies of council flats and bright offices lit up with people at computers in the windows, and, up above, a black starry sky with now and again a jet. As a swimmer, I felt connected to everyday life in a way I never do in an indoor pool. (317)

The immersion in water seems oddly continuous with an immersion in the 'everyday life' of the city and yet it seems to revitalize that everyday life as well. It seems balanced ambiguously between presence and suspension, intimacy and hiatus. Like the riverine localism of the Confluence project that frayed the edges of the places it connected along the route of the river, the identity of place becomes a slippery thing, always ready to be reconstituted by fresh ways of looking. Deakin's sense of enchantment is always grounded in local detail, but the local itself is a Heraclitean and replenishing thing.

In a review of a number of New Nature Writing books, and responding to a conference in Cambridge in 2007 on 'Passionate Natures' (organized and run by Robert Macfarlane in memory of Deakin), David Matless addresses 'questions of affect, enchantment and animation' that were becoming characteristic of the form (2009: 185). He proposes setting out a continuum of 'wonder' on which books of the genre might be placed, with 'Wonderful!!!' at one end and 'I wonder???' at the other (184). His concern is that 'for all its joy and elation, [enchantment] can carry a submissive quality' and his words are directed at Deakin's (and Macfarlane's) boyish and exuberant prose style (185). However, there is also room here for a nuanced understanding of enchantment in a modern context. Jane Bennett has recently made a claim for enchantment as, in fact, 'a state of interactive fascination, not fall-to-your-knees awe' (2001: 5). She concedes that the charge of 'naive optimism' that is most often raised against it does suppose 'links between enchantment and mindlessness, between joy and forgetfulness' but adds that sometimes 'a certain forgetfulness is ethically indispensable' (10), especially in pulling us out of 'enervating cynicism' (13). *Waterlog* seems to operate in that space of 'interactive fascination' and it gives the book an individual but strong moral charge that will no doubt encourage its readers, not only to take pleasure from, but also to care for, their local rivers. Its connection to Common Ground's 'Confluence' project is a reminder of that – emerging from a convergence of the arts and the conservation movement – it is a book that poses a challenge to more top-down projects of chorography or the urban preoccupations of picturesque tourism, the agendas of which have been related to stabilizing or homogenizing aesthetics of national identity.

Dart

In December 2003 Robert Macfarlane published something of a call to arms in defence of British nature writing. He began this by offering a strong defence of Alice Oswald's book-length poem *Dart* (winner of the 2001 T. S. Eliot Award) from an attack by A. N. Wilson. For Macfarlane, *Dart* might have been a long poem rather than a prose work but its vivid and innovative representation of place aligned it with a resurgent interest in the literature of landscape, place and nature. In a gripe over the relationship between poetry and nature, Wilson had 'blamed Wordsworth' for the expectation that 'poets ought to be country dwellers' and 'lovers of unwrecked England'. The vitriol was surprising. Wilson goes on:

> When the radio performance of Dart was over, I sat down and read the book through. For half an hour, it produced in me the novel sensation of wishing, quite passionately, that the rivers of England could be filled with nuclear waste and the countryside concreted over. Of course the feeling evaporated. But it reminded me that there are more ways than one of being corrupted. (2003: n.p.)

Macfarlane was curious about where this was coming from and traced it back to Stella Gibbons's *Cold Comfort Farm*, a 1932 parody of the popular rural novel that planted suspicion of rural representations generally in the British psyche. This, of course, speaks to the kinds of warnings offered by Williams in *The Country and the City* as well but what Macfarlane suggests is that this prejudice had eclipsed a whole body of work that explored what he called 'sanctity in the human relationship with the natural world at a time of cultural cynicism and disconnection' (2003: n.p.). A certain prejudice was preventing people from acknowledging the world of difference between, for example, the stereotypes of Mary Webb's rural novels (it was Webb more than anyone, though also the lingering influence of Hardy and Lawrence, that *Cold Comfort Farm* was attacking), or the distant, idealized urban perceptions of the countryside that Williams was so careful to historicize, and a more sensitized, intelligent tradition of which Macfarlane felt Oswald's *Dart* was a part. He mentions a handful of British and Irish authors for whom landscape and place have featured importantly in subtle and complex ways, and who have themselves featured importantly in the post-war canon, among them Seamus Heaney, Geoffrey Hill, Ronald Blythe, Gavin Maxwell and Bruce Chatwin.

Macfarlane's argument recalls the agenda of *Second Nature* twenty years on, though also, perhaps, it suggests how that earlier work was slipping from memory. In fact, a subsequent series of essays that he published in *The Guardian* in an attempt to revise and revitalize the popular perception of landscape writing is collected on *The Guardian*'s website as his 'Common Ground' essays now in a nod of allegiance (Macfarlane 2005a). That he singles out Alice Oswald (as well as, it should be added, Roger Deakin and Richard Mabey) is no surprise. As a poet Oswald has shown that same experimental search for new perspectives, new ways of thinking about and writing about place and this is nowhere more evident than in *Dart*. She reflects, in a Ted Hughes Memorial Lecture, on her desire to break down a sense of distance that she attributes to a 'lyrical, romantic, pastoral tradition of "Nature poetry"', one that she suggests feels 'as if the poet was sitting on a rock on a hill looking at the world through a telescope' (2005b: n.p.). Again, then, we have an author writing about landscape anxious about the particular 'Nature' tradition she draws on. Hughes was a great influence on her attempt to break down this distance, but so too had been Sue Clifford and Angela King with their work on Confluence, though this is less well acknowledged. In fact, Oswald had contributed two 'river poems' to Common Ground's anthology *The River's Voice* edited by Clifford and King and published as a part of Confluence in 2000. One of her poems had even been illustrated and printed on a postcard for the project's publicity. *Dart* itself also makes reference to two of the more obscure sources from a reading list on rivers published by Common Ground as a part of the project, but perhaps most striking is the fact that in its draft stages Oswald was also thinking about *Dart* in musical terms. Early on she described her attempt 'to orchestrate [the poem] like a kind of Jazz, with various river-workers and river dwellers composing their own parts' (1999: n.p.). This immediately brings to mind the participatory musical events that Common Ground had been choreographing along the Stour, the choirs writing new watery ballads and drinking songs, the musical plumbers and the local history groups, all collaborating together on new musical works celebrating the river and the cultures and working landscapes that it has drawn to its banks.

The reason for drawing this connection with Common Ground is not to undermine the originality of what Oswald was doing – the poem goes far beyond these connections and takes the voice of the River Dart in the poem in its own remarkable direction – but rather it is to see the poem's use of a heteroglossic or polyvocal form not, as some critics have suggested, as drawing on Eliot's *The Waste Land*, but within its rightful context of collaboration between the conservation movement and the arts, a collaboration that helped to shift the British literary aesthetics of landscape away from a generalized nationalism towards more experimental practices working in thoughtful ways with real people and emerging out of distinctive place cultures. Oswald no doubt saw the value in Confluence's multifaceted approach to the Stour catchment, its locally distinctive assemblage of cultural history, wildlife and natural energy and, much as Clifford and King would have wanted, her poem emerged as something of a parallel project in the catchment of the Dart. She does something very different with *Dart* in the end but the imagination and community participation in the 'Confluence' project do seem to have inspired something in her.

Dart is one long book-length poem that follows the West Country river from its source in the upper reaches of Dartmoor down through the villages and towns of south Devon to the sea on the south coast at Dartmouth. Like Michael Drayton's seventeenth-century *Poly-Olbion* it is articulated in the first person and Oswald claims in an introductory note that 'all voices are to be read as the river's mutterings' (Oswald 2002a: ii). However, the voice is based upon a carefully crafted composite of tape-recorded interviews that she conducted with people along the river:

> I decided to take along a tape-recorder. At the moment, my method is to tape a conversation with someone who works on the Dart, then go home and write it down from memory. I then work with these two kinds of record – one precise, one distorted by the mind – to generate the poem's language. It's experimental and very against my grain, this mixture of journalism and imagination, but the results are exciting. Above all, it preserves the idea of the poem's living voice being everyone's, not just the poet's. (1999: n.p.)

This is language figured collaboratively and with an unusual self-restraint ('very against my grain'). The craft itself becomes a matter of negotiating between artistic vision and real voices, an inclusive balancing act.

The poem begins in the mode of a question – 'Who's that moving alive over the moor?' – and continues with an animalistic curiosity nosing its way into sense like Ted Hughes's 'Wodwo', less an articulation of meaning than one long listening inquiry.[4] Deryn Rees-Jones has noticed this parallel too, as both

---

[4] What am I? Nosing here, turning leaves over
Following a faint stain on the air to the river's edge
I enter water. Who am I to split
The glassy grain of water looking upward.

(Hughes, 'Wodwo' in 2003: 183)

poets use a voice not their own but a voice emerging as consciousness and language at the same time. She quotes Leonard M. Scigaj who suggests that 'Wodwo' discovers 'itself *as* it discovers the world' (2005: 235). Like 'Wodwo' then, *Dart* must discover itself through articulating what it encounters, in this case the language of others. It is a fugitive voice in search of its own continuity, moving from being to being: 'I depend on being not noticed, which keeps me small and rather nimble, I can swim miles naked with midges round my head, watching wagtails, I'm soft' (2002: 7). This 'soft' listening voice of the poem was there right from its methodological beginnings in research. As the ferryman between Dartmouth and Kingswear said when asked if he recognized his own voice in the poem, 'she's used her skills to stand aside and allow people who are part of the Dart a say in her poem' (Oswald 2002b).

One of the particular achievements of this method is to bring to bear in the poem a range of surprisingly intimate working vocabularies and turns of phrase: from the poacher's dialect term 'voler' meaning the 'unique clean line a salmon makes in water' (2002a: 38) to the water abstractor who describes the way sewage is 'stirred and settled out and wasted off, looped back, macerated, digested, clarified and returned to the river' (2002: 30). Or the following drawn from conversations with a worker at the woollen mill:

> tufted felting hanks tops spindles slubbings
> hoppers and rollers and slatted belts
> bales of carded wool the colour of limestone
> and wool puffs flying through tubes distributed by cyclones.
>
> (19)

In each there is embedded a distinct way of thinking about and apprehending the river in which the river's cultural meanings begin to proliferate in intricate ways. The poacher's predatory and quiet watchfulness, the water abstractor's machinic efficiency or the wool worker's bouncing, kinetic energy: each reveals a dialogue with qualities that the river affords for different communities of people. This micro-localism is so very far removed from the riverine chorography of Michael Drayton's *Poly-Olbion*, even subversively so. By choosing to present the many voices of the poem as the river's one voice, *Dart* emulates Drayton's own many-voiced, many-rivered Britain, but the difference is one of scale. While Drayton gathers the many regions into one voice, Oswald shows even the one region to be intricately composed of disparate voices, striking up an interesting intertextual dialogue with *Poly-Olbion*. A closer look at the way this dialogue plays out shows a curious tension at work in the way that Oswald inflects the traditions she is working within.

Poly-Olbion was published in parts from 1612 onwards, following a wave of chorographical writings[5] and Christopher Saxton's *Atlas* of 1579, the first collection of county maps of Britain. However, while it fits in with these other projects that helped to bring the nation as a whole under the purview and control of a centralized authority, *Poly-Olbion* was also subversive in the way it asserted its own authority and in this sense it does bear closer comparison with Oswald's *Dart*. Drayton is preoccupied with rivers, most of his text being given over to their description in one way or another. He is quite conscious of their capacity to be, as Andrew McRae suggests, 'at once evocative of place yet curiously placeless' (2008: 508). A river is a slippery character in all manner of ways and therein perhaps lies some of its appeal to the subversive author, as in this dynamic descriptive passage early on in Drayton's poem:

> I view those wanton Brookes, that waxing, still doe wane;
> That scarclie can conceive, but brought to bed againe;
> Scarce rising from the Spring (that is their naturall Mother)
> To growe into a streame, but buried in another.
>
> (1612: 5)

Richard Helgerson sees *Poly-Olbion* as a radical text with an important part to play in chorography's shift from an England whose authority lay with the crown to an England whose authority lay with the land itself. In the first edition of Saxton's *Atlas* (commissioned by the queen's privy council) the frontispiece bears an engraving of Queen Elizabeth I 'enthroned, surmounted by her arms and an emblem of her rule, flanked by figures of cosmography and geography, underscored by verses celebrating the accomplishments of her benign reign. ... As we turn the pages we are invited to remember

---

[5] William Lambarde's *Perambulation of Kent* (1576); William Harrison's 'Description of England', published as a preface to Raphael Holinshed's *Chronicles* (1577 and 1586); Richard Carew's *Survey of Cornwall* (1602); George Owen's *Description of Pembrokeshire* (1602–1603); and William Camden's *Britannia* (1607).

that Cornwall is the queen's, Hampshire the queen's, Dorset the queen's and so on' (Helgerson 1986: 54). By 1612 in *Poly-Olbion,* maps of Saxton's that had previously held the royal insignia were now adorned instead with multiple sea nymphs and decorative boats and the frontispiece bore not the image of the queen, but of Great Britain herself in just the same posture and frame. 'Positive value', Helgerson continues, 'is invested in an implicitly antimonarchic image, an image of the headless (or, better, the many-headed) body of the land' (78). The River Dart became, for Drayton, one of these many heads invested with a new importance (the Dart is even a queen herself in the poem).

What we see then, in these 'curiously placeless' river narratives, is an emphasis on change, fluid boundaries and shifting authority. In Drayton's Britain the land itself is privileged, and its 'many-headed' network of regional voices, though all speaking with a nationalist unison, are a challenge to the single head of sovereign power. Oswald, then, takes one of what were many voices united under the myth of the nation state in Drayton and recreates it as *itself* many voiced. At a glance this appears to be a challenge to nationalist chorography in favour of local allegiances, but it is worth remembering that this does also seem to be in the subversive tradition of Drayton himself and we might argue that just as Drayton asserted land over monarch, Oswald is challenging an externally imposed national unity with an intricate and inclusive localism. Oswald is writing her poem in the immediate wake of the referendums on devolution and amid a growing atmosphere of discontent in terms of national unity. Raymond Williams had identified this sense as early as 1984 when in an interview with Philip Cooke he had asked:

> What are the genuine alternative units capable of developing a politics speaking to the interests of the people rather than the unjustified units of a presumed nation-state? Where there is a national entity such as Wales or Scotland, there is already a measure of self-definition, a real base. But it does not only occur in such places. (1989: 239)

Totnes is perhaps the most notable urban centre on the River Dart and as the heart of the Transition movement it comes coded with a certain significance regarding autonomy and dynamic localism. It is hard to ignore this when we consider the shifting political landscape alluded to in *Dart*'s relationship with *Poly-Olbion*. This becomes all the more intriguing when we consider that not only is Totnes a site of pioneering localism but, according to Drayton, and Geoffrey of Monmouth before him, it is also the site of the landing of the first humans in Britain. After the Trojan war, Brutus and a group of soldiers took flight in search of somewhere to found a new civilization and eventually landed at Totnes and made their mark by killing the last of the uninhabited archipelago's ogres called Gogmagog nearby (in fact the inhumanly over-large footprint that Brutus first imprinted when they made landfall is preserved in concrete as a tourist attraction in the town centre). This story of nation-founding arrival is the one aspect of Drayton's account that Oswald chooses to retell in her own way in *Dart*.

Oswald retells the Brutus myth, but what is most interesting in her version is its situation between the voices of the sewage worker and the stonewaller. Her tale of Brutus begins: 'It happened when oak trees were men/when water was still water'. The latter phrase recalls Ivan Illich's 'historicity of matter' as it recalls the previous sewage worker's 'macerations' (1986: 30). The epigraph for *Dart* is also from Ivan Illich actually: 'Water always comes with an ego and an alter ego.' Perhaps as strange as the water's 'alter ego' here though is that 'oak trees were men'. Here she seems to be challenging the idea that Britain was unpopulated before Brutus and his men arrived from Troy. In fact, Oswald is very careful to represent the river as busy with life as Brutus arrives: cormorants, sparrows, salmon, oysters, shelduck, heron, river crabs, foxes and seals, not to mention the 'skirts of the trees' and perhaps most importantly the repeated 'race of freshwater' (2002: 31–2). The implication is that the myth of nationhood that builds up around Brutus and secures a classical origin for the British eclipses these pre-existent 'races' of wildlife. There is also the implication that the infrastructure of the nation requires that we materially reconstitute that 'race of freshwater' (abstracting water into its alter ego) to serve such needs of the nation as sewage processing and waste disposal. Perhaps for this reason then, Brutus and his men are described, in the same breath, as 'outcasts of the earth, [*and*] kings / of the green island England' (30). This is a curious juxtaposition of phrases that addresses Englishness in a surprising way. One cannot be English and of the earth since the two are opposed here.

After the retelling of the Brutus myth, she moves into the voice of the stonewaller in a stiff gear-shift of voices between the metred lines of the heroic narrative and the slow prose of the stonewaller obliviously at work. The hinge between Brutus and the stonewaller, though, is the giant Gogmagog himself who, we know already, is to have his 'throat slit' (2002: 31).

> At Totnes, limping and swaying,
> they set foot on the land.
> There's a giant walking towards them,
> a flat stone in each hand:
>
> stonewaller
>
> You get upriver stones and downriver stones. Beyond Totnes bridge and above Longmarsh the stones are horribly grey chunks, a waste of haulage, but in the estuary they're slatey flat stones, much darker, maybe it's to do with the river's changes. (32)

The stonewaller *is* Gogmagog. The shift from the more classical, rhymed quatrains to prose is also a shift in perspective from a hot-headed gang gearing up for war to someone going about their daily business. The daily business, of course, is a local one, working closely with the land. Stonewalling, unlike bricklaying, requires the careful use of the pre-existent order of shapes to make its lines. It engages with the forms of the land carefully to make its own narrative. And the stonewaller is under threat from the origin myth of the nation about to impose itself. These new kings of England are outcasts of the earth and the stonewaller, for his attention to the earth, becomes an outcast of England.

Dart is a poem that uses a river's indeterminacy – its doubleness, at once placed and placeless – to look at locality. Like Common Ground's 'Confluence' project it shows the local to be an intricate and ongoing performance that commends itself to wider appreciation, but one that is sometimes at odds with the ambitions of the nation at large, or at least caught in a tension between the two. What both of these projects, and Deakin's *Waterlog*, show through their interactions with rivers is that a recuperated indeterminacy itself can be an asset and a resource for the renewal of identity. The rivers are material presences passing through the local here, but they are also metaphors for the Heraclitean energy of place as an open-ended experiment in living; and for the way these experiments are connected and in dialogue with other experiments in other places too. Figured in this way, the contemporary sense of the local that this chapter is exploring, in fact, meets Timothy Morton's argument for 'a poetics of anywhere' in which place is always interrupted by its own 'uncanny' double (2010: 50–2). But the point of the uncanny is that it is both at the same time, the energy arising from the tension between the two identities. The recession of the familiar into the unfamiliar can reveal, for sharp moments of clarity, the excess that lies beyond our conventional ways of apprehending or of living out locality and stretch the imagination to do things differently, or just deliberately. But this means not seizing locality too tightly, not asserting it so much as working with the indeterminacy in ways that can be outward-looking and inward-looking, forward-looking and backward-looking at one and the same time.

What better example of the slippery indeterminacy and excess lying in wait beneath the familiar apprehension of place than this passage in *Dart* when the river speaks to the canoeist, trying to lure him out of his canoe into the rough water? There is danger and mortal dread to it, certainly, but there is also an anarchic *genius loci* seducing the tourist away from his comfortable distance towards a sea-change:

> come falleth in my push-you where it hurts
> and let me rough you under, be a laugh
> and breathe me please in whole inhale
>
> come warmeth, I can outcanouvre you
> into the smallest small where it moils up
> and masses under the sloosh gates, put your head,
> it looks a good one, full of kiss
> and known to those you love, come roll it on my stones,
> come tongue-in-skull, come drinketh, come sleepeth
>
> (Oswald 2002: 15)

The passage is an upward radiation and a lure downwards at one and the same time. Its plays on language show a voice capable of bending the structures and rules of language to its will. It is a voice speaking across the slippery line between the familiar and the unfamiliar, between place and placelessness, that site of creative energy in which the local may be redreamed and remade.

Four Fields

Fiona Stafford's writing on the literature of the Romantic period has explored the way in which, towards the end of the eighteenth century, a cultural shift took place in the British literary tradition in which 'local detail ceased to be regarded as transient, irrelevant, or restrictive, and began to seem essential to art with any aspiration to permanence' (2010: 30). Recourse to values, feelings and meanings that were grounded in distinctive cultural geographies began to be understood as what authors and works and even publics, wherever they might be, had in common. Far from dividing and isolating people, locality came to be understood as the very difference that we share. It is true that not all forms of localism operate in such an outward-looking way and she warns that 'if the indigenous becomes the goal rather than a starting point, local art is in danger of seeming divisive or oppressive' (9). But we can see in the kinds of work that this chapter has discussed so far that, for some, the local offers a source of enchanting beauty and social energy that radiates upwards and outwards. We have seen that those qualities which can make the local so vulnerable to being marginalized and overlooked – its subtle and intricate distinctiveness, its difficulties and complexities – can also be precisely those that give an art founded on such qualities its enduring meaning. In the Confluence project and in *Waterlog*, locality was bound up with an intimate process of rediscovery, a way of being, thinking, listening and writing with fresh eyes for the elements on which it, and we, depend. In *Dart*, locality was revealed in the overlooked fine grain of a place and the underappreciated lives that make up its social and cultural fabric. The poem attempted to do justice to this, even to the extent of expressing an argumentative relation to the more homogenizing movements of nationalist art. In each case, the vividness and inventiveness with which the authors commend these places to their readers, the confidence that they have in the value of local detail, make them easy to appreciate and relate to elsewhere.

We might think of this as 'parochial' in the sense that Patrick Kavanagh famously suggested, in that the word might refer to someone 'never in any doubt about the social and artistic validity of his parish' (2003: 237). It is in this sense of the term 'parochial' that Stafford describes 'the life-giving work of local artists' that 'grows unshowily from the ground, quiet, unobtrusive, but ultimately strong enough to resist the distortions of an invasive regime, and sufficiently mobile to reach out to those who can respond sympathetically' (2010: 11). She recalls, for example, James Currie, who assembled the first edition of Robert Burns's work in 1800, praising the poet's ability to convey his attachment to Ayrshire and 'marvelling at the thought of his songs being sung on the banks of the Ganges and the Mississippi as well as the Tay and the Tweed' (123). There is an intriguing relationship here between Romantic literature's arrival at an awareness of its global circulation and the much later 'new localism' that emerged from the environmental movement's emphasis on thinking globally and acting locally. The sense of an international community rooted in local attachments and the authenticity of personal experience that arose in the Romantic period established for the much later localism of the environmental movement some of its grounded and moral weight, its ethic of autonomy and individual responsibility. One example of this at work is to be found in Elizabeth Kolbert's *Field Notes from a Catastrophe* (2006) which sets out to show global warming at work by making localized visits to places that are suffering the worst effects. Locality is a scale at which evidence is registered in its indisputable authenticity and communicated to an international community.

Tim Dee's *Four Fields* is a book that works in the midst of this relationship as well, energizing the local with the international and the international with the local. The 'four fields' of the book's title are in the reclaimed but shifting terrain of the fens of eastern Britain near his home in Cambridgeshire, in the bush and scrub of Zambia on a lapsed farmstead, in the prairie-become-battlefield-become-farmland near the border between Montana and South Dakota and in the poisoned and abandoned landscapes of the Exclusion Zone around Chernobyl in northern Ukraine (2013: 208). Each in its own way is a landscape with a complex recent history of change in which human and animal, and commercial and elemental, forces are in a tension that is shaping the world of the field. The book describes a year in its structure and form, beginning with the fens in springtime before moving out to Zambia (and Kenya), returning to the fens for summer, travelling to North America, returning to the fens again for autumn, travelling again, to Ukraine, and returning one last time to the fens for winter. In doing so it offers an internationally punctuated pastoral calendar of the fens bringing in, or travelling out towards, a much wider world alive with fish and birds and large mammals but fraught with unstable human economies, violent clashes of civilization and devastating pollution. The places are opened up and connected by natural and by social forces – migrating birds seem to move between them like a common backdrop; people cleared from one land move into another as an occupying force – and yet each is given to the reader in its distinctive qualities of weather, wildlife and topography. What the fields have in common though is that they are *made* landscapes. Like Common Ground's central theme of 'local distinctiveness', fields offer a way of thinking about the human relationship with the natural world that refuses to separate 'Nature' as an object isolated from everyday human affairs.[6] Kathleen Jamie goes so far as to suggest that the book 'is proof that really, there is no such thing as "nature writing"', if we are to understand nature writing as being concerned with only non-human affairs (2013).

The fens are a cluster of places that Dee shows, at various times, have been either ocean floor or forest or farmed fields. Evidence of the different layers rises to the surface from time to time, as when a Mesolithic farm tool is found sunk in a freshwater peat brick on the ocean floor by fishermen (2013: 22), or when the ancient, preserved trunks of oaks are found lying 'beneath a wet treeless place' (216). The subtle ways in which this is a constructed landscape are there under the fields but they are there in the language of the area too: 'Drains beneath the grass vein the ground, while pumps and ditches and a thousand cuts (reaches, eaus and lodes, conduits and leams, fosses and sewers, washes and sluices) fetch rain and river water from the fields and beyond and bear it away' (19–20). There has even been talk of rewilding initiatives in future intended to bolster the area's biodiversity and that will no doubt add another layer of meaning to the story of the place (46). In this sense Dee gives the fens to us as a vertical landscape that we forage down through, its story one that is read through its interpenetrating strata of natural resource and human resourcefulness.

Dee never forces the comparisons between the places but their juxtaposition invites speculation. In Zambia the English farmer of a tobacco plantation has

---

[6] In fact, Common Ground had promoted their own investigation of fields in a three-year project called 'Field Days' in the mid-1990s which toured an exhibition of ideas for investigating and celebrating fields and published a 'Manifesto for Fields' and an anthology of poetry about fields (Clifford and King 1997).

recently died leaving no money to plant the prepared fields and no money to pay the workforce which lives uncertainly nearby in their one-room huts. On the farm next door, the failure of a pension scheme and the unstable price of wheat on the global market lead to tensions and a crop of seven hundred tobacco plants is destroyed in the night. This farmer is experimenting with a dam and irrigation system now and encouraging a local chief to give away land to the people in the hope that they might take on a sustainable stewardship of its woods. The fields here are as unstable as the fens in different ways, dry bush and scrub ready to creep back in like the water of the fens if they're left alone. They are the outcome of perpetual negotiation, the expression of strained labour relations and local imagination in adversity.

In Montana, a very different story reveals the battlefield sites of war between the Sioux and the American armies, representative of a wider landscape change where the deep history of prairie gives way to the wires and fences of the settlers. Today 'less than five percent of the original tall grass prairie (the eastern prairie type) remains. A few unploughed acres rise above the surrounding land, like the islands of wet undrained fens in Cambridgeshire that are higher than the farmland around them' (123). The fens and Montana are also bound by a shared history of enclosure, Dee suggests. 'Landless but enclosed people left one continent for another and there sought fences. ... We, the Europeans, wanted the grass the Indians had, and if we could convince ourselves that they didn't actually own it (since they weren't subduing the earth enough, as God commanded man to do in Genesis) it made taking it from them that much easier' (126). The theological underpinnings of the acts of enclosure, giving to the capitalist thrust of 'improvement' an air of transcendent virtue and sublimation, were redeployed in a North American context to justify what would become genocide. For Dee, this is written into the enclosure of the prairie and the making of the fields.

In Chernobyl, he is put to work by research scientists counting grasshoppers in the Exclusion Zone. He is told he is safe, that the background radiation is less powerful than an X-ray in a hospital, but he is also told not to chew grass stalks, or his own nails, since 'ingesting radiation is the best way to absorb it' (191). The Exclusion Zone is a place that is pervaded by a generally invisible threat that he finds 'ineffably strange: to be in a calm clearing that could kill you, where soil is dangerous, where the air might violate you, where standing under a blue sky is risky'. Occasionally the threat visibly reveals itself in traces of startling uncanniness: a forest has been turned red by the radiation (188); catfish in the cooling ponds around the reactors grow to ten feet long in the heat (211); some swallows have their toes facing the wrong direction (185); and the abandoned buildings of towns and villages nearby have filled with little walled forests (199). In a passage searching for some kind of historical parallel to this most modern of disasters in Prypiat, the empty town where the nuclear plant's workers used to live, Dee searches for the underlying feeling of the place:

> Piranesi's Roman ruins; Mayan temples lost in the jungle; monkeys overrunning other gods in India; Max Ernst's vegetable-slime paintings; the ever renewing Golden Bough; Ozymandias's instructions to the deaf desert; the revenge of Gaia – it all crowds in as thick as the pressing trees but nothing can truly assist with the profoundly unsettling task Prypiat puts before you. To stand in the forest that was once a town is to look *after* us. Down the wooded streets of Prypiat's arrested past you are bowled into the aftermath of man, into a future that has already arrived. (209)

Enthusiasts for rewilding are excited by stories of wildlife pouring back into the Exclusion Zone '*after* us', since the humans have vacated the area, but the scientists he is with are more critical and Dee himself reminds us that this is a 'poisoned rewilding' of sterile eagles and swallows with visible tumours (209). It is something that informs his understanding of rewilding more generally and we might think back to his reservations about such projects in the fens where 'what is proposed is a description of our profound separation from the fens and the fields, a terminal version of the pastoral' (51). He even describes such fenced rewilding as an 'exclusion zone … an enclosure beyond enclosure, the darkest arcadia' (51). Such extreme versions of rewilding forfeit the heritage of fields as a part of our cultural history (good and bad) and clear them of the human knowledge, skill, interest and meaning that have been an important shaping influence. The challenge for Dee is not to withdraw from the field but to become conscious of, to struggle with, to redeem and refine *the art of the field* wherever that field might be.

Four Fields explores a tension between, on the one hand, fields as 'a few hundred acres standing for the world' and, on the other, fields as 'site-specific, idiomatic and accented' (17). Dee is alert to the distinctive qualities of each of the fields he is exploring while at the same time looking for 'the common ground they make, the *midfield*, as he calls it (4). What do these disparate places have in common? What, through their 'idiomatic' differences, connects these fields, and connects us as citizens of the fields internationally? The answer is not an easy one, and not an easy one to hear, and perhaps the only cheering news is that in a world of fields that are ever on the move in the Heraclitean sense – with inundation, reclamation, enclosure, evacuation, migration, colonization, agriculture, technology and conservation all wrestling their different shapes into the shapes of the fields – the people local to those fields are among the agents of their future. Whether those people wish to recognize this or not, whether they wish to act in response to this recognition, whether they are even empowered to act in response to this recognition, is an open-ended question. In this sense, Dee comes to write fields as opportunities all too often overlooked and taken for granted: they are

> old but apt; imposed but giving; made in proportions that fit the Earth and us, that bring us together, that allow us to belong, that take the oldest and most searching human measurement – how much land does a man need? – and say, this can be yours, these acres, this plot, your field, man's not nature's, but the best thing of man, and the thing of his that is nearest to becoming nature. (13)

Fields are long braids of human history and the elements there to be read, there to be worked and written over, but they do not wait for anyone to work them. They change and grow to exist at all. Dee is drawn to the particular fields he writes about because 'each is now at a more angled point in its life' (14). And its life is our life too. This is the local as volatile, vulnerable, but full of potential as well.

Towards the end of the book, Dee draws out a character from the historic Cambridgeshire landscape as an unlikely figure to be so well equipped to apprehend the shifting shapes of fields. John Ray, author of the first ever county *Flora* (of Cambridgeshire), was one of the earliest parson-naturalists in England. Unlike many philosophers of the natural world who saw their work as collecting and reproducing knowledge from book to book, his method was to get outdoors and look with his own eyes, to undertake field work, *simpling* as he called it (a word Dee tells us Ray used to describe searching for – especially medicinal – flowers) (233). Writing in the seventeenth century, Ray's work preceded (and would influence) Carl Linnaeus and therefore preceded some of the organized certainty with which Linnaeus would help the Enlightenment lay out the known species of the natural world. Ray was working in a period when, as Dee describes, 'Plant nomenclature and taxonomy were as unstable as the ground,' the ground, that is, in the watery fens (234). The uncertainty with which Ray was faced at this time required of him a resourcefulness that was a mixture of careful attention and imaginative improvisation and it is this that makes him, we are told, an author from whom we can learn a great deal today. Dee describes his work as 'stuffed with looking and thinking about looking' and as 'beautiful in both its precision and its vagueness'. The combination of 'precision' and 'vagueness' speaks to the stretched imagination and the attempt to rediscover the local beyond the usual conventions of representation that we have explored throughout this chapter. Dee dramatizes a lengthier example of Ray's technique:

> Look at the bunch he has picked of 'small foxtail grass' and 'lesser bastard Fox-tail-grass' and 'small rough-eared bastard Fox-tail-grass'. See how sometimes on the fen even the great naturalist was lost for words, or rather flooded with them. Pay attention to 'Water-grasse'; 'Float-grass'; 'Great water Reed-grasse'; 'our great Reed-grasse with chaffie heads'; and 'the marsh soft Rush with a round blackish head', you know the one. (235)

These carefully differentiated and improvised names represent a searching for new descriptions, new ways of apprehending the local and Dee edits them into a syntax here which seems to emulate a curious child. There is an innocence to it, but one that has made a serious and resourceful art of its innocence, alert to the revelations of that 'undiscovered country of the nearby'.

It is an art we have seen privileged as the guiding orientation of the authors commissioned to produce new writing for Common Ground in *Second Nature* and one that was put to work in the community of the Stour on the Confluence project. We have seen it inform Deakin's intimate and watery counter-map of loved places in *Waterlog* and we have seen Oswald break out into a whole new form of inclusive and socially engaged poetry using such an art. For Ray, the book knowledge of the naturalist's discipline was insufficient to the fields as they were to be found outdoors and he hoped to offer a more intricate account based on fieldwork. For Dee, it is about extending the range of the nature writer's prose to speak to a *midfield* that is worldly and local at once; a *midfield* that, today, is also more fluid, constructed, contested and imperilled than it is often thought to be. A local art, in this sense, is not only about searching for a fresh way of seeing but it is also about weaving together the complexity of the freshly seen, and doing so in a form that does justice to its difficulty and its richness at one and the same time.

2

The Wild

In Seamus Heaney's translation of *Buile Suibhne*, the old Gaelic tale of *Sweeney Astray* first written down in the seventeenth century, the Irish king Sweeney is exiled from human society by the Christian priest Ronan. When, in a rage, Sweeney throws the priest's psalter into the sea, kills one of his psalmists and cracks the bell he hangs around his neck, Ronan places a curse upon the king, turning him from the protection of the social sphere to a life naked and mad in the wilderness: 'Bare to the world he'll always be' (Heaney 1992: 92). Exiled and exposed to the elements, he roams without rest and from time to time is described as half-bird as well, literally 'bird-brained' and taking refuge in a hawthorn tree. Sweeney's curse is to occupy these paradoxical layers of living ambiguity, neither one thing nor another: king but exiled; free but mad; man but bird. They are liminal conditions that Heaney himself comes to identify with as a poet: 'It is possible to read the work as an aspect of the quarrel between free creative imagination and the constraints of religious, political, and domestic obligation' (87).

Always on the outside, Sweeney's is a life of restless suffering under one or another form of elemental discomfort:

> shivering; glimpsed against the sky,
> a waif alarmed out of ivy.
> Going drenched in teems of rain,
> crouching under thunderstorms.
>
> (97)

And yet, there are also times when 'the Bann cuckoo' is 'sweeter/than church bells that whinge and grind', when, Sweeney reflects:

> I prefer the scurry
> and song of blackbirds

> to the usual blather
> of men and women
> ...
> the squeal of badgers
> in their sett
> to the hullabuloo
> of the morning hunt.
>
> (96, 104)

Jane Bennett has written of such ambiguous 'crossings' between the animal and the human in literature, suggesting that 'under propitious conditions, you might find that their dynamism revivifies your wonder at life' and that 'their morphings inform your reflections upon freedom' (2001: 32). Sweeney's are rarely 'propitious conditions' but there are certainly moments of vivification, and it is the 'sweeter' birdsong here that reveals, by contrast, the unpleasant noise of human matters ('whinge', 'blather', 'hullabaloo'). Beyond the social order of domestic obligations (and yet somehow still peripherally influenced by it), such moments of enchantment that come from encounters with the non-human can have lasting effects that might yet be meaningfully fed back into reflections on those very same obligations. Bennett goes on: 'Their charm energizes your social conscience, and their flexibility stretches your moral sense of the possible' (32).

Again, this is enchantment understood less as a quality of submission and more as 'a state of interactive fascination', as we saw in relation to Roger Deakin in the last chapter (Bennett 2001: 5). If Chapter 1 drew attention to the vital and fluid indeterminacy that is often overlooked in relation to the local – but that can be a powerful resource for reimagining (or continuing to imagine) what the local might be – then this chapter will look a little more closely at the point of contact between the human and the indeterminacy of the wild. I will argue that, for a number of authors, a critical attention to activity at the human/non-human interface leads wildness to yield subtle reflections that can unsettle and revitalize the human sphere as well. This interface between non-human and human has the *potential* to challenge the social order and open new avenues of thought and feeling, provided the non-human is not domesticated and appropriated beyond all recognition. It is helpful, in this sense, to think of the wild as a qualitative effect felt in the mode of relationship rather than as an identifiable space or place.

On the surface there might be something slightly counter-intuitive about a chapter on the wild in a book about place in Britain and Ireland. Could there, for example, be something oxymoronic to the idea of a 'wild place' if we take place to be the known, inhabited and familiar? Of recent years, the book that perhaps takes to the subject in the most committed and passionate way is Jay Griffiths's *Wild* (2007). For Griffiths, the wild is a subject that takes her to the Arctic, the Amazon, the Indonesian Ocean and to West Papua. It is a subject unbounded by national or regional allegiance; in fact, it is often shaped and determined precisely in resistance to regional and national administration full of the kinds of localized tensions we explored in the previous chapter. If Griffiths does hold true to any allegiance, it is to those, especially women, who have spoken up for the wild, and who have been often very violently attacked for doing so. In the sense that the wild might be what precedes or resists a violent, colonial or corporate intervention, Griffiths draws attention to the plight of people involved in such battles.

In Britain, however, true to the very relative and contingent nature of wildness, authors have treated the subject very differently and in this book I am concerned with the British and Irish landscape in particular. Britain and Ireland present landscapes long deforested and developed for agriculture, with difficult histories of clearances and enclosures, and on a scale very small and densely populated relative to other countries. As Jamie Lorimer has argued, in contrast to the United States, 'The imagined purity of wilderness is less significant' in Europe because 'the valued baseline tends more toward the premodern than the prehistoric' (2015: 22). Britain and Ireland offer intensely layered historical landscapes rife with cultural and political tensions that, as we have seen, problematize the idea of nature, let alone wild nature. In a broad review of the New Nature Writing as a form in 2008, Boyd Tonkin warned that 'an innocent quest for the beauty of wild things' in this 'densely-peopled heartland of vandalistic industry' is, and should be, a complicated pursuit (n.p.), all of which has meant that a distinctive and at times quite uncertain version of the wild has grown up in recent years that reveals its close intertwinement with human society. The contemporary existence of the wild, for example, is not something that is taken for granted and in some of the books this chapter will consider, authors find themselves making an argument for its recovery or resuscitation. The 're-' of 'rewilding' is articulated especially strongly in Britain with an acute awareness of what has been lost and of our role as humans in intervening.

Influenced by Jane Bennett's work, queer theorists have recently been turning to the idea of 'wildness' as a productive interruption of discourses of state power that seek to control and produce sexual or racial identities. The disruptive ambiguity of the wild holds a politically radical, anarchic and emancipatory appeal and, for Jack Halberstam, it offers a 'space/name/critical term for what lies beyond current logics of rule' (2014: 139). Halberstam reflects on wildness in an essay dedicated to the late Michael Taussig whose death brings to the fore of Halberstam's mind 'a wild space of unmeaning and un/being where darkness and light, self and other, order and chaos slip out of their orderly opposition and the symbolic order of signification itself falters and collapses' (139). She quotes Taussig who argued that wildness can bring on a revelation in which 'objects stare out in their mottled nakedness while signifiers float by. Wildness is the death space of signification' (137). It becomes a space for what she calls, after José Esteban Muñoz, 'disidentification', through which subjects, as well as objects, can appear in their 'mottled nakedness', in styles of being that underlie their social signification as black, white, heterosexual, homosexual and so on (143).

This tradition descends via Bennett from Henry David Thoreau and his famous decision to 'live deliberately' in the woods at Walden Pond. In Bennett's first book, about Thoreau's idea of wildness, she sees the liminal place of his cabin as open to the 'sensuous intensity' which he nurtured 'as a counterforce to the powerful lure of convention, tradition, normality' (2002: xxiii). This is not a reading of Thoreau as getting 'back to nature' as much as it is a reading of him looking ahead in an ambitious thought experiment. In fact, the personal and deliberate nature of *Walden* as a whole venture situates it halfway between a thought experiment *and* a lived place; the life lived in the place is as much a part of the project of writing the book as the book is a part of the process of living there. For Thoreau, for Bennett and for some of the authors that this chapter will discuss, wildness is concerned with just such a deliberate experiment in place and in writing, one that endeavours to unlock what Bennett calls the 'eccentric and decentering potential within any object of experience' (xiii).

For Robert Macfarlane, British life in the early 2000s calls out for precisely such an 'eccentric and decentering' experiment in alternative thought. Macfarlane turns to the Sweeney myth and finds that the mad king's 'journeying from wild place to wild place, his wintering out, his sleeping close to the ground' make 'inspiring sense' in a modern context (2007d: 46). Under the priest's curse, Macfarlane suggests that Sweeney 'became "revolted" by the thought of "known places," and ... "dreamed strange migrations"' (45). Such 'strange migrations' might be understood as a queering or, in Muñoz's term, a 'disidentification' of normative organizations of space and a search for a revitalized understanding of place in its own 'mottled nakedness'. Towards the end of his first book *Mountains of the Mind* (2004), Macfarlane describes some of the 'known places' from which he is trying to shake free: 'Most of us exist for most of the time in worlds which are humanly arranged, themed and controlled. One forgets that there are environments which do not respond to the flick of a switch or the twist of a dial and which have their own rhythms and orders of existence' (275). He comes to see these 'themed and controlled' environments as a form of 'amnesia' (275). 'So many forces', he suggests in a later article, 'now warp us away from direct experience of the land on which we live. Urbanisation, habits of travel, modern farming practices, footloose industries, the internet' (2007a: 13). The echo of Thoreau is apparent here too as the search for wildness is aimed at puncturing these modern organizations of space, loosening their hold on our experience. Macfarlane's 2007 book *The Wild Places* becomes, itself, a thought experiment in the form of a domestic travelogue attempting to decentre a conventional spatial orientation of Britain and Ireland. The first part of this chapter, 'Inter-animation', traces a movement in Macfarlane's book from an initial, rather straightforward, search for these 'wild places' to a more careful reflection on wildness itself. I argue that this move is an important one in understanding the relationship between wildness and place in a British context.

Placing the wild is no easy matter and doing so begins to lean precariously close to the more dubious idea of wilderness, one that has come under fire from, particularly American, historical geographers. In William Cronon's memorable critique of the idea in the United States, wilderness emerges as, contrary to popular wisdom, 'a product of civilization' (1995: 69). For Cronon, the meaning of wilderness is historically loaded, produced and reproduced in the land itself by various means. In fact, it might be understood as the social, cultural and spatial *formalization* of wildness itself, which is of course a paradoxical act of domestication that others have read in Foucauldian terms of utopian and heterotopic discourses (Whatmore 2002; Chaloupka and Cawley 1993). At different times, Cronon shows us, this has involved the development of an aesthetically coded mythology of national heritage, the establishment of projects and processes of bureaucratic conservation, even the violent dispossession of Native American peoples and the erasure of historical and archaeological evidence (1995: 71–80). As we will see in the second part of this chapter, 'Intertwined', Kathleen Jamie has brought an equally critical eye to the Scottish landscape, one that has come into conflict with Macfarlane's *The Wild Places* and in doing so has arrived at a different way of thinking about the wild. For Jamie, understanding the wild has meant challenging assumptions about spaces deemed to be wild, and challenging assumptions about spaces deemed to be domestic, in ways that are inflected by gender and national identities. 'Wild and not-wild is a false distinction, in this ancient, contested country,' she writes, echoing Boyd Tonkin's concerns above (2008a: 25). Here, I explore this complication of wildness through a reading of her prose and poetry together.

In the third part, the chapter builds on both Macfarlane's and Jamie's explorations of the wild in relation to George Monbiot's controversial manifesto for 'Rewilding', *Feral* (2013). Monbiot critically evaluates conservation policy and practices in Britain by broadening the temporal scale at which they set their baselines. Rewilding emerges as a future-oriented and experimental practice being led by individuals and groups of pioneers self-consciously collaborating with the non-human. What we see is Monbiot exploring the real-world implementation of many of the ideas that emerge in Jamie's and Macfarlane's books. I conclude by returning to other writings by these two that have explored issues over community land rights to suggest an emergent politics of wildness that extends the previous chapter's exploration of dynamic localism. Rewilding shows very clearly how wildness in Britain is about interface and interconnection between the human and non-human. Lorimer has even recently argued that we might 'think of the wild as the commons, the everyday affective site of human-nonhuman entanglement' (2015: 11). These books on wildness show an intensification of activity out on the frayed edges of place, temporally, spatially and conceptually, that can feed the imagination as it destabilizes convention.

Inter-animation

Robert Macfarlane's *The Wild Places* begins by setting out an agenda to counter the sense of landscape in modern Britain that has arisen through car culture and the mentality of the road atlas. 'There are now thirty million cars in use in Britain, and 210,000 miles of road on the mainland alone. ... The roads have become new mobile civilisations in themselves: during rush-hours, the car-borne population across Britain and Ireland is estimated to exceed the resident population of central London' (2007d: 10). He feels that this has given way to a certain landscape psychology that ignores most of what it passes through:

> Maps organise information about a landscape in a profoundly influential way. They carry out a triage of its aspects, selecting and ranking those aspects in an order of importance, and so they create forceful biases in the ways a landscape is perceived and treated. ... The road atlas makes it easy to forget the physical presence of terrain, that the countries we call England, Ireland, Scotland and Wales comprise more than 5,000 islands, 500 mountains and 300 rivers. It refuses the idea that long before they were political, cultural and economic entities, these lands were places of stone, wood and water. (10–11)

The Wild Places begins as an extended attempt to recover this 'physical presence of terrain', to gather it back in as a corrective geography to a blurred, distanced and alienating motorway vision, a vision so pointedly attacked in J. G. Ballard's *Crash* (1973) or *Concrete Island* (1974) and in Iain Sinclair's *London Orbital* (2002). In fact, *The Wild Places* might thoughtfully be read in relation to these works as a book in a very different form of dialogue with the same modern Britain.

As a foil to such speed the book sets off in search of any remaining wild places in Britain and Ireland, challenging a whole list of authors who, like the American William Least Heat-Moon, have found in Britain only 'a tidy garden of a toy realm where there's almost no real wilderness left and absolutely no memory of it' (qtd. in Macfarlane 2007d: 9). In a culture predicated on the vision of space underpinning the road atlas, Macfarlane feels, it becomes all too easy to pre-emptively call time on the wild when a counterculture that might nurture slowness and distinctiveness not only draws attention to the remaining wildlife, but begins the process of caring for it too. Macfarlane is very much influenced by Roger Deakin in this book, both by the style and motivation of *Waterlog* and, more literally, in person as Deakin was a good friend. Deakin features quite prominently as a guide and mentor in parts of the book, he accompanies Macfarlane on some of his journeys and the book is dedicated to his memory. *The Wild Places* opens by searching out the rare and remote across the north-western edges of the archipelago but it later performs a homeward narrative arc. Following the late T. S. Eliot, the final chapter claims 'to arrive where we started/And know the place for the first time' (qtd. in Macfarlane 2007d: 313). In the end, the search for wilderness in remote places is replaced by a revelation about the more immanent and omnipresent wild as a living process that subtends everything. The wild is discovered to be our more intimate neighbour if we just take the time to look. Though 'set about by roads and buildings, much of it menaced' (321) it is still there with 'the sheer force of ongoing organic existence, vigorous and chaotic', a reminder of 'luxuriance, vitality, fun' (316). The book becomes an act of conjuring forth this 'sheer force', in rich and kinetic prose and in experimental journeys on foot that imitate Sweeney's 'strange migrations'. The challenge is to find new interactions between body and land, mind and place, language and the wild, as self-conscious and deliberate as Thoreau's own thought experiment living in the Maine woods.

In an essay called 'Nightwalking' that forms part of an early version of the chapter on 'Ridges' in *The Wild Places*, Macfarlane writes of a night spent in the snow in mountains under a near full moon. It is a startlingly vivid essay that captures something of the intense exposure to the night sky that comes with visiting such a high and remote place in the winter, though where exactly the place might be is not apparent. It is the immediacy of the bodily experience of cold mountains and clear sky in winter that really matters here rather than the wider sense of orientation that the road atlas might give us. Lying on his back on a frozen tarn, watching the hail fall 'like pills, then like tiny jagged icebergs' Macfarlane remembers August Strindberg's experiments with night photography when he 'laid large photographic plates, primed with developing fluid, out on the earth, hoping they would take slow pictures of the stars' movements' (2005c: 220). There is, in this photographic exposure, a resonant metaphor for Macfarlane's particular method of putting himself out in the land and waiting to see what comes.

However, Macfarlane reminds us that, in fact, the photographs Strindberg took were not pictures of the stars as such, but were rather strange, chemical blemishes brought about by frost. It was a coincidence that they looked like stars, the outcome of a complex and unpredictable series of reactions precipitated by the temperature of the exposure (221). But this makes the anecdote all the more interesting for Macfarlane. It recalls Rebecca Solnit's claim that 'walking, ideally, is a state in which the mind, the body, and the world are aligned, as though they were three characters finally in conversation together, three notes suddenly making a chord' (2000: 5). Note the interesting social and musical metaphors of a 'conversation' and a 'chord' here, contrasting the idea of simple receptivity with one of emergent, creative interaction, a busyness at the interface with the wild. What we see is a realization that the 'direct experience' he is looking for is about an exchange and experiment with things that Solnit calls a 'conversation'. Rather than a passive receptivity, this becomes the book's search for corrective experience.

It is also interesting to consider, then, some subtle changes that take place between the writing of this essay for *Granta* in 2005 and *The Wild Places* in 2007, changes that also might be related to a trajectory of thought about what constitutes 'direct experience' in the first place, and how its articulation might be related to a certain political feeling for how we relate to place and the land. One of the most notable things about this 'Nightwalking' essay in *Granta* is the total absence of any place name. We are told it is the north-west of England; it appears to be mountainous, we hear of a 'tarn', so perhaps we assume it is the Lake District, but we are not told so, and we are certainly not told whereabouts in the Lakes. In *The Wild Places* there is more room to elaborate and we are informed it is near Buttermere in the mid-western fells, but in this earlier version we are given only the cardinal directions long after an eerily rich and lucid account of the immediate orientation:

> There was the moon, fat and unexpected above the mountains. Just a little off full, with the shape of a hangnail missing to black on the right side, and the stars swarming around it. ... Snow perpetuates the effect of moonlight, which means that on a clear night, in winter mountains, you can see for a distance of up to thirty miles. (2005c: 218)

It is as if Macfarlane is suggesting that we have all the orientation we need in the immediate, intimate account, as if the vivid and carefully articulated perceptual field were enough to serve as a counterbalance to the road atlas.

This is not completely unprecedented. He has suggested elsewhere how influential he feels J. A. Baker's *The Peregrine* (1967) has been on him and one of the techniques he admires is Baker's stripping away of place names from the Essex landscape and his use simply of 'the South', 'the North' and so on: 'He inhabits a cardinal landscape ... he steers himself only by landform and feature' (Macfarlane 2005b: xiv). In fact, Baker does this out of an extreme dislike for the human world. 'My pagan head shall sink into the winter land and there be purified,' he claims early on (2005: 41). The sins of which he is searching to be 'purified' are those of environmental damage, in particular the use of toxic pesticides in agriculture, which reduced the peregrine population in Britain to just sixty-eight pairs between 1939 and 1962 (Macfarlane 2005b: v). So when Macfarlane withdraws the place names in this early essay we might read this as an experiment with Baker's 'pagan' anger and its flirtation with the wild, an attempt to 'disidentify' place with its human history. As Macfarlane suggests: 'Baker hopes that, through a fierce, prolonged, and "purified" concentration upon the peregrine, he will somehow be able to escape his human form and abscond into the "brilliant" wildness of the bird' (viii). Here too, of course, we find the flicker of the memory of Sweeney, and we are reminded of Bennett's description of an 'energise[d] social conscience' (2001: 32).

A similar technique has been employed more recently to different effect by Thomas A. Clark in his exploration of the Western Isles of Scotland (a book Macfarlane refers to in *The Old Ways* (2012)). Each of his short poems paints an extraordinarily vivid and often quite magnified view of, for example, the flowers on a clifftop or the parting mists on the sea, but never discloses a place name, in fact, never even uses a capital letter.

> a sea mist closing
> every distance
> cliffs falling away
> from the edge of a world
> only half accomplished

(2009: 8)

Or:

> a path through the gold
> of bird's foot trefoil
> delayed by the pink
> of thrift or campion
>
> (16)

Interestingly, the title of this collection is *The Hundred Thousand Places* (2009), though 'places' here suggests something beyond, or rather below, the conventional understanding of 'place' as a defined and stable geographical entity. Clark's book demonstrates a *proliferation* of places by way of careful and close attention. Myriad places are always replenishing, always boiling away, under the mapped and named place itself, if only by acute moments of perception. It suggests writing as in some way complicit in the process too, as a way of bringing these places into being *as places*, though there is nothing permanent and named about them. They are as fluid as the 'conversations' that Solnit associates with walking above. They exist to swell up, disrupt and surprise us, almost to defamiliarize and disorientate like Oswald's seductive *Dart*, but they do so in such an immediate way that they already suggest *re*familiarization and *re*orientation. There is something of what both Baker and Clark are doing in the way Macfarlane is framing his narrative here: 'absconding' into 'brilliant' wildness but also interrupting the familiar with a busy and plural *re*orientation that has an echo of the uncanny to it.

Macfarlane does include place names when he comes to publish *The Wild Places* and each chapter is very carefully situated and named on the map in the end. Not to do so might have come a little close to a reactionary retreat from human affairs, which was never the task Macfarlane set himself. But in the chapter titles – 'Island, Valley, Moor, Cape, Summit, Ridge, Tor' – we can hear an echo of Baker, that close eye on the 'landform and feature' that a bird might steer by. And in the highly particular and vivid prose descriptions, we can hear something of a desire to recognize the proliferating nature of place, of *the places beneath place*; to record one modest moment's view of something much more Heraclitean and, in short, wild. Both of these approaches have different qualities of the wild to them, troubling and resisting a rather blasé glossing over of place as known and somehow done with.

In this recuperation of the physical presence of landform and its close relationship to the body, Macfarlane is also showing the influence of Christopher Tilley's *A Phenomenology of Landscape* (cited in the bibliography at the end of *The Wild Places*). Drawing on both Martin Heidegger and Maurice Merleau-Ponty, Tilley explores the way in which landscape occurs somewhere between objectivity and subjectivity in a way that places an emphasis on the body and its presence in the land: 'Perceptual consciousness is not just a matter of thought about the world, but stems from bodily presence and bodily orientation in relation to it, bodily *awareness*' (1994: 14). Key to this is what David Morris calls 'the crossing of body and world', crossing serving simultaneously as a location and an activity, something suggestive of landscape as a practice to be performed (as opposed to just a representation alone) (2004: 26). For Tilley 'subjectivity and objectivity connect in a dialectic producing a *place* for Being in which the topography and physiography of the land and thought remain distinct but play into each other as an "intelligible landscape", and "a spatialization of Being"' (1994: 14; Tilley's emphasis). We might think of this as the type of place that is being described when Macfarlane uses the term 'wild places', provisional and played out between body, thought and land. This conflation of 'land and thought', their crossing as simultaneously an 'intelligible landscape' and 'a spatialization of Being' is really the ultimate achievement of *The Wild Places*, one captured by the often-quoted realization that 'certain landscapes might hold certain thoughts, as they held certain stones or plants' (2007d: 115).

Macfarlane describes here the 'thought' that plays out in the interplay of large, flat, limestone pavements and their deep, linear grykes on the west coast of Ireland in the Burren: 'Limestone, I found during my time in the Burren, demands of the walker a new type of movement: the impulse to be diverted, to wander and allow the logic of one's motion to be determined by happenstance and sudden disclosure. We learned, or were taught by the ground, how to walk without premeditation' (166). In this sense, a close attention to the limestone might be understood to 'queer' the normal walk from A to B to C. Such prompts from the ground might, in time, prompt instances of place lore and folk culture. In the chapter on 'Forest' he considers the relationship between forests as cognitive spatial experiences and the literature of forests where, in fairy tales, they so often become a space where worlds meet.

There is no mystery in this association of woods and otherworlds, for as anyone who has walked in woods knows, they are places of correspondence, of call and answer. Visual affinities of colour, relief and texture abound. A fallen branch echoes the deltoid form of the streambed into which it has come to rest. Chrome yellow autumn elm leaves find their colour rhyme in the eye-ring of a blackbird. Different aspects of the forest link unexpectedly with each other, and so it is that within the stories of forest, different times and worlds can be joined. (98)

What is being alluded to here is something close to what James J. Gibson describes as the 'affordance' of an environment, that is, 'the specific combination of the properties of its substance and its surfaces taken with reference to an animal' (where the animal here is a human) (1977: 67). For Gibson, certain features have given meanings for certain animals that arise out of the relationship between the perception of the body and the perceived substance and surface of a given object; this is what the object or landform 'affords'. One ought to be wary of universalizing here and open to the possibility that the thoughts 'found' in a landscape might vary depending on cultural background, or might be affected in different ways by, for example, blindness, deafness or age but such differences are something that might represent 'variations on a theme' that will only help proliferate the value of a given place.

For Macfarlane, this affordance runs right up to the level of our imaginative cultures – art, literature, music – and the fact that forests and other 'wild places' 'can kindle new ways of being or cognition in people, [and] can urge their minds differently' leads to a powerful argument about what he calls 'inter-animation' (2007d: 111). As an idea and philosophy about conservation, this 'inter-animation' shows a memorable intersection of the humanities and ecology at work. It is an argument not only about the way our lives are underpinned in an everyday way by the wild, but it adds a qualitative cultural layer of value to conservation discourse: 'Thought, like memory, inhabits external things as much as the inner regions of the human brain. When the physical correspondents of thought disappear, then thought, or its possibility, is also lost. When woods and trees are destroyed – incidentally, deliberately – imagination and memory go with them' (100). Of course, not all thought inhabits external things, and not all thought inhabits external things in such sensitive and careful ways, but Macfarlane's book does argue for a productive rediscovery of this important relationship. And doing so might even suggest ways to *stimulate* the cultural value of the wild in terms of its contribution to heritage, both heritage as our history and heritage as a potential that places might have, tapped or untapped. This is not an argument that should be offered instead of one about intrinsic value but it is a strong supplement that might broaden its appeal. It also does so without capitulating to the accountancy language of the Ecosystems Services movement, which has been criticized for its weaknesses in addressing the question of cultural value (Coates et al. 2014). Macfarlane's spatialization of thought in *The Wild Places* achieves something of considerable value that may well prove yet more important in future. Its interactions and inter-animations of diverse and distinctive landscapes map out intimate topographical experiences that lend themselves to translation and dialogue with other areas of limestone, forest, moorland and so on, wherever they are in the world. His work foregrounds a cultural depth to place on the outer edge of the familiar. It reveals meanings, correspondences and dialogues that are there for the finding in a variety of different ways of *being* in place.

Intertwined

> When a bright, healthy and highly educated young man jumps on the sleeper train and heads this way, with the declared intention of seeking 'wild places', my first reaction is to groan. It brings out in me a horrible mix of class, gender and ethnic tension. What's that coming over the hill? A white, middle-class Englishman! A Lone Enraptured Male! From Cambridge! Here to boldly go, 'discovering', then quelling our harsh and lovely and sometimes difficult land with his civilised lyrical words. (Jamie 2008a: 26)

So wrote Kathleen Jamie in a 2008 review of Macfarlane's *The Wild Places*. Until then Jamie and Macfarlane had been spoken of in the same breath as writers somehow collaborating in 'The New Nature Writing' as a movement.[1] There are obvious similarities in their work, of course. They are both concerned with

---

[1] When *Granta* had published their special edition on 'The New Nature Writing' earlier that year, both Jamie and Macfarlane were foregrounded, as they were in The Wildlife Trust's slightly dewy-eyed *Nature Tales* anthology, and later in the more progressive *Towards Re-enchantment: Place and Its Meanings*, an anthology published by the group Artevents.

the quality of attention that we bring to our environments. And they are both trying to challenge conventional representations of place, to get under the familiar map and rethink certain cultural assumptions. Nonetheless, looking a little more closely, there has been some considerable difference in how they went about these things and this was what the review brought out, reminding readers that, however far we get from the human into the wild, landscape is still a genre fraught with identity politics.

Jamie does herself admit early on to what she calls 'a huge and unpleasant prejudice', but nonetheless, the review prompts a closer examination of what becomes a conflict over the contemporary meanings of 'wild' (2008a: 26). There are various threads that can be drawn out of this quoted passage and followed. Both class and gender have an uneasy relationship with 'nature writing' but perhaps the most relevant issue at stake in Jamie's critique of *The Wild Places* is the 'ethnic tension' that comes from the way the book uses the archipelago as a theatrical space to perform its realization about the wild. *The Wild Places* owes a debt to the form of a bildungsroman, a novel through which the protagonist undergoes a life-changing epiphany in a coming of age or wisdom. There is, at the beginning, the slightly quixotic endeavour of a boyish mountaineer looking for the remaining wild places in Britain and Ireland: remote edges, uninhabited silence, *contact!*, as Thoreau might say (1972: 71). But to a degree Macfarlane sets this up to perform the shift in consciousness to the much more modern and productive idea that we have looked at in detail.

This change comes to a head in a journey to Ben Hope, one of the most northerly and one of the 'least accommodating places' (Macfarlane 2007d: 156) that he travels to: 'There could have been nowhere that conformed more purely to the vision of wilderness with which I had begun my journeys,' he suggests. 'This place refused any imputation of meaning' (157). Here dawn cannot come quickly enough to begin the descent and the return home to the more humanly arranged landscapes of the south. It is after this bleak encounter with what he calls the 'gradelessly indifferent' (157) that he begins to see the wild as something more miniature and closer to home. Another formative trip (this time with Roger Deakin) comes soon after this. In the Burren in Ireland they lay together, belly-down on the limestone pavement staring into one of the flower-filled grykes and Deakin seems to steer the 'Lone, Enraptured' mountaineer's gaze into his more developed realization: 'This, Roger suddenly said as we lay there looking down into it, is a wild place. It is as beautiful and complex, perhaps more so, than any glen or bay or peak. Miniature, yes, but fabulously wild' (168). This leads to the later realization that wildflowers emerging through cracks in the urban pavement back home might also be emissaries of a planetary wildness lying in wait beneath the shell of modernity. Macfarlane borrows a term from Gary Snyder who senses what he calls 'a ghost wilderness' that 'hovers around the entire planet' (317). This 'ghost wilderness' becomes the image of the elemental archipelago itself subtending our human civilization on top of it. The wild stops being about the spatially remote, about the Scottish north, and becomes about a living omnipresence (but in this case it is realized in the homely southeast). 'This was a wildness quite different from the sterile winter asperities of Ben Hope,' he suggests, 'and perhaps, I thought for the first time, more powerful too.' 'Ach weel,' replies Jamie, perhaps with another groan (2008a: 27). Of course, she admires his revelations of intimate local distinctiveness such as in the chapter on the holloways in Dorset, but for her there is still an uncomfortable spatialization of this narrative that is freighted with a long tradition of English incursions into a Scottish 'wilderness'. In the end, her attack on *The Wild Places* seems a little unfounded and, as she admits, 'prejudiced' given the book's acknowledgement of a shift in the narrator's understanding of the wild emulating that bildungsroman. There is a vulnerability to the inner drama of *The Wild Places* that is tapping into more than just Macfarlane's own confessed innocence about the wild, the likes of which it seems a little rough to judge. Nonetheless, it does draw attention to a broader tension at work in the Scottish landscape for Jamie.

In her 2005 book *Findings*, and in other essays of around the same time, Jamie articulates several challenges to the idea of the wild.

> Sometimes you hear this land described as 'natural' or 'wild' – 'wilderness', even – and though there are tracts of Scotland north and west of here, where few people live, 'wilderness' seems an affront to those many generations who took their living on that land. Whether their departure was forced or whether that way of life just fell into abeyance, they left such subtle marks. (2005b: 126)

Some of these 'subtle marks' are the 'findings' of the book's title. This passage comes at the end of a chapter in which Jamie walks up into the hills in search of shielings, or shieling grounds, clusters of huts that were once occupied during the warmer months when transhumance structured the year and the cattle were brought up into the hills for summer grazing by the women and children. When she arrives at the markings on the map there is 'nothing to be seen' and she checks and rechecks her bearings. Soon though, she gets her eye in and begins to make out a 'rough rectangle of stones' here, a 'green knoll' suggesting a gable-end there, 'small dry-stone humble thing[s], no taller than myself' (120). What she finds here in the Central Highlands is 'not a great vista of peaks and ridges, but a contained place, almost domestic and serene' (120–1) (the whole glen with its river and green grass she comes to describe as 'girlish' (126)). For Jamie, these 'subtle marks' are as hard to recover beyond the idea of a Scottish 'wilderness' as Macfarlane's topographical affordances are to recover beyond the British road atlas.

The relationship between place and the wild is an historically complicated relationship in Jamie's writing, and one inflected by gender as well. The shielings would have been a place of women and children, she tells us, while the men worked the farms down below, before harvest time. Jamie finds herself 'nodding an acknowledgement to the woman of the house' as she enters the ruin of a hut through a gap in the stone wall (124). The book is full of such nods to the domestic that resist the pull of a wilderness aesthetic and this chapter in particular becomes an exercise in empathy, decoding the distinctive associations each lived place might have had from what remains: one has a boulder of shining quartz by the door; another is the nearest hut to the river; some have stone recesses built into the walls, 'cool places to stand butter and cheese' (124). The practice of transhumance died out in the Central Highlands in the latter half of the eighteenth century 'at the time of the Improvements' and these ruins are often all that remains now on the edge of memory with only the slightest of clues to a whole way of life (122). 'What a loss this seems now,' she wonders, 'a time when women were guaranteed a place in the wider landscape, our own place in the hills. ... The presence in this valley of another woman [today] would have surprised me' (122). So wildness, or at least, wilderness, for Jamie, is bound up with a masculine (and often English) ideal imposed on a historically 'cleared' and 'improved' landscape. And it carries with it the risk of erasing an ordinary history of women living together.

William Cronon, writing in 2003 about the Apostle Islands in Lake Superior, observes a related problem that troubles the idea of wilderness in the United States in a way that speaks to this contemporary Scottish context as well. The National Park Service, at the time he was writing, was making recommendations for the designation of the islands as 'wilderness' which, under the 1964 Wilderness Act, would mean they were protected. However, exploring the language of this act, Cronon identifies an important problem in that 'the National Park Service will seek to remove from potential wilderness the temporary, non-conforming conditions that preclude wilderness designation' (n.p.). This includes 'demolishing historical structures' (n.p.). It also includes 'implying that dramatically altered landscapes are much more pristine than they truly are' and the refusal to interpret for park visitors 'the human history of places designated as wilderness' (n.p.), all of which poses a serious problem for a place with a rich history of Norwegian immigrant settlers, French traders and a centuries-old population of Obijwe people for whom the area served as a spiritual homeland. As Cronon has shown, for the 1964 Wilderness Act 'nature' is something to be made 'untrammelled' and 'pristine', even if it is neither (n.p.). While this presents a case more extreme than the example given by Jamie, it nonetheless reveals a parallel concern for the survival of marginalized histories in an apparently wild landscape. Jamie shows that even before the official work of designation, there are ways in which the imaginative conventions and genres of landscape can intrude on our experience of it.

Jamie's particular interest in this issue might be traced to an essay published the same year as *Findings*. In an edition of *Granta* in 2005, Jamie describes a trip to the mining landscape where her family lived for several generations before she was born. All the mines are decommissioned, she finds, most of the houses have been demolished and there is only farmland, moorland and an opencast site filled with 'sullen green water' (2005a: 92). A local farmer shows her the site of No.41 Darnconner, the house of her great-great-great-grandparents, and she notes her 'astonishment' at its near disappearance into 'the open moor of dun-coloured grasses and moss' (94). On the way around she describes how 'my foot slipped and released a few flakes of coal slag, so I put them in my pocket, with a notion to take them home to my mother' (95). The flaking off of the coal becomes an intimate moment of recollection, another 'finding' that really belongs to the wider book itself, but more personal this time, almost a recovery of a family heirloom, preserving an ordinary working history against erasure (the place is soon to be buried under a 'biomass' willow plantation to be cropped for fuel for power stations) (97). For Jamie, wild and human landscapes do not come to us separately. They are bonded in the history of labour, whether by the seasonal rhythms of transhumance or the mining community gathered on a geological seam of coal. The always intertwined nature of this history troubles the more literary and aesthetic traditions of the wild as remote.

This tension finds itself played out intriguingly elsewhere in this essay as different layers of landscape history interrupt one another. On her way up to Darnconner, she describes 'hen harriers and busted tellies; a liminal place, the edge of the moor', and it is liminal in a number of senses: on the cusp of old and new certainly, wild and human, definitely, but also liminal in the sense of being caught between genres (92). Looking around the opencast, she recalls Robert Burns rather ironically to herself: '"Ye banks and braes," I thought, "how can ye bloom sae fresh and fair?"' (92). The question takes on new meanings over and above the Romantic, unpacking some of that astonishment she felt at the erasure of her family history: how can you grow over what was here, it seems to ask, or how can you enfold this blighted, industrial landscape with such an incongruously pastoral scene? This was a working place for her family, the site of a tough, poor existence in conditions that had prompted the union men to recommend closure of the mines. From somewhere, though, adding another layer to this already complicated space, 'I'm Forever Blowing Bubbles' drifts into her head, perhaps an ice cream van on an estate nearby, she guesses later (92). What begins to emerge here and elsewhere is the sense of landscape as always an interrupted form, interrupted by history, family, modernity, the wild and even the landscape genres themselves. These interruptions are part of the cultural geography of place for Jamie and they prevent what she sees as the 'lone, enraptured, male' experience of the wild. It is not that she does not look for those moments of rapture; she does,[2] but they are punctured and

---

[2] In *Findings*, describing a rare bird sighting, she writes: 'Like some medieval peasant granted a vision, I was kneeling in a field, fixated by this uncanny cross in the sky. Then, as it moved slowly out of sight, I raced for home excited as a child, holding its image in my head like a bowlful of blue water – mustn't spill a drop' (2005b: 42).

complicated for her by other factors and those punctures and complications are an important part of the structure of her experience.

Findings is run through with such interruptions, often related to family issues: 'Nana, slipping into dependency, and mother who was adjusting to life at home having been paralysed by a major stroke, and my scared heroic dad doing his best; there were the needs of our small children to be met, and then my daughter had missed her first ever day at school because she was in hospital,' not to mention her husband contracting pneumonia which forms the central chapter of the book (2005b: 164–5). For Jamie, landscape as an interrupted genre is part of being a woman. In an interview on Radio 4 she suggested, with a certain sense of humour: 'So many relationships, women of a certain age, it's all we seem to do, manage relationships, a part of our own ecology if you like' (2006). In her poetry too, enraptured solitude is complicated by relationships and again this finds itself woven into the representation of place in an interesting way. She is as critical of her own tendencies towards Romantic wanderings as she is of Macfarlane's, careful always to make poetry out of what is there rather than what she would like to be there. In the poem 'The Buddleia', when she pauses 'to consider/a god, or creation unfolding in front of my eyes', she describes how her close attention begins to evoke

> the divine
> in the lupins, or foxgloves, or self-
> seeded buddleia,
> whose heavy horns flush as they
> open to flower, and draw
> these bumbling, well-meaning bees
> which remind me again,
> of my father ... whom, Christ,
> I've forgotten to call.
>
> (2004: 27)

Landscape never fully unravels itself from the complications of family, community, work, the home. That comma before 'of my father' brings the syntax to a peak before dropping it into the bathos of the ordinary domestic experience of forgetfulness. The 'god' of the beginning of the poem is lost to the expletive 'Christ' of the penultimate line. This is the poet caught again in Heaney's and Sweeney's 'quarrel between free creative imagination and the constraints of religious, political, and domestic obligation' but played out at the very ordinary scale of a garden (Heaney 1992: 87).

It is a theme that she revisits elsewhere. As far as she tries to wander off, and as far as we expect her to wander off, into the enraptured experience of the wild, she is always pulled back elastically by familial connections 'without whom', she suggests (in the title poem of the collection *The Tree House*),

> we might have lived
> the long ebb of our mid-decades
> alone in sheds and attic rooms,
> awake in the moonlit souterrains
> of our own minds; without whom
> we might have lived
> a hundred other lives
>
> (2004: 42)

The Romantic notion of the writer in solitude hinted at in those 'moonlit souterrains' is a myth for Jamie, her desire for which she slightly parodies in 'The Buddleia'. 'The Tree House' describes 'our difficult/chthonic anchorage/ in the apple-sweetened earth', but the anchorage she is describing is our relationship to family as much as our relationship to the planet (2004: 41–2). It is the whole difficult ecology of relationships that forces her to claim that 'wild and not-wild is a false distinction' (2008a: 25). They come at once together. She describes hoisting herself up into a literal tree house in this poem while her children and husband are out, and feels a 'complicity' with the tree 'like our own, when arm in arm / on the city street, we bemoan / our families' (2004: 42). But by the end of the poem we see things from the perspective of the tree, and *we* are the family that *it* makes sacrifices to sustain. Our home, with its garden tree house, a 'dwelling of sorts' is 'a gall / we've asked the tree to carry / of its own dead' (43). Limbs are wrapped around limbs, perspectives shift, lives are intertwined: these are the 'difficult' shapes of our relationship with the wild that we encounter in *Findings* and *The Tree House*.

In the central chapter of *Findings*, Jamie's husband Phil gets pneumonia and is hospitalized. The writing does not shy away from this, and her fear and horror at the prospect of losing him are written as carefully and as sensitively as her earlier explorations of peregrines or corncrakes. She does not distinguish between domestic and natural environments, or rather, she is quick to show their deep intertwinement since it is within that intertwinement that her own very different version of the wild is to be conjured: 'To give birth is to be in a wild place, so is to struggle with pneumonia' (2008: 27). 'Nature isn't just daffodils and trees and birds,' she explained on Radio 4. 'Growths and cross-sections of the brain, this is also nature. We are incarnated, we are natural creatures, and so I guess if I take nature at its widest definition what else is there?' (2006). In a passage coming to terms with the medical information she has been given about her husband's lungs, she is sat on her back step and there is an imaginative landscaping of the human body that explores a beautiful but unnervingly vulnerable state of intimacy with corporeal wildness:

> The alveoli, we're told, if they were unpacked from our lungs and spread out, would cover an area the size of a tennis court, 78 feet by 27. Or from the wall to the hedge breadthwise, and the bench to the shed longways. An area the mellow sun was now casting with long afternoon shadows. I stood with my back to the shed and surveyed the area, tried to imagine, what? ... A fine, fine cobweb, exchanging gases with the open air? And what of our nerves? There are hundreds of miles of neurones in our brains. I tried to imagine them, all that nerve, all that awareness and alertness spread out around me. All that listening. (2005b: 104–5)

The lungs, the nerves, the marriage, the garden, the sunlight are all revealed in such close quarters here, interpenetrating and interdependent. This is not a morbid image but one of total vulnerability and exposure, one of frightening intimacy. It is unsettling, but also a healing prayer of sorts ('Isn't that a kind of prayer? The care and maintenance of the web of our noticing, the paying heed?') (109). It is a recovery of the wildness within us that lies sometimes a little close for comfort beneath our usual domestic life.

In a later chapter she turns to Playfair Hall at the Royal College of Surgeons in Edinburgh to look at the specimens in jars as an antidote to the idea of nature 'out there', and she finds just as compelling and mysterious 'the forms concealed inside, the intimate unknown' (2008b: 141). In an essay for *Granta*'s *The New Nature Writing* she describes being shown various human body parts under the microscope at the pathology lab in Ninewells Hospital in Dundee. Looking down into a human liver she comments:

> I was admitted to another world, where everything was pink. We were looking from a great height down at a pink river – rather, an estuary,

with a north bank and a south. There were wing-shaped river islands and furthermore it was low tide, with sandbanks exposed. It was astonishing, a map of the familiar: it was our local river, as seen by a hawk.

'It's like the Tay!' I said. (41–2)

The movement in this short passage is one from estrangement ('another world') and distance ('a great height') to a metonymic familiarity and intimacy ('our local river'). The body becomes as far reaching as a familiar landscape, the land as close as the organs inside us. These two passages, one a projection of the inside of the body onto the land and the other a projection of the land onto the inside of the body, speak of the intimacy we share with the wild in Jamie's very different version.

Rewilding

Macfarlane's exploration of a relationship with the wild based on 'inter-animation' and Jamie's own very careful articulation of something more 'intertwined' and interrupted in form seem to share the conclusion that the wild is closer to home than we might think – even than we might like, at times. It is how they arrive at this that differs. What sets out the separation between the human and non-human is a matter of culture and the way it conditions perception: either entrenched personal habits of perception bred of our immersion in a hyper-mediated society or more focused expectations associated with certain aesthetic genres. In their written work, both develop forms that attempt to reach beyond these and to refresh and revitalize the tradition of nature writing with experiments that *try out* (the original meaning of 'essay') something new. In this, the wild takes on some of that 'counterforce to the powerful lure of convention, tradition, normality' that Jane Bennett reads in Thoreau (2002: xxiii). These works are experimental in challenging their readers to pick apart certain assumptions, to question what they might take for granted and to open their eyes to a richer complexity in plain sight. George Monbiot's *Feral* takes this same cultural work a step further and asks how we might challenge assumptions and intervene in material ecosystems themselves to stimulate some of their stymied or overlooked potential. The book articulates the same challenge to perception, arguing that we need to 'open up the ecological imagination' (183) and resist the idea that 'the dim, flattened relic' (89) of a landscape we live in is the best we could hope for. The book has now even grown into a visionary and controversial charity called 'Rewilding Britain', which is addressing the ecological damage that has been written into land and sea since the deforestation of the late Bronze Age thousands of years ago.

Surprisingly, one of the groups that comes under attack from Monbiot is conservationists themselves. Conservationists, he argues, have been as guilty as anyone of limiting their perception of ecosystems, as the result of cultural norms and uninterrogated assumptions. One of the most striking ideas that the book proposes is that of a phenomenon (coined by fisheries scientist Daniel Pauly in the 1990s) called 'Shifting Baseline Syndrome', something that has been shaping our understanding and our conservation of ecosystems in powerful and perturbing ways for decades (qtd. in Monbiot 2013: 69). This 'syndrome' describes a situation in which, 'when fish or other animals or plants are depleted, campaigners and scientists might call for them to be restored to the numbers that existed in their youth: their own ecological baseline. But they often appear to be unaware that what they considered normal when they were children was in fact a state of extreme depletion' (69). Monbiot scales this idea right up to address the much broader way in which deep views of landscape history such as paleoecology are ignored by conservation institutions like the National Parks Association. Because of this, his argument goes, landscapes that have been devastated by deforestation in the distant past, and excessive grazing that continues into the present, are now being carefully maintained as if that state of damage was their healthy 'natural' state and all they are capable of. There is something quite arbitrary about the levels at which the baselines are being set.

Perhaps the most striking example he gives of this is in contemporary Wales in the upland heath of the Cambrian Mountains. This is an area that was colonized by Neolithic farmers between 6,000 and 4,000 years ago (66). They deforested the land, cleared and burned it back and it has been heavily grazed by sheep and cattle ever since, bar some short periods around the plague years. This grazing, he argues, has depleted the nutrient base of the soil so thoroughly that trees will not grow, plant and animal life is at a minimum and some in fact now describe it as the 'Cambrian Desert' (64).

Nonetheless, the Countryside Council for Wales describes the area's Claerwen nature reserve as 'perhaps the largest area of "wilderness" in Wales today'; the Cambrian Mountains Society describes it as a 'largely unspoiled landscape' adding 'there is nothing to compare to the wilderness and sense of utter solitude that surrounds these vast empty moorlands'; and the chairman of Cambrian Active (invested in the tourism of the area) describes it as 'one of the largest wildernesses left in the UK' (66–8). For Monbiot, this is based on a misunderstanding about what constitutes a healthy ecosystem. His argument here is related to Jamie's critique of Scottish wilderness but on a far greater scale of time. Like Jamie, Monbiot is calling for a better acknowledgement of what thriving ways of life have been forgotten and erased from now empty and denuded areas labelled as 'natural', 'wild' or 'wilderness'. When we take into consideration the way this 'Shifting Baseline Syndrome' can inform regional and national conservation policy, 'wilderness' as it is understood here, can take on a surprising meaning that, in *Feral*, begins to run exactly counter to the meaning of 'wild' itself. The change that *Feral* promotes then is, first, one of scale. It contemplates a much deeper sense of time, challenging that European tendency that Lorimer observes of thinking in terms of 'premodern' landscapes rather than of 'prehistoric' landscapes (2015: 22). This is, again, a process of what Muñoz calls 'disidentification', but for geography rather than subjectivity (qtd. in Halberstam 2014: 143). It calls to the surface a shadowy prehistory that destabilizes contemporary signifying practices.

In many ways, *Feral* is unlike Macfarlane's and Jamie's books. It is more research-led and closer, on the whole, to popular science and journalism. In fact, it is the chapters of personal narrative, in their attempts to animate his agenda, that feel the weaker of the book's strategies for making its case. Likewise, the argument for rewilding based on his own personal sense of being 'ecologically bored' seems a little self-absorbed when juxtaposed with the book's wealth of research elsewhere and its overall vision (2013: 7). Nonetheless it does contribute to the same cultural reappraisal of the role of wildness in our individual and collective lives as Macfarlane and Jamie. *Feral* is rethinking the meanings and social order of place where place interfaces with the non-human, is under the influence of the non-human and is in collaboration with the non-human. In doing so, the book's real strength is in the accounts it gives of the work of key pioneering individuals who have taken on the replanting of trees, the reintroduction of species and the rehabilitation of land simply out of a personal sense of care. In this there is a wonderfully ordinary vision of rewilding as a force for change that takes root in disparate, localized and self-willed initiatives of the dynamic kind we considered in the previous chapter.

The book's shift in scale is in both directions at once: it demands we think at a much greater timescale about large ecosystems in deep time, while also showing that those beginning to do this are working on small-scale, localized projects at a time when national bodies are not.

Monbiot introduces Alan Watson Featherstone who began the charity 'Trees for Life' which has so far bought up 10,000 acres of the Scottish Highlands for reforesting. According to Featherstone, so overpopulated is much of the area of the Highlands with deer, serving the interests of wealthy landowners and the hunters they draw in, that vast areas once densely forested centuries ago are completely denuded of trees despite the fact that, left ungrazed, they would reforest themselves quite independently within a decade or two. It is in the interests of the landowners that these areas remain denuded in this way and so they do, with a whole Highland wilderness aesthetic that has grown up around them. Featherstone has experimented by simply putting a fence around certain areas to keep out the grazing deer and, as a result, grassland has given way to plants and saplings, plants and sapling have given way to trees and trees to forest. Another pioneer in Wales, Ritchie Tassell, worked in forestry before he and others began collaborating to buy up land, fence it off to prevent grazing by sheep and where necessary to replant the area with native trees, or with trees well adapted to the particular type of soil. Featherstone hopes later to reintroduce wolves and Tassell to reintroduce beavers, because, as keystone species, these animals can have the effect of creating habitat for a whole range of other plants and animals. The book also draws attention to the fact that, in what they are doing quite independently, these projects are also engaged with a much wider global rewilding movement. Again and again, Monbiot draws attention to how strangely resistant Britain has been to rewilding projects that have been almost ubiquitous in Europe. Beavers have been reintroduced 161 times in Europe since 1924, but it is proving a considerable struggle to support even their very minimal reintroduction in Britain, despite the history of British place names suggesting their long association (Beverley in Yorkshire,

Beverston in Gloucestershire, Barbon in Cumbria and Beverley Brook, which flows into the Thames) (79–80). These small-scale, pioneering projects are not the exception when seen in the broader context. In fact, such a shift in scale shows British national policy to be the exception. It is in *Feral* that we begin to see the political implications of landscape practices that are informed by wildness.

What distinguishes the work of these eccentric pioneers of rewilding from traditional conservation practices is a particular approach to the question of agency. Conservation projects focused on the careful control and maintenance of a particular landscape type, such as upland heath, endeavouring to keep it within given measures and parameters, tend to endorse a distinction between powerful, intelligent human beings on the one hand and passive, pliant 'Nature', which they control, on the other. But as Sarah Whatmore has argued, the thinking behind such 'fortifying' conservation practices risks 'eras[ing] all but "humans" as agents in the making of these wild places' (2002: 13–14). For Jamie Lorimer, the recognition of the Anthropocene has brought just such a rarefied conception of 'Nature' to an end for conservationists (as it has also brought such a rarefied, separate and 'objective' view of the 'Human' to an end) (2015: 9). The challenge of the Anthropocene, with its revelation of a much more complicated epoch, he argues, has the potential to 'catalyse modes of "stewardship" based on diverse, reflexive awareness of the always-entangled nature of humans with their environments' (4). For both Whatmore and Lorimer, the idea of 'wildlife' is offered up to replace the idea of 'Nature', describing as it does for them 'a relational achievement spun between people and animals, plants and soils, documents and devices in heterogeneous social networks' (Whatmore 2002: 14). Lorimer goes on: 'Here, wildlife is vernacular, everyday, and democratic. It provokes curiosity, disconcertion, and care. It demands political processes for deliberating discord among multiple affected publics' (2015: 11).

These corrective descriptions of wildlife conservation 'in the Anthropocene' chime with Monbiot's suggestion that in these pioneering localized projects of rewilding there might be 'no fixed objective' (2013: 83). They are concerned with 'allowing' a 'self-willed' ecosystem to 'find its own way', and of course helping it to do so (10). As Featherstone tells Monbiot in Scotland, in phrases reminiscent of Macfarlane's own exploration of the wild, 'I asked myself: what's the message in the land? What's the story it's telling us?' (qtd. in Monbiot 2013: 105). Such rewilding initiatives explore ways to foreground and promote the agency of animals and plants themselves. In so doing, they also challenge the cool, scientific objectivity of the 'Human' agent as well, and instead tend to suggest the everyday, local, political authority of Lorimer's 'multiple affected publics'. Conservation understood in such 'post-Natural' and hybrid terminology goes beyond 'the instrumental desire to secure the delivery of ecosystem services' and may well find itself considering qualitative cultural values and community heritage as local distinctiveness becomes a more important and defining measure (Lorimer 2015: 9). Stimulating the abundance of forests or animals in a place can have powerful implications for the sense of personal and collective identity and can connect with the processes of dynamic localism considered in the previous chapter.

Scotland offers an excellent example of this overlap between dynamic localism and conservation practices. Featherstone's work in the Highlands has been helped along by changes in land ownership law that came about after the new Scottish Parliament set out the Land Reform Act of 2003. This act was initiated to change a very old and unequal system in which it has been estimated that only 432 people own half the rural land in Scotland, though this number has to be estimated because there is no public record of land ownership in Scotland yet (Monbiot 2014: n.p.). In an effort to change this state of affairs, the new act stipulates that when an area of land comes up for sale in Scotland, the local community themselves should not only have first refusal to buy it, but if they organize themselves to do so, government money will be made available to help them from a new Land Fund.

Kathleen Jamie has herself described an example of this process in action when the community she lives in pooled their money to buy a loch and its surrounding woodland after it was put up for sale by Scottish Water in 2007 (2015: 26). Jamie describes the long process of assessing the community interest, raising the money and voting on the issue which, as it happened, overlapped with the 2014 Scottish referendum on independence. Though Scotland voted 'no' in the referendum, the community around the loch voted 'yes' to buy the land, 95 per cent in favour. 'Our loch is, so to speak, a drop in the bucket,' Jamie says. 'But it's our drop, and maybe it will someday be our bucket' (26). There is a curious collision that happens on that 'our' here, between community, country and nation, the outcome of which is to imagine the community land trust as somehow its own country devolving from Britain and steering its own fate. It will be interesting to watch how local groups in Scotland who buy their land choose to manage that land and whether they might be more inclined or less inclined to explore imaginative and experimental initiatives, perhaps even reforesting areas of open land and reintroducing species like Featherstone. There is a suggestive relationship here between rewilding and a form of re-commoning, in which connection to the land is stimulating questions about the protection of private or corporate interests that have been taken for granted for too long.

Robert Macfarlane has explored a Scottish community land initiative in an essay published in 2010 by Art Events that has since come to feature prominently in his 2014 compendium of topographical language, *Landmarks*. In this case, it was over the issue of whether a vast wind farm should be placed on the Isle of Lewis by the engineering and energy company AMEC. What is particularly interesting about this case is the way that the recovery of a language and a cultural history at the very intersection of human/non-human interaction became the focus of attention. As part of Scotland's drive to source 40 per cent of its energy from sustainable alternatives by 2020, AMEC filed an application in 2004 to site Europe's largest onshore wind farm down the middle of the north of the island. The journalist and former editor of *Granta*, Ian Jack, took the side of AMEC in this dispute, describing the area known as The Brindled Moor, in language reminiscent of eighteenth-century agricultural improvement, as 'a vast dead place: dark brown moors and black lochs under a grey sky all swept by a chill wet wind' (qtd. in Macfarlane 2010a: 124). In response to this and other descriptions of the moor as a 'wasteland', the leader of the opposition to the planning application, Finlay MacLeod, called for a language to challenge Jack's and AMEC's representation of the moor. He called for the following, from which Macfarlane takes the title of his essay: 'What is required is a new nomenclature of landscape and how we relate to it, so that conservation becomes a natural form of human awareness, and so that it ceases to be underwritten and underappreciated and thus readily vulnerable to desecration. What is needed is a Counter-Desecration Phrasebook' (qtd. in Macfarlane 2010a: 124).

This idea of a 'Counter-Desecration Phrasebook' becomes an important one to Macfarlane since it prompts an investigation of language akin to those particular 'thoughts' that might be 'found' in the landscape through processes of 'inter-animation'. This too is a question of perception but it draws language into the debate as well. For MacLeod there is an intrinsic link between the 'under-written' and the 'under-appreciated'; for Macfarlane, this is a vicious circle: 'Language-deficit leads to attention-deficit' (115). As words such as 'catkin', 'conker', 'brook', 'minnow' and 'bray' are being eroded from the *Oxford Junior Dictionary*, his argument goes, so, gradually, is our ability to see and hear such things (116). There is also a form of Shifting Baseline Syndrome at risk of going on in this loss of detailed and localized topographical language. The argument is a nuanced version of the structuralist belief that 'nothing is distinct before the appearance of language' (Saussure 2010 [1916]: 856). To counter such desecration the Lewisians collected a detailed vocabulary of local terminology into a glossary and phrasebook: *Mòine dhubh* is 'the heavier and darker peats that lie deeper and older into the moor,' for example; and *éig* refers to 'the quartz crystals on the beds of moorland stream-pools that catch and reflect moonlight, and therefore draw salmon to them in the late summer and autumn' (Macfarlane 2010a: 109). Such a glossary of terminology seems to offer more than just nomenclature; it suggests those particular affordances struck between people and land through long acquaintance, but in this case it resists universalizing them by showing their close association with local history and a particular community.

Macfarlane's *Landmarks* (2014) borrows this idea from Lewis and attempts to scale it up to a national glossary. The book is another image of the nation at large that is heterogeneous, intricate, inclusive and open-ended, founded in vernacular localism but showing its diverse parts in dialogue with one another, like Mabey's *Flora Britannica*. We can also see this book as a form of cultural rewilding, drawing attention to the linguistic space at the intersection of the human and non-human. Macfarlane draws attention to where the language has thinned, and is thinning still, and attempts to rehabilitate it. In this sense we can understand its composite landscape vision as political, as about identity and the different ways people identify with place, as a part of their intangible heritage. However, it is not immediately clear what one might do with, or how one might read, *Landmarks*. Perhaps this is part of its particular beauty. Like Monbiot's projects of rewilding the book seems to have 'no fixed objective' beyond putting things into circulation, getting things growing again

(2013: 83). It is unlikely that many terms will find their way into the *OED*, but that might make *Landmarks* all the more important as a book, an historical snapshot of an ambiguous, changing, vernacular language that exists on the outer edge of language in its written conventions and form. Like Sweeney under his curse, the language of this 'counter-desecration phrasebook' is between worlds, beyond the security of the normal social sphere yet still connected to it tenuously by ways of seeing and thinking. Like the projects of rewilding and community land initiatives, the uncertainty that comes with this 'word-horde's' (Macfarlane 2014: 3) connection to something beyond our control, and often beyond our everyday perception, is precisely what makes it so vivid and what might make it in the end, to quote Jane Bennett again, 'stretch our moral sense of the possible' (2001: 32).

3

Edgelands

Patrick Keiller's 2010 semi-fictional documentary film *Robinson in Ruins* turned a sharp eye on the cultures of landscape and place in Britain. The film takes an unusual form of narrative that, like Keiller's previous two films, uses the fictional character 'Robinson' as its central device. Robinson is a melancholic flanêur of England's cities, industrial estates, dockyards, suburbs and ruins who, in this film, turns his attention to the countryside of the south of England. His name looks to Defoe's shipwrecked and island-bound *Robinson Crusoe*, as it looks to the verb coined by Rimbaud: *robinsonner*, 'to let the mind wander or to travel mentally' (Coverley 2010: 68). As Robinson wanders from place to place reflecting on what he sees, there is also a gesture to Defoe's own *Tour through the Whole Island of Great Britain*, a national survey developed from several years of travel (1724–6) and in the tradition of earlier chorographical works such as Saxton's *Atlas* (1579) and Drayton's *Poly-Olbion* (1612). However, the story that the film has to tell about the English countryside is one fraught with very modern contradictions in which picturesque scenes hide histories of enclosure and violent insurrection, in which agricultural labour has been determined by global agents and economic crisis, and in which the uplifting experience of the kinds of wildlife explored in the last chapter is undermined by figures about biodiversity loss and climate change. One of the ways in which the film unearths these contradictions is by choosing particularly ambiguous edgeland spaces from which to look into this uncertain countryside: motorway embankments, decommissioned quarries, retail parks, even a disused military base. Robinson himself is very often to be found taking refuge in such dilapidated edgelands, in terrain that jars with the more conservative literary and artistic conventions of the rural.

'A few years ago, while dismantling a derelict caravan in the corner of a field, a recycling worker found a box containing 19 film cans and a notebook,' the film begins. 'A group of researchers have arranged some of this material as a film, narrated by their institution's co-founder with the title *Robinson in Ruins*'. Robinson, it seems, shot these reels before he disappeared. Typically absent, he never speaks himself, but what we watch through the lens of an always completely stationary camera is through his eyes, and what we hear are excerpts from his journal in the voice of a narrator (in this case Vanessa Redgrave) trying to piece together what might have happened to him. Early on, Martin Heidegger's notion of dwelling and his philosophy of 'the fourfold' are employed in a typically paradoxical fashion. The narrator speaks while the camera is fixed on a boarded up and derelict building where Robinson has been living, if not 'dwelling':

> Despite his increasing insubstantiality, Robinson had returned from Lidl with two bottles of Putinoff vodka and several own-brand items in illustrated packaging that recalled the dwelling of black forest farmers which, for Heidegger, let Earth and Heaven, divinities and mortals, enter into simple oneness with things. For which simple oneness Robinson began to search by visiting a well.

The satirical juxtaposition of Heideggerean dwelling and the marketing strategies of 'own-brand' budget European supermarket goods bring the idea of 'simple oneness' into question. And yet our protagonist sets off quite innocently in search of exactly this, oblivious, so it seems, to the irony. After finding the well that Robinson is inspired to go in search of, though not, perhaps, the 'oneness', there is a sudden change in the weather and he recalls 'the purpose of his undertaking': 'The next day ten leading climate scientists published a paper warning that then current CO_2 targets were too high for humanity to preserve a planet similar to that on which civilisation developed and would lead, instead, to irreversible disaster'. The narrator moves on but for many the lingering, contradictory experience will be a familiar one: the desire for an innocent connection with the world shot through by an awareness that in our most ordinary behaviour – in our use of supermarkets and energy, for example – we have long undermined the prospects of such innocence. The camera remains staring at the boarded up, derelict building where Robinson has been living. It is a liminal space, not quite a home, not quite a place at all really, in the conventional understanding of the word, neither rented nor owned, just occupied provisionally by this mysteriously vanished character. It is walking distance from both a budget supermarket and a well and, like the derelict caravan where the recycling worker found these film cans, we place it mentally in that terrain on the edge of the city, a liminal, ambiguous and paradoxical place, one that might trouble any static or stable idea of place itself.

The term 'edgelands' was first coined by the landscape historian Marion Shoard to describe the 'interfacial rim' that lies between city and country, often a very large zone in which planning regulations are relaxed to allow for the building of infrastructure necessary to life on either side of it (2002: 117). 'Waste landscapes' or 'drosscape' are other terms that have been used to describe these difficult-to-define places (Berger 2007). Another helpful term is the French phrase *terrain vague* used by the architect Ignasi Solà-Morales Rubio to describe the vacated and derelict sites in and around a city (1995). 'Edgelands' and *terrain vague* are not quite interchangeable but, as Joanne Lee has pointed out, thinking about edgelands as *terrain vague* encourages us to see the 'edge' of 'edgelands' as plural and labyrinthine rather than as a straightforward border between city and country (two concepts that are themselves already deeply intertwined) (2015: 14). It encourages us to see edgelands as *intricately*, rather than *simply*, liminal. In this sense, military ruins in remote areas, and wastelands in the heart of a city, might also be considered edgelands for the simple fact that they have fallen out of currency. For Rubio, *terrain vague* is, and is not, a place. It is in some sense the undoing of a place like the derelict caravan or boarded up building that Robinson occupies. *Terrain vague* is 'after' a place in the sense that Richard Jefferies's *After London* (1885) imagines a city that has been overrun by wild nature. In this sense the 'edge' is a temporal and historical one as well.

Terrain vague as a term also helps to envision edgelands as a space in their own right rather than as merely defined by what is on either side of them. In this sense it is helpful to think of edgelands as a *type* of *terrain vague*, one with very distinctive characteristics which contrast the power and activity, the overdetermined functional space, of a city. They represent a space which is 'void, absence, yet also promise, the space of the possible, of expectation' (Rubio 1995: 119). But promise and possibility are rarely permitted to remain promise and possibility for long without being 'realised' as something else, so these are also often sites of conflict and change. They beckon, for example, to the developer and the conservationist alike to reinvent and restore. It is perhaps this clash of promise and conflict that has seen artists and authors gravitate towards them in recent years.[1]

Edgelands are spaces in which the 'event' of place is in unusually dynamic flux, often both in terms of wildlife and modernity (Massey 2005: 140). Far from the careful mediations of the human and non-human in the previous chapter's exploration of the wild, here wildlife and modernity overlap in sprawling, feral and unbalanced ways. On the one hand they are spaces where the pesticides of large-scale agribusiness are not employed. They are not 'productive' land in the agricultural sense and so they are often left alone meaning that biodiversity can come to thrive. The photographer Edward Chell, for example, has spent time recording the proliferation of rare wildflowers in the ribbons of motorway embankment (the 'soft estate') between roads and the surrounding farmland (Smith 2014). On the other hand, as Marion Shoard has argued, the relaxation of planning regulations in the edgelands has meant that they have become 'the ultimate physical expression of the character of our age, unmediated by the passing tastes of elite groups' (2002: 141). Incinerators, sewage works, gasometers, warehouses, or 'big sheds', and retail parks sit side by side with marshland, coastline, flood relief channels and 'restored' nature reserves (former gravel pits or quarries). The composite of ecology, topography and human geography has intensified in these zones in singularly modern ways that reveal and illuminate tensions and contradictions that exist in our conventions of landscape and in our understanding of place. Writing about edgelands is therefore very often a process of self-consciously renegotiating our relationship with landscape and place through complex hybrids of genre, convention and form. It is perhaps for this reason that we so often find Robinson in the edgelands, walking, watching, living, trying to make sense of the conflicts and contradictions of this island-bound existence in his own fugitive way. This chapter will take a closer look at several works by authors and artists who are doing likewise. It will begin by considering 'Modern Nature' through Richard Mabey's *The Unofficial Countryside* (1973) and it will continue with an exploration of 'Feral Modernity' through Paul Farley and

---

[1] For example, see 'Ruin Lust' (4 March–18 May 2014). Tate Britain, London. 'Soft Estate: Art of the Edgelands' (8 March–3 May 2014). Spacex, Exeter.

Michael Symmons Roberts's *Edgelands: Journeys in Britain's True Wilderness* (2011). However, the account of edgelands that emerges between these two begs a question about not only the contemporary status of edgelands, but also the kinds of history they contain and the kind of future they might have. These are, of course, questions of heritage. In the final part, through a reading of Ken Worpole, and Jason Orton's *The New English Landscape* (2013), the chapter explores the possibility of an edgelands heritage and asks what we might learn about heritage more widely by thinking about it in relation to such ambiguous places.

Modern nature

> There, where the tapering cranes sweep around,
> And great wheels turn, and trains roar by
> Like strong, low-headed brutes of steel –
> There is my world, my home; yet why
> So alien still? For I can neither
> Dwell in that world, not turn again
> To scythe and spade, but only loiter
> Among the trees the smoke has slain.

In the early pages of Richard Mabey's *The Unofficial Countryside*, we are given these lines from George Orwell's 'On a Ruined Farm Near the His Master's Voice Gramophone Factory' (1973: 19). They describe a particular moment of reorientation in between the country and the city. Orwell is resistant to both of them and stands his ground, circumspect and clear-sighted. The city is a place of modernity, development and ambition but one in which he feels he cannot 'dwell'; and yet there is no going back to a long-past agricultural way of life either. The moment's pause in which he comes to 'loiter' reveals a landscape of its own, a difficult and uncertain space which would not easily conform to the usual literary conventions. This is the *terrain vague*, beginning to break out of the old country/city binary, that Mabey himself sets out to explore, an edge in many sense of the word: between country and city, between past and present, and even between the literary conventions of the rural tradition and the modernist city. Orwell's loitering inspires Mabey to try something new, to find his way into the gaps, or under these conventions, sniffing out the state of the natural world where it has often come to thrive against the odds. Beneath both country and city, Mabey finds a surprising environment of animals and plants that suggest a prehistoric resilience haunting the edges of an all-too-human world. In so doing, a space is revealed that has almost nothing to do with the country and the city, and yet it is one that subtends both. Mabey's 1973 book is an attempt call up that landscape through the gaps between the worlds which have been laid over it. As he does so, the places he writes about find a purchase in the public imagination and a record is made of their distinctly modern shape and qualities.

The Unofficial Countryside was published the same year as Raymond Williams's *The Country and the City* and between them they represent something of a change in the climate of the literature of the British, and especially the English, landscape. What both Orwell and Mabey are resisting here is a retreat into the idealized notion of the countryside, one that Williams suggests is, in fact, a 'myth' associated with the pastoral idea of a 'golden age', a recently vanished era when everything might have been simpler (1973: 37). F. R. Leavis and Denys Thompson had offered a modern example of such a myth in their idea of 'organic community' in the 1930s. This was a way of life in which social relations were based on craftsmanship and the rhythms of nature, one that was the recent victim of industrialism, urbanism and modernity and yet also, paradoxically, 'right and inevitable' (qtd. in Williams 1958: 252). This is not to say that social relations based on craftsmanship and the rhythms of nature ought not to be something to aspire to but rather that 'organic community', much like the 'dwelling' of Heidegger's Black Forest farmers, somehow misremembers and idealizes a life based on agriculture in the middle of the twentieth century. Such a backward-looking ideal can end up blinding people to the contemporary reality which, as Mabey was to find, offered a remarkable story of its own that was going untold. Williams does concede that a 'myth' like this can serve as a radical call to arms against capitalism, but argues that this is often for those with little experience of rural life, and generally at the expense of an understanding of the actual history of feudal and pre-feudal social organization. It is more often the case, he suggests, that 'an idealisation, based on a temporary situation and on a deep desire for stability, served to cover and to evade the actual and bitter contradictions of the time' (1973: 45).

In an essay examining the environmental tradition 'after organic community', Martin Ryle has argued that our 'sense of loss ... is also a cultural resource' and that, 'rather than dismissing it, we need to confront and understand it' (2002: 22). By doing precisely this and exploring the difficult modern relationship to the urban and suburban environment, Mabey begins to reorient himself in relation to the living landscape free of the nostalgia that Williams warns us against. And it is interesting to note that this begins with loitering. 'Loiter' comes from the Dutch to wobble or wag about with particular reference to a loose tooth. The *OED* suggests that the word began to be used in its modern meaning as slang introduced to England by foreign 'loiterers' themselves. Loitering is what you do when others believe you should be elsewhere doing something else. It is to be displaced, then, and without purpose, or perhaps more accurately, it is to appear to be without obvious purpose. It is not working or travelling, waiting or resting. It is as liminal and ambiguous as the edgelands themselves, not one thing or another. Loitering is often the behaviour of 'suspect' characters, workshy, malicious ('loitering with intent'), obstructing the flow of purposeful life – all of which no doubt looks back to certain xenophobic anxieties about immigrants, tramps, travellers, outsiders. The more industrious, even industrial, a society, the more suspect the loiterer. But loitering might also, in fact, be about acclimatization or reorientation. We might think here, too, of Keiller's use of stationary camera positions in which there is no zooming, no panning, no movement of any kind.

Like the style of writing itself, the style of walking through, watching or apprehending a place read the land differently and can therefore be read themselves as a choreographed (or unchoreographed) performances might be, from a hike along an ancient byway to a local trespass in a landscaped garden; from a search for a folkloric site to the observation of nesting birds from a kitchen window. Mabey begins *The Unofficial Countryside* with this reference to loitering as an expression of his anxieties and uncertainties about how to travel in search of a landscape beneath the usual conventions. He describes planning to 'journey in an erratic circle around London, tacking towards and away from the centre' but soon decides this is a 'ludicrously inappropriate formula' (1973: 26). In fact, he suggests that he wants to distance himself from previous, ambitious expeditions and their subsequent national or regional 'surveys', like Defoe's or William Cobbett's. These, he suggests, are the modes of travel of the 'official countryside', and after feeling quite embarrassed by carrying the usual day-sack and binoculars in a highly populated suburb he suggests:

> Rambling ... was certainly no natural activity in the built-up areas. It tempts you to try and make an adventure out of something whose most important meaning is altogether more intimate and homely. If I wanted to catch that sense it would more likely be in lunch-hour strolls, weeds found in a garden corner, a bird glimpsed through a bus window. It was a change of focus that was needed, a new perspective on the everyday. (30–1)

The 'new perspective' that Mabey discovers comes through a certain resistance to convention, resistance *both* to the countryside ramble with its memory of landscape tourism and the picturesque, and to that of the industrious metropolitan flow of crowds. But it doesn't come easily at first, or from any one sustained style or method of investigation. It comes from a whole spectrum of very ordinary ('intimate and homely') ways of looking and moving.

The book's opening pages describe an author 'locked-up, boxed-in, and daydreaming morbidly', stuck in gridlocked traffic driving out of London. In response to this though, rather than taking to the usual hills and valleys, Mabey heads down to the canal towpaths and gravel pits, the wastelands and municipal parks within the M25. He watches sand martins in a temporary sandbank raised by road works in Middlesex from a Greenline bus as it passes daily (1973: 33). He pulls over in his car to explore an explosion of giant hogweed (*Heracleum mantegazzianum*) among rows of factories (82). He allows himself to get lost and ends up knee-deep in mud on Hampstead Heath. He emerges from the heath for a pint in a pub, filthy, 'feeling smug about my hard morning down t'park' (the turn of phrase playfully juxtaposing traditions of work and recreation, industrial and designed landscape) (115). Essentially, there is no prescribed method but opportunism to get off the beaten track and under the conventional myths. Routes feed out in any direction from the daily routine at the insistence of chance encounters.

There is an obvious parallel here. In Paris, Guy Debord and the Situationists had been developing experimental tactics for a highly politicized walking of the city since 1958, tactics that challenged the usual flow of people and consumption. Mabey's careful consideration of the way in which he was going to approach these modern landscapes, the improvisation according to sudden chance encounters, does connect to the idea of the *dérive*, or the 'drift', in which ambience or happenstance would lead the walker away from the usual flow of the crowd. Mabey's self-conscious search for a new perspective strikes a chord with that 'moment of life concretely and deliberately constructed', the very 'situations' that gave the Situationists their name (Debord 1958: n.p.). However, just as Mabey attempts to discover a form more singularly adapted to these places than the narratives of the 'official countryside', so he diverges from the deliberate constructions of urban psychogeographers as well. Mabey's real source comes less from post-war Paris than from eighteenth-century Hampshire, from Selborne, and a naturalist whose own extraordinary way of looking at the world broke new ground for the science. Gilbert White, about whom Mabey would go on to write a prize-winning biography, advanced our contemporary knowledge of migrating birds and, by way of the most unquenchable and minute curiosity, discovered numerous species of wildflower and insect in the landscape around his home. It is to White more than anyone that Mabey is directing our attention with the structure of his book as a seasonal year. He here describes White's unorthodox methods, in which there is something of his own search for a new perspective based on 'the intimate and homely'. Mabey describes:

> the patient, inquisitive watching, the changes of focus as questions multiply; the answers dawning, from flashes of intuition or plain hard reasoning, and these forming a framework to test against yet more watching. And all these processes not rigidly ordered but advancing together in a kind of continuous feedback loop. (2006a: 81)

This collision of the naturalist and the psychogeographer throws a curious light on a book that was very much of its time in 1973.

Stephen E. Hunt has suggested the term 'psychoecology' for work like Mabey's, and later works by Macfarlane and Deakin. Hunt draws on affinities shared between these nature writers and Iain Sinclair and Will Self, and emphasizes the 'agency of the writer in constructing as well as describing the natural world' (2008: 76). The particular construction of the natural world in this book comes from turning an eye on a very modern version of 'nature' that an emphasis on either country or city had overlooked. While some might have assumed no wildlife would survive in edgelands, Mabey recognized its resilience and adaptability, its 'dogged and inventive survival in the face of all that we deal out' (1973: 23). *The Unofficial Countryside* offers startling observations or images, visions almost, of the human and non-human worlds tangled together, before which Mabey describes himself at times as 'morbidly elated' (29). We see a heron building a makeshift nest 'on the roof of a captive heron's cage in the nearby Zoo', pointing up an absurd disjuncture between the bird as a spectacle and the bird as a more neighbourly and everyday sight (108). We see 'a calling cuckoo caught in a Lido fence' where the play of alliteration on the c's and l's oddly aestheticizes a disturbing scene: a real, modern cuckoo and the cuckoo of pastoral convention collide (29). There are grebes like 'obsolete Spanish aristocrats' against 'the tasteless backcloth of bulldozers and extraction machinery', a tragi-comic image which brings the wildlife to the foreground and sees the human development recede (62–3). There is the noise of a tree full of starlings 'well nigh blotting out the grind of the concrete mixers a few hundred yards away' (46). Each one offers something of an imagist poem stitching together wildlife and modernity. There is a very particular version of nature here, but it is a long way from 'Nature' as a non-human objectified other 'out there', pristine and untrammelled (Morton 2007: 6).

This book's introduction explored the way 'Nature' has become a problematic term in light of recent developments in environmental criticism. Bill McKibben has argued that the effects of human development have had such far-reaching effects on our atmosphere and oceans that 'our mistaken sense of nature as eternal and separate will be washed away' (1990: 7). Timothy Morton has gone so far as to suggest that it is the very concept of 'Nature' as something 'other' and 'out there' that is holding us back from a truly ecological form of thought (2007: 5). Jamie Lorimer proposed that in light of critical deconstructions, 'multiple natures' might be possible and 'multinatural' thinking necessary for understanding them (2015: 2). Mabey has been a passionate defender of the use of the term 'nature' but he rarely means by it something 'eternal' or 'out there'. The particular nature he offers in *The Unofficial Countryside*, for example, is distinctively placed in the *terrain vague* of Greater London in the 1970s. Kate Soper has endeavoured to balance both 'nature sceptical' and 'nature endorsing' arguments to arrive at some productive thoughts about the idea. On the one hand, she has argued that the nature that ecologists are attempting to conserve is also the nature that has been dominated and destroyed in the name of a certain *natural* order of relations, rights of ownership and forms of exploitation (1990: 250–1). Here she points out the hypocritical ironies of essentialist arguments that ascribe a moral value to nature. Nature in this sense has always been something conceptually constructed, and historically contingent, and people have often endeavoured to hide its constructed form with such appeals to an organic essence. On the other hand, though it is true that much of what we refer to as 'natural' has been shaped and developed by the human hand and the modern world, nonetheless 'that activity does not "construct" the powers and processes upon which it is dependent for its operation' (249). It is this latter version of nature as power and process, related to the previous chapter's exploration of the wild, that Mabey is exploring beneath the conventions of country and city.

In 2011 Tim Dee suggested of the 'New Nature Writing' that there were some surprising challenges to be faced by the authors in coming to terms with a contemporary sense of nature:

Country diaries survive in some newspapers but DDT, species losses, and Ted Hughes' gore-poetics saw off the nice in the 1970s, while nature itself – under the human heel – has been pushed, bloodied, shrunken and ruined to the front of the stage ever since. There, even enfeebled, it has called for new descriptions, fresh thoughts. (22)

Far from being something 'out there' offering an escape from modernity, Dee suggests that a new version of nature has emerged, shot through and through by modernity, entrenched with the same complexities and anxieties. If a version of modern nature is showing itself here, it is a long way from the natures (plural) of the past: from, for example, the endlessly replenishing divine nature of the eighteenth-century physico-theologists; or the carefully ordered taxonomies of Carl Linneaus's *Systema Naturæ* (1758); or even the deified, tutelary 'Nature' of Wordsworth. This is a particular, late-twentieth-century version of nature, and Mabey's *The Unofficial Countryside*, like Hughes' 'gore-poetics' contributed to its reappraisal. Abject and vulnerable perhaps, but also bearing up strikingly under the pressure, this modern nature is a bruised and resourceful survivor. In Mabey's 'new descriptions, fresh thoughts' there is a particular historical perspective. This is, again, a construction of nature based upon historically contingent ways of looking and their concomitant forms of representation, but it is one founded on such values as concern, admiration and curiosity, arising out of the conservation and environmental movements of the time. Watching those sand martins nest and rear a family of chicks in a pile of sand on a roundabout that would only be there for a matter of weeks before being used in construction, Mabey learns something new about familiar wildlife, about its gall, opportunism and toughness. The book brings this to light, enriching a public understanding of wildlife, connecting that understanding with contemporary experience rather than letting it rely too heavily on the conventions of another era.

Tracing the animals and plant life in and around a city also refreshes ways of thinking about the space of the city as well. That the first summer after the Blitz there was rosebay willowherb flowering on over three-quarters of the bombed sites in London, 'defiant sparks of life amongst the desolation', is a reminder of the earth's capacity for renewal, always just a foot or two beneath the pavement (1973: 35). Kestrels too are found to be nesting quite 'democratically' in 'the Savoy Hotel, gasometers in the East End, Nelson's Column, the House of Lords, various power station chimneys and a ventilator shaft in Broadcasting House' (101). A very different perspective on London emerges inflected by the wildness, both at its heart and on its edges, both under it and surrounding it. Modern nature, as much as it lies 'under the human heel', seems ready to sprout back up and over it as well and there is something consoling and inspiring to admire in its resilience. Far from posing an escape from modernity, an 'out there' to our 'in here', this particular nature, when watched narrowly through Mabey's naturalist's eye, underpins modernity, runs right through it and shows itself in lively and contemporary dialogue with it. The ambiguous *terrain vague* of edgelands allows this distinctively modern nature to emerge, to erupt, in fact, with all its fascinating paradoxes through the landscape traditions and conventions of another era.

Feral modernity

In 2011, the two poets, Paul Farley and Michael Symmons Roberts, collaborated on a book called *Edgelands: Journeys into England's True Wilderness*. The object of the book was to explore, like Mabey, those overlooked and in-between places such as wastelands, business parks, container ports, motorway bridges, sewage works and power stations: landscapes they felt had been largely ignored by the more conservative traveller in search of picturesque scenes. 'Sometimes they are written off,' they suggest, 'as part of the urban (or suburban) human landscape that has to be escaped, or transcended' (8). Farley and Roberts owe a debt to Mabey but they also develop and grow the project in an interesting way all their own. Marion Shoard argued in 2002 that edgelands offer an unexploited opportunity to connect with the functioning architecture of the ordinary needs on which our day-to-day lives are based in their raw state, and that for this reason they are to be celebrated. For Shoard, a greater appreciation of these landscapes would be beneficial since they represent the reality of our footprint on the immediate environment. Were schoolchildren to encounter the waste dumps and car crushing facilities that are hidden away on these sites, so her argument goes, it might make them more conscious of the impact that they as individuals, and as members of families, are having on the land in which they live. That in Britain and elsewhere all our necessary ugliness is hidden in areas that are largely ignored has led to an embarrassing sense of disconnection with reality, an 'alienation and puzzlement' symptomatic of a bourgeois consumer attitude to place (2002: 142). It is precisely to Shoard's call for an appreciation of these places, then, that Farley and Roberts were responding with their book in 2011.

Early on the authors quote a few lines of poetry by the eighteenth-century Quaker poet John Scott who once described the wildflowers clustered over an enclosure ditch. A friend of the poet struggled with the 'shameless modernism' of remarking on the ditch since it suggested a politically and economically constructed landscape that did not square with a pastoral or a picturesque aesthetic. Farley and Roberts wonder 'how would he have coped with barbed-wire fencing or the IKEA car park?' and with this in mind they set about making such 'shameless modernism' their project (2011: 32). The more they travel through such 'complicated, unexamined places' (10), the more they find they 'admire them' (9). Tim Edensor has argued that the editing out of such reminders of contemporary life is a tactic still largely employed in the representation of rural England in magazines, observing that 'there are no pylons, mobile phone masts, new buildings or telegraph poles to be seen', all of which are essential to our most basic infrastructure needs (qtd. in Worpole and Orton 2013: 28). Ken Worpole suggests that such omissions may have 'substantially contributed to the confusion we experience today' (28) when it comes to modern landscape aesthetics, a confusion no doubt related to that 'alienation and puzzlement' that Shoard suggests is a result of our overlooking edgelands (2002: 142). Farley and Roberts were attempting to adjust their aesthetic sensibility, to align it more closely with the state of the land as it is used and encountered by hundreds of thousands every day, walking dogs on the edge of town, driving around industrial estates, looking from the window of a train, or the raised viaduct of a motorway. They are framing what we might see every day but seldom inquire after. Scenes that would never ordinarily find themselves framed or appealing are lifted out of the obsolete and offered up in short passages of poetic prose.

In a strange and playful way then, this is landscape tourism and the picturesque in a modern literary guise, though all is not as straightforward as it seems. Take the following passage, for instance, where the love of ruins and a curious preoccupation with finding surprising new compositions might have been written by William Gilpin himself were it an abbey rather than a factory:

> Have you seen the sudden, filmic light effects of low winter sun across a ruined factory, the hard-cut shadows and blinding reflections off broken glass? Late-afternoon sun on a clear day throwing giant shadows like ink fields on the scrubland behind power station cooling towers? Or milk morning sun brushing the tops of willowherb, nettle, thistle, in the unkempt field behind the car-crushers? (2011: 257)

The adjustment in aesthetics here cannot help but remind us that there was also an adjustment in aesthetics taking place in the early days of the picturesque. An artistically minded, largely urban population were beginning to tire of the familiar tamed and productive agricultural landscapes and to travel further afield. Mountainous, craggy and wild landscapes like the Lake District had been described by Ralph Thoresby in 1697 as full of 'dreadful fells, hideous wastes, horrid waterfalls, terrible rocks and ghastly precipices' (qtd. in Thomas 1983: 258). In the second half of the eighteenth century, however, they were beginning to be highly valued and written about by, for example, the poet Thomas Gray, who visited on his own in 1769, and of course later Wordsworth and Coleridge. The taste for such landscapes was changing and the rise of the tourist with his or her Claude glass saw the beginning of their consumption as scenery. In their chapter on 'Water', Farley and Roberts seem to be encouraging a subsequent change that might echo this of the eighteenth century, and though the style of landscape is qualitatively different, the appeal to a class of aesthetic tourist seeking novelty to consume seems oddly identical.

'Water' begins with Alfred Wainwright's much loved 'Innominate Tarn', itself among the Lake District's 'Haystacks', before taking us, by way of contrast and by way of preference, to two other pools in their own 'True Wilderness': one on the edge of the Naylorsfield housing estate north of Liverpool and one on the outskirts of Peterborough, just beyond 'a well-used dogging spot' (2011: 72–5). The latter pool is described as a pond 'rich in detail, a Pre-Raphaelite vision with the focus now screwed tight and sharp, now scrimmed and soft, touched by the colours of wild flowers in the summer months' (75). The poets end that particular part reminding us that 'all over England, ponds just like them have claimed the lives of children, on summer afternoons separated by decades' (75). As with all good picturesque landscapes, the rich aesthetic is brought into tension with a background sense of danger or drama, something to bring about what Gilpin called a 'pause of intellect' (1972 [1792]: 50). It is something familiar to the pastoral tradition too, the *memento mori* often spoken by death himself: *Et In Arcadia Ego* ('Even in Arcadia am I') (Dubrow 1999: 194). Farley and Roberts frame the most unlikely of places using well-known landscape conventions. In part there is a nostalgic celebration of a type of edgelands place in which they and many others will have spent childhood afternoons, weekends or summer holidays but the celebration is complicated by the feeling that this also seems to parody the picturesque itself as well. Can it be both a celebration and a parody? Again, the exploration of edgelands unearths a paradox in our attitude to landscape. Childhood nostalgia and adult scepticism can inhabit us at the same time and the uncertainty as to what the edgelands are, what they should be – that sense of conflict and possibility – brings this out.

Mabey's inventiveness in *The Unofficial Countryside* is most apparent in his way of looking and exploring, but with *Edgelands* the inventiveness is most apparent in the written form itself. The book is divided into chapters with edgeland themes or features for titles, such as 'Canals', 'Bridges', 'Pallets', 'Retail', 'Mines' and so on, but each chapter is further broken down into an idiosyncratic structure of smaller sections, and a distinctive form begins to emerge. Part annotation, part sketch, part diary entry, these are often not more than a page, and never more than three pages, long. This prevents the sense of a continuous journey or a polished, conventional narrative, and feels more reflective, more like a collage of set pieces with the emphasis on thinking and inquiring rather than on a finished thought or an answered question. It is a form that captures something of that 'loitering' Orwell describes above, but the book lacks any of the melancholy and instead sets out to embrace the modern in prose that is heterogeneous and experimental in its figures. The short set pieces become routines, flurries of conversation that try out an idea before receding into silence again. The rhythm seems oddly reminiscent of Samuel Beckett's dialogue at times, punctuated unevenly by pauses as a subject runs out and a new one is concocted. In fact it becomes frustrating to read. You could be forgiven for asking, from time to time, 'what are they doing? Where is this going?' But this is the moment that you are also tuning in to the form. This is not a book that has set out to go anywhere. Like Mabey's, perhaps even more so, it is resistant to the 'going a journey' narrative. In an early review, Geoff Dyer wrote:

> It's not just that there is no sense of a developing argument; there is an absolute lack – and I mention this as a shortcoming precisely because I am the kind of reader for whom this is not a priority – of any kind of narrative drive. Two-thirds of the way through, it becomes evident that Edgelands is never going to be more than the sum of its parts – but the parts are often terrific. (2011: n.p.)

The book toys with expectations and forces the reader into a halting disorientation, never quite sure what might be encountered next. In the end its perpetual shifting comes to emulate the ambiguity of the places themselves, ever changing their character depending on what they are being used for (a rough playground for children, a sleeping spot for the homeless, an area to walk dogs or watch birds, meet for casual sex, view stars, get fit, cycle, graffiti or host a rave). This is what Rubio calls *terrain vague* again, in which there exists intensely 'the space of the possible' (1995: 119).

If we take, for a moment, the definitions of space and place given by Michel de Certeau, an unusual relationship between them begins to open up here. In de Certeau's largely urban conception, 'space' is what we create within the 'place' of a city by moving across it (Buchanan 2000: 102). Space is the performative assertion of our freedom within and against the restriction of such freedom by the architecture and legal discourse of streets, alleys, towers, stairways and subways that make up the *place* of a city. De Certeau's understanding of place is one at odds with the understanding of place that this book is arguing for, but it might be instructive to consider the relationship to space that he puts it in for a moment. In the edgelands it is precisely this static conception of place that de Certeau gives that has come undone as the built environment lapses into *terrain vague*, making the freedom of the individual's creation of space all the more free and possible. For de Certeau, the walk is a creative act and is described, in terms akin to language itself, as an 'enunciative focalisation' (1984: 116). This casting of lived space as an assertive, signifying act is particularly marked at moments in the book when surprising things occur in the edgelands, when they become miniature theatres for strange human behaviour. In the following from the chapter on woodlands, after reading about a rise in people hunting deer in edgelands in Scotland they imagine the following:

> A hunt in the postmodern forest might begin with the weapons being inspected and made ready, the dogs quietened in their car cages. Next, a few lines of grey cocaine are chopped out with a supermarket loyalty card on the back of a CD case, and, suitably emboldened and excited, the caravan of 4 × 4s switches to full beam and enters the scratchy woodland. Leaving the vehicles at the car park, the party then moves ahead on foot, quietly through a dark scented with honeysuckle, wild rose and nightshade, over stiles and along footpaths, deeper into the woods, until the shout goes out and the dogs are let loose. The whole thing is recorded on cameraphones. (2011: 169)

An oddly anonymous nocturnal group is involved in activities for which we do not seem to have a frame of reference. Conventionally, hunting is undertaken in parkland or the Highlands by landed gentry, the wealthy, even the aristocracy. We do not readily associate hunting with this environment, or with drugs, loyalty cards and cameraphones, but the neglect to which edgelands have been left has opened up the potential for a certain transgressive freedom. And this comes across through the movement from reportage into fictionalized narrative as well. It is a textual liberty that emulates the taking of a certain spatial liberty. Everything about the passage transgresses. Even the 'honeysuckle, wild rose and nightshade' hint at a postmodern subversion of sylvan pastoral.

In a later passage, the pastoral and postmodern collide again in the oddly transgressive behaviour of another anonymous group of people. Again the border between non-fiction and fiction melts away. It is one of the shortest entries in the book from the chapter on 'Weather', reproduced here in full:

> The spring of 2010, and the first signs that iPhone birdsong apps are being abused, as people begin to play the pre-recorded warblings and alarm bells of various confused species back into the trees and bushes. We see the first occurrences of a new kind of edgelands flash mob: at first light, hundreds gather in the silent places outside of towns and cities, lit by the firefly glow of their phone screens, and at the preordained exact moment play the songs of their chosen birds, a digital dawn chorus made possible by lightweight flash-memory technology. (259–60)

There is a morally ambiguous curiosity that we feel at this, part imagined, part based on news reports. Fiction seems to take over from reportage, picking up and dramatizing the scene about halfway through again. It is exciting, bizarre and concerning all at the same time. This nocturnal troupe, enabled by new technology, challenges a passive, romantic absorption of the dawn chorus by interacting with it, by participating in it. The lines between nature and technology, human and animal, fiction and reality, all become blurred. The flash-mob performance creates a momentary space of enchantment and bacchic frenzy that appears suddenly and recedes just as quickly. In this and the hunt scene above there are playful, barbed and provoking images of anonymous human behaviour at the wild edges and they are offered up without comment before a change of subject. There are no judgements in the edgelands, they seem to be saying. This is Rubio's 'space of the possible' pushed to a space of carnivalesque lawlessness and anarchy, a behavioural as well as a spatial hiatus from the ordinary running of society. These passages present an interesting comparison to Mabey's visions of wildlife tangled up with land developments: visions of feral modernity that complement his own visions of modern nature.

However, the admiration that Farley and Roberts hold for edgelands as *spaces* (in de Certeau's definition) is, in the end, as difficult as their adoption of the picturesque and pastoral modes. It is subversive and imaginative, but it is also oddly detached. The nostalgia arising out of their childhood experiences in edgelands emphasizes the spatial possibilities and freedoms, but in doing so they somehow fail to connect with the contemporary status of edgelands as *places*. 'The edgelands now need something beyond a merely subjective celebration of their identity,' wrote Shoard in her review of their book. 'Far more than our towns and countryside, they are being subjected to ceaseless change. Wild space is being prettified at the expense of its character and creatures. Industrial ruins are being cleared away' (2011: n.p.). The detachment with which Farley and Roberts admire the edgelands sits somewhere between the modernist detachment of the flâneur and the visual detachment of the landscape tourist. The book will no doubt be a powerful tool in making arguments for the conservation of edgelands, but how that conservation might take place – how the ambiguity and vagueness of them as places might be protected without being made into something less ambiguous and less vague – is a difficult discussion that they avoid. For example, they are quick to sniff out the hypocrisy of a community woodland group who damage the edgelands ecosystem where they plant their trees. Nonetheless, they seem to welcome the retail village or the industrial estate, even in one case provocatively proposing a 'Premier Inn on top of Ben Nevis and a Little Chef on Scafell Pike' (2011: 166).

With the latter of these, they are provoking a reaction from those who mountaineer out of a desire for solitude, but there is a certain anonymous and homogenized design that comes with these forms of development, and an unfortunate and wilful disregard for history. What industrial ruins, picturesque pools and edgelands wildlife were bulldozed to make room for the Trafford Centre outside Manchester, or Birmingham's Fort Shopping Park, places that they find 'beguiling in their honesty'? (217). The imposing architecture of retail parks, shopping centres and container ports is an example of the spatial deterritorialization and feral modernity that they admire too. Shoard herself questions where the workers in such superstores or offices can go in their lunch hour, suggesting that 'the absence of any community space deprives people of their right to live fully' (2011: 132); and she takes issue with the fact that 'councils neglect to provide the most basic public facilities they would automatically provide in a town' (131). These are important issues for the future of edgelands too. In their race to appreciate these places, Farley and Roberts at times seem to ignore or excuse bad design, and the question is begged as to whether celebrating edgelands as an unadulterated expression of our historical moment needs to mean celebrating even footloose and profiteering short-termism. The community woodland they criticize is led by local people invested in the place. Its failures might more kindly be viewed as part of a learning curve, while no such curve will exist on sites owned by global corporate interests unless people demand it. *Edgelands* offers a subversive aesthetic that will no doubt generate interest in these exciting spaces, and it does so in a curiously playful relationship with the conventions of landscape aesthetics, but the book, at times, quite knowingly lapses into a mode that is a symptom of modernity rather than a thoughtful interaction with it.

An edgelands heritage

Ken Worpole and Jason Orton's *The New English Landscape* offers a very different approach to edgelands as it explores a more localized view in the area of the Thames estuary. For Worpole and Orton, influenced by the principles of the European Landscape Convention (which the British have been quite late to sign), our understanding of landscape and place goes to the heart of 'politics, public aesthetics and cultural identity' (2013: 11). They too confront and challenge the tradition of the picturesque from within its own terms – they offer Worpole's critical essays accompanied by Orton's carefully composed photographs – but the critique they articulate is one guided by local histories, among them histories of the communities of artists, intellectuals, socialists, anarchists and Tolstoyans who moved to Essex land colonies associated with the 'back to the land' movement of the late nineteenth and early twentieth centuries. This is a view of the edgelands not merely as free, creative space to visit and think in, space to explore on foot and admire, but as sites where lives were made and utopian experiments lived out. Together they explore the remaining traces in the landscape and document the coming change as large-scale developments move in. Marion Shoard has suggested that at some point people will have to carefully consider the kind of 'relationship' they want to see in the long term 'between our activity in the edgelands, their epic infrastructure, their unique wildlife and industrial archaeology, and their peculiar place in our imagination' (2011: n.p.). If Mabey pioneered new ways of exploring modern nature in these places, and if Farley and Roberts have begun to make arguments for appreciating their feral modernity as well, then Worpole and Orton explore both their third, historical dimension, but also the way these three aspects might be related to one another culturally. They have responded to Shoard's suggestion here by beginning to articulate a distinctive form of heritage for these unusual landscapes, where heritage has recently come to be described (by Rodney Harrison) as 'a form of social and cultural action ... as a form of 'work' which helps to produce a culture' (2010: 36). It is not an easy issue to articulate in relation to edgelands. Putting a fence around such places and signposting them is not the solution; but doing nothing and leaving them to fall prey to future development as the empty wastelands they are often assumed to be is equally unsatisfactory.

In 2014, Worpole and Orton's project website showed a photograph of a small shed nestled among buddleia bushes, accompanied by text describing it as the site of the former Joseph Wells Fireworks Factory near Dartford, Kent. It is one of a number of corrugated iron sheds, 'which for obvious reasons were spaced apart from one another'. They ask, 'How do structures like these feature in debates about what should be preserved in landscapes which are earmarked for regeneration?' The answer, of course, is that presently they do not. 'Unfortunately, planners and developers frequently see landscapes like these as blank canvases that can be cleared or levelled flat. The specifics of place are something they would prefer not to have to address when making their decisions on the future of such ambiguous places' (Worpole and Orton 2014: n.p.). Like Mabey's work, and to an extent Farley and Roberts's, their combination of fieldwork, research, writing and photography helps to unearth a new way of thinking about this area near Dartford, but one that is based on a more careful investigation of historical depth. The insecurity of the place's identity – far from being liberating, as it seems to be for Farley and Roberts – in fact invites a closer scrutiny, one that coaxes more meaning out of the place. Such scrutiny of the insecure heritage of the area has been sustained over several years and continues to grow in their ongoing work. This work can be understood as heritage work insofar as it 'helps to produce a culture', as Harrison suggests; not in the outmoded sense of what was critiqued as 'museumification' in the late 1980s, where the abiding image was of the past under a 'bell jar ... into which no ideas can enter, and, just as crucially, from which none can escape'. This is heritage work insofar as it presents a way of thinking critically about the past as a way of understanding its meanings in the present and for the future (Hewison 1987: 144).

They also admire the work of architect Peter Beard, and in particular his vision for the wildlife sanctuary around Rainham Marshes. They read this designed landscape as, to borrow Jonathan Bate's description of Central Park in New York, 'a representation which we may experience' (2000, 64).

> The complex network of boardwalks, bridges, bird hides and viewing platforms ... has a strong philosophical basis in the art of pathfinding and memory of place, weaving in references to prehistoric brushwood riverside tracks (the exquisite carved wooden *Dagenham Idol* from 2400 BC was found here), the medieval field system and the rusting ruins of military infrastructure – all combined together in a subtle open air theatre of memory. (2013: 77)

The key here is the way Beard draws attention to the plural nature of the landscape for them, the capacity with which he attempts to hold together wildlife and prehistory with medieval and modern military traces. This phrase – 'a subtle open air theatre of memory' – seems to resolve some of the difficulty of the edgelands without closing it down. It suggests a connection to the past but only in the sense that it is being performed in the present. There is a slant reference here to Raphael Samuel's *Theatres of Memory* (1994), a book instrumental in the heritage debates of the 1980s and 1990s again, and a book that also challenged the abstract separation of the past from the present, the representation of memory as 'merely a passive receptacle or storage system, an image bank of the past', and argued for a recognition of memory as rather 'an active, shaping force ... a way of constructing knowledge' (x). This relationship to the past challenges the perception of edgelands as empty. It endeavours to draw out the many different layers of history vying for place in the present and, in doing so, it can invigorate the sense of promise that they offer.

With its emphasis on traces, ruins and history, *The New English Landscape* begins to articulate an important question: what might a heritage of the edgelands look like? The answer is important for two reasons: first, it offers a frame of reference for an increasing number of people who care about such places; but second, the singularly provisional, ambiguous and contested nature of edgelands suggests that a form of heritage that emerges from them might be of interest to the study of heritage itself more widely. Anxieties have been voiced among heritage researchers about the different forms of 'authorised heritage discourse' and their top-down administration by national or international bodies (Smith 2006). Increasingly, attention in critical heritage studies has been turning to alternative forms of heritage practice. Nuanced themes such as intangible cultural heritage, contested heritage and heritage and climate change have been foregrounded for the challenges they pose to heritage workers. There are very distinctive questions that arise in the work of the authors this chapter has discussed about the way constellations of meaning reveal themselves and about how we can interact with them.

The final chapter of *The New English Landscape* is 'Modern Nature,' a term that stems from a conversation between the artist and film-maker Derek Jarman and Maggi Hambling about Jarman's garden near the power station in Dungeness.

> She said: 'Oh, you've finally discovered nature, Derek.'
> 'I don't think it's really quite like that,' I said, thinking of Constable and Samuel Palmer's Kent.
> 'Ah, I understand completely. You've discovered modern nature.' (Qtd. in Worpole and Orton 2013: 76)

The fact that Jarman and Hambling are discussing gardening is important here, in that gardening suggests an involvement with the landscape, a relationship of co-creator, invested in the place beyond its consumption as spectacle. But the type of landscape is important here too. The fact that Jarman's garden is in the shadow of a nuclear power station on one of the most bleak and alien stretches of shingle beach in Europe might perhaps make it doubly an edgeland. Like Mabey's startling visions of resilient wildlife, this too is a version of a precarious, living world involved in complex relations with humans and modernity. It is a place that in its vulnerability chimes poignantly with Rubio's description of *terrain vague* as 'both a physical expression of our fear and insecurity and our expectation of the other, the alternative, the utopian, the future' (1995: 121). Such a singular form of gardening, in this simultaneously recuperative and prospective sense, becomes a metaphor for a wider argument about landscape heritage, landscape aesthetics and the interactions they might have with the practices of planning and design. In a sense, Jarman's garden can be read as a metaphor for the work of all of the edgelands authors, artists and film-makers that this chapter has discussed, nurturing difficult but meaningful forms out of the most unlikely of places, and working at that ambiguous interface between the revealing of meaning and the making of meaning. New senses of place, each in some way slightly recuperative, emerge from new ways of looking and writing here that are struggling out of old conventions. Through the work of these writers, artists and film-makers, edgelands have become sites in which a certain self-reflexive attitude to place has emerged in Britain today; and they have become places to which we might turn to explore a similarly self-reflexive approach to landscape heritage itself more widely.

4

The Periphery

In 1972 a young and successful artist by the name of Timothy Drever moved with his wife from the bustling metropolitan art world of London to the Aran Islands off the west coast of Ireland, where they would live and work for over ten years. In the early 1980s they moved back to the Irish mainland, to the fishing village of Roundstone on the coast of Connemara where they still live today, though by that time the artist had become a maker of detailed maps too and, perhaps more importantly, he had become the author Tim Robinson. As the artist Timothy Drever in London, he had been preoccupied with abstract and geometrical forms and with the social and public spaces of exhibition as they were beginning to be picked apart by the land art movement in Britain and the United States. As the author Tim Robinson, he would find that these very preoccupations with space would intensify and unfold through the poetics of writing about place. Since this dramatic move west he has created several editions of new maps of the Aran Islands, the Burren and Connemara (what he calls his 'ABC of earth-wonders') (1996: vi). The Aran maps in particular were the first to have been made since the Ordnance Survey had attempted to do so as a part of the British government's colonial administration in the mid-nineteenth century. The research undertaken for the maps soon led to what he called the 'world-hungry art of words' and he is now the author of a two-volume study of the Aran Islands, a three-volume study of Connemara, two editions of miscellaneous essays mostly exploring the same places and a volume of short fiction and experimental writings. These works, as John Elder has suggested, have earned Robinson 'a permanent place on the shelf that holds the scientifically informed, speculative and at the same time highly personal narratives of such earlier masters as Gilbert White and Henry David Thoreau' (2014: 1).

Thanks to recent developments in 'regional modernisms', it has become increasingly apparent that the twentieth century saw an abundance of modernist artists and authors turn their backs on the city and the security of mainland life in search of fresh perspectives from the periphery, although most seem to be clustered around the 1920s and 1930s (e.g. see Alexander and Moran 2013). As John Brannigan has shown in *Archipelagic Modernism* (2014), small islands in particular seem to have worked a magical gravity as authors as various as Michael McLaverty, Peadar O'Donnell, Hugh MacDiarmid, W. H. Auden and Louis MacNeice all found themselves experimenting with island tropes in diverse ways. For some, islands were '"hard-edged" microcosms of continental or mainland life'; for others they were remote 'alternative worlds' (145). In asking what drove this islomania, Brannigan suggests an historical and cultural tension identified by Pete Hay that appears to run to the heart of the island experience at the time: that between 'vulnerability and resilience' in which islands are figured as either the 'victims of change' or as 'uniquely resourceful' (qtd. in Brannigan 2014: 147). Such a curious and uncertain tension, Brannigan argues, may well have appealed to authors during the 1920s and 1930s, when

> the very notion of the 'wholeness' of 'Britain', 'England', or the 'United Kingdom' was undermined politically and culturally by the emergent sovereignty of the Irish Free State (1922) and its constitutional claim to the 'whole island of Ireland' (1937), by the Scottish Renaissance of the 1920s, by the formation of Plaid Cymru (1925) and the Scottish National Party (1934), and by the palpable decline of British imperial power across the globe. (147)

Given such political instabilities, a fascination with islands as sites where authors might confront and work out feelings about 'insularity', 'security', 'remoteness' and 'rootedness' seems quite plausible. The literature of islands of this period, he goes on, promised, in various ways, 'not just a corrective but an alternative to the dominant conceptions of identity and belonging to the past' (148).

Robinson's move in 1972 might certainly be seen in this same tradition – and we will explore his particular inflection of post-imperial space – but there are some important differences as well. In fact, it was less this island literature that lured Robinson out west than it was Robert Flaherty's film *Man of Aran*.

Though this was made in the period Brannigan explores (1934), Flaherty was an American film-maker and his interest in life on the islands fitted a much wider concern with global anthropological film-making that included other well-known features of 'docu-fiction' set in the Canadian Arctic (*Nanook of the North* 1922), in Samoa (*Moana* 1926) and in Polynesia (*Tabu* 1931). For Robinson, who had been living and working in Istanbul and Vienna prior to London, drawn away from the UK by what he has called 'sheer Romanticism' (buoyed by Patrick Leigh Fermor), *Man of Aran* framed the islands as an exposed and elemental extreme, the edge of a whole continent, comparable aesthetically to the northern remoteness of the Canadian Arctic, and yet relatively close to home as well (Smith 2013: 5). Atlantic waves pounded sea caves at the foot of huge, windswept cliffs, diminutive figures of women hauled baskets of seaweed, men hunted a basking shark in a canvas currach (though in fact this was a recreation of a tradition long since passed for the purposes of the film). *Man of Aran* projected a precarious life lived between rough limestone and a thousand miles of ocean on the outer edge of Europe. Such powerful imagery of these Atlantic islands in the 1930s may well have generated another layer of historical meaning about the quality of peripheral exposure when it was seen in a cinema in 1972.

It was from 1968 onwards that the first images of the whole planet framed from space were popularized provoking anxieties about precisely the 'vulnerability and resilience' of not just island life, but the planet as a whole. 'Earth Rise' and 'Blue Planet', taken from the Apollo 8 and the Apollo 17 missions, offered an historic iconography for how finite, fragile and endangered people were beginning to feel life on Earth really was. Buckminster Fuller's influential concept of 'Spaceship Earth' (1968) and James Lovelock's 'Gaia' hypothesis (1972) both responded with urgent and scientific forms of system-based ecology that began to conceive of the Earth as a whole in need of careful monitoring and control. Not to mention the fact that the coastal edge of Aran that the film showed the islanders looking out from was one that was nested on the line of the European continental shelf, a geological feature itself visible from space. When Robinson set out for the periphery in 1972 then, the sense that this coastal edge connoted was not only one of a national periphery (i.e. the edge of Ireland), nor of the slightly larger sense of an edge to the Irish and British archipelago, but a sense of periphery based on a geological edge visible from space, a periphery of vulnerability on a planetary and cosmic scale.

A unique opportunity is afforded by Robinson's work to explore the whole oeuvre of a man who moved between visual art, map-making, and writing as if they were points that help to triangulate the elusive nature of place in his career. This chapter will do just this, tracing his careful investigation of place as it is braided with scales of spatial register from the cosmic, through the imperial and national, right down to the local, communal and personal. One crucial shaping factor in Robinson's work on place is the idea of the margin or the periphery. What level of detail has escaped the eye looking out from the centre? What sits precariously on the outer edge of perception or cultural memory? What new horizons open when one's periphery becomes centre and what do these do to a sense of place on the periphery? Robinson's sense of scale is challenged by what he comes to call 'the view from the horizon' but as much as it is enlarged it is, at the same time, miniaturized (1997). The horizons of the place multiply internally in curious and exciting ways. The idea of regional and national periphery is supplanted by the idea of fractal horizons at the intersection of space and place.

For Robinson, place is a secular but nonetheless metaphysical concept through which to contemplate our wider relationship with the spatial cosmos.

> Imagine that in a few hundred years' time humanity has put aside all its misguided supernatural beliefs and turned its religious instincts to the Earth, the true author of our being. Then a rite will be called for to celebrate this thoroughly realist and romantic-materialist cult of the Earth. This rite will be the Visiting of Places, to contemplate them in all their particularity. (2003: 51)

This description of a 'rite' associated with the secular contemplation of place presents a very telling knot in Robinson's thought. He is, of course, an atheist who dismisses religion's 'misguided supernatural beliefs' here. Such beliefs are, for him, too transcendental, too dependent on any other world than this. However, there is some lingering devotion or asceticism in the religious outlook that holds his fascination. Though religion itself is not for him, there is nothing wrong with our 'religious instincts' which might simply be redeployed into this 'realist and romantic-materialist cult of the Earth'. The subtitle of his first book is *Pilgrimage*, but as the book goes on to explain, it is a pilgrimage 'with eyes raised to this world rather than lowered in prayer' (2008: 25). There is a pattern here. While he rejects the supernatural, there lingers a ritualized exploration of place that suggests veneration for its hidden dimensions, for its more-than-immediately-apparent meanings. The key to understanding his distinctive, secular metaphysics, however, is in his fascination with space, not place: 'I prefer this body of work to be read in light of "Space" ... somatic space, perceptual space, existential space and so on,' he describes, 'ultimately there is no space but Space, "nor am I out of it", to quote Marlowe's Mephistopheles, for it is, among everything else, the interlocking of all our mental and physical trajectories, good or ill, through all the subspaces of experience up to the cosmic' (1996: vi).

The relationship between Robinson's map-making and prose is well known and something that he has reflected on frequently in his books. However, there has been little reflection on the relationship between all *three* aspects of his career – the maps, the writing and the earlier visual art.[1] This is despite his having exhibited at some quite prestigious galleries in the 1960s and 1970s,[2] his selection for exhibition at a John Moore's Biennial in Liverpool by a panel of judges featuring Clement Greenberg in 1965 (Robinson 2001: 44) and despite there even being a print of his still to be found in the Tate Gallery archives in London today. By looking a little more closely at the relationship between this neglected alter ego, Timothy Drever, and the more familiar Tim Robinson, a comprehensive picture appears of the developing practice of a quite singular, inquiring mind, one capable of very striking leaps of faith in pursuit of his elusive subject matter: 'Space'. When we understand his career as more than writing alone, as a practice that has art at one end, map-making in the middle and writing at the other, we see that this 'Space' itself, with all its 'interlocking ... trajectories', is not only the subject but the *medium* with which he has been working all this time. His move to the periphery in 1972 might be understood as a way of intensifying this experience of space and place where they intersect. Islands especially have often been thought of in these terms as sites of pioneering cultural work. Damian Walford Davies has

---

[1] The exception to this is an autobiographical essay in *My Time in Space* and the slim volume issued from Coracle Press in 2012 called *The View from the Horizon*, both of which I will be drawing on here.
[2] The Walker Art Gallery, Liverpool (1965); Signals Gallery, London (1966); Lissom Gallery (1968); and Kenwood House (1969).

explored the original and diverse creativities at work in the island writing of the naturalist (who like Robinson might also be described by so many other disciplinary titles) Ronald Lockley, a man who made his island world on Skokholm an 'experiment in a way of living' (Lockley qtd. in Walford Davies 2016: n.p.). And John Brannigan draws to our attention a description of the Rathlin of Michael McLaverty as a 'laboratory for the study of cultural process' (J. D. Evans qtd. in Brannigan 2014: 148).

If Robinson's move to the Aran Islands is to be understood in such a tradition of 'experimental' living on the margins, we might think of his experiment as one in what would later come to be called, appropriately enough, 'deep mapping'. The three aspects of his work that this chapter discusses took place largely before the (practice-led) theorization of 'deep mapping' by figures in Europe such as Ian Biggs (2010, 2011), Mike Pearson, Clifford McLucas and Michael Shanks (Pearson and Shanks 2001). These aspects of his work even precede the moment when the idea of 'deep mapping' was called forth from the work of Wallace Stegner by William Least Heat-Moon in the American tradition. Nonetheless, the way that deep mapping, in the UK especially, has formulated itself *in practice* does suggest a reflection on the curious historical relationship between it and Robinson's work (Least Heat-Moon 1991). Not least of all because, for Ian Biggs in particular, Robinson is singled out as a figure who 'anticipates' deep mapping, part of a thread that Biggs traces back through John Cowper Powys to Thoreau (2011: 11). Deep mapping is at heart a form of place-making or place-transformation. It recognizes that the identity associated with place is not a matter of essence, stability and boundedness but of work, life and creative energy. It explores new dialogues between the variety of often marginalized perspectives with which a place is invested, past and present, though with an emphasis on 'constructive reconciliations in the present' (Biggs 2010: 5). The terminology associated with the practice of deep mapping – and it is crucially to be understood *as practice* – can be read along a continuum of verbs that enact an engaged cultural work associated with this transformation. Drawing on Biggs again, deep mapping 'intervenes', 'challenges', 'destabilizes', 'mediates' and 'reconfigures' 'existing territories and presuppositions' (5). It offers a form of resistance to prevailing conventions of place representation and a recovery of the rich but underappreciated cultures going overlooked. As such it has to it a fundamental inclusiveness of attitude and often a quite radical 'heterogeneity' of outcome (Pearson and Shanks 2001: 166). In the United States a 'deep map' might consist of a place-based prose work that combines a variety of stylistic forms grounded in personal experience. However, in the United Kingdom it has tended to involve a wider combination of place-based conversations, oral history work, writing and performance. The deep map becomes the whole process of research, investigation, creative composition and performance.

Unlike other chapters in this book which take a variety of authors as their subject, this chapter considers only Tim Robinson, but it explores the three very different aspects of his career as he moves from the centre to the periphery and as they break down the idea of the periphery into a deep map of place with intricate horizons and edges. In the first part of this chapter, 'A Bridge into the Real World', I show how his early experiments with the geometrical spaces of autonomous abstraction in a particular strain of modernism in the visual arts expand in conflicted ways out into the public and social sphere at a crucial time of political awakening. In the second part, 'Making Amends', I then show this conflicted expansion to be the guiding influence in his navigation through a very unusual exploration of map-making in Ireland which begins to challenge the conventional sense of cartographic space and suggest more inclusive and non-standardized forms. In the third part, 'A Quest for Space', this same line of developing spatial thought and practice is traced from cartographic to linguistic forms of space as language is found to be able to do what neither the art nor the map could. Throughout these parts a sense of a place on the periphery is shown to be established and eventually supplanted by a fractal geography of place underpinned by the 'interlocking trajectories' of 'all the subspaces of experience up to the cosmic' (Robinson 1996: vi).

'A bridge into the real world'

In 1996, Robinson was asked to take part in an exhibition at the Irish Museum of Modern Art in Dublin. It had been nearly twenty-five years since he had left the London art world and turned to map-making and the literary essay. Nonetheless, the work he chose to exhibit brought together his earlier visual art with his mapping and writing in an interesting way that demonstrated a certain surprising coherence of thought. In the middle of the room, scattered on the floor like large pick-a-sticks were what seemed to be surveyors' rods, some with equidistant black and white stripes, some just white with a single inch painted grey at different points on the rods, and above them, suspended by a splayed rainbow of thread, was one more yard-long white rod. The lines on the black and white rods were not, however, all equal, suggesting a certain divergence from the standard that they brought to mind. On the walls around them were two of his intricate, hand-drawn maps of the Aran Islands and of Connemara, and between them were some twelve extracts from his books *Stones of Aran: Pilgrimage* and *Setting Foot of the Shores of Connemara and Other Writings*. After visiting the exhibition, a friend described the surveyor's rods on the floor as 'measure become organic' (1997: 11). It is an interesting phrase in which there is a sense that the measure has somehow lapsed or that it has been overcome from the inside. The phrase has an echo of 'gone native' to it, since what use is measure if it is not answerable to a universal standard? There is something absurd and paradoxical about these surveyors' rods, each with its own measure and none of them bound by the same proportions. The white rods with a single inch painted grey at different points were called 'Inchworm', a name for the caterpillar form of the geometer moth, so called because, according to Robinson, its movement in small loops seems to 'measure the Earth' (57). Again, there is something absurd about the idea of an animal that might measure to no purpose other than travel. The measurement is not recorded or abstracted but simply performed. Life as lived is the only measure of which these rods speak. They *are* a standard rather than appealing to one. There is something very strangely prescient in this installation, the rods of which were created originally before Robinson left London in 1972 and had been in storage all the while. They seem to have within them the kernel that would grow into his remapping of the Aran Islands, the Burren and Connemara, refusing the standards of the nineteenth-century Ordnance Survey and asserting a form of spatial autonomy.

The level of abstraction and the subtle but philosophical commentary on space that we see in the rods here was characteristic of Robinson/Drever's London work of the time, though of course without the accompanying maps and writing. In the 1960s, modernism had returned to the London art world reconstituted by American intellectuals like Clement Greenberg who, since 1939, had been defending a purist abstraction and the avant-garde in a way that we might imagine could appeal to Robinson's background in mathematics. For Greenberg, abstraction narrowed and raised art 'to the expression of an absolute' in which 'subject matter or content' had become 'something to be avoided like a plague' (1999: 531). This led, he suggested, to 'free and autonomous' work, pure painting or sculpture, 'valid solely on its own terms' (531). As mentioned, Greenberg had been among the judges who selected Robinson/Drever to exhibit in the John Moore's Biennial in Liverpool in 1965, and other exhibited works of his from around the same time also show a fascination with geometry and mathematical proportions. For example, the print that remains in the archive of the Tate Gallery in London is one, the form, composition and proportions of which were produced by a strict adherence to certain geometrical principles and rules (Drever 1969). As he describes in an exhibition catalogue from the time, 'Aesthetic choices were progressively replaced or limited (and so made more crucial) by geometrical demands' (Drever, Herring and Joseph 1969: 15).

However, there was also an emergent pull away from the 'autonomy' of abstraction at this time and it is this subsequent tension between the two that would propel him out of London in 1972. For an exhibition in the summer of 1969, he and the artist Peter Joseph published an essay in *Studio International* called 'Outside the Gallery System'. In it they voiced their dissent at an art world bound up with commodity fetishism, suggesting that this 'increasingly isolates the artist from the public', channelling work 'at best into a museum, at worst into an investor's cellar', leaving the artists themselves to a 'comfortable enervation' (255). Robinson/Drever and Joseph set about challenging this by holding their exhibition outdoors in the grounds of Kenwood House. Not only this, but the art they exhibited relied on the interaction and participation of visitors to be fully realized. 'Consideration of the environment is essential,' they declared: 'The scale and dynamics of the work must relate to the area in which it is shown. Thus, it seems natural that "environmental art" should be not just the latest fad of the art-world, but a bridge into the real world' (255). Robinson's own exhibition piece was a series of large, flat, coloured shapes produced, again, according to geometrical rules, but here they were set down on the lawn and he invited the public to move, reorder and experiment with new compositions to bring the work alive (see Figure 4.1). This echoed a previous interactive installation that he had exhibited indoors at

Figure 4.1 Timothy Drever. 'Four-Colour Theorum', Kenwood House, 1969.

Kenwood House the same year called 'Moonfield', where visitors were invited to enter a darkened room with a black floor only to find their feet knocking black wooden shapes on the floor which they were encouraged to turn over revealing a white underside. As people made their way through the room new patterns of black and white emerged dependent on their physical interaction. 'Moonfield is thus a new surface to be explored, and this exploration creates its topography,' the exhibition catalogue claimed (Drever, Herring and Joseph 1969: 5). This topography that was 'created' through the interaction between artist, artwork and public was described as a 'real space both in philosophic and social terms' (17).

Both the outdoor work at Kenwood House and 'Moonfield' demonstrate the fascinating paradox of an artist working in forms of autonomous abstraction while at the same time expressing a yearning for the social engagement and interaction that abstraction had spurned. In the case of the outdoor exhibition, there was also clearly a disillusionment emerging with the conventions of the gallery-oriented metropolitan art world. (Deep mapping itself can be seen to emerge from a similar uncomfortable feeling about the lines drawn between an 'art world' and a 'real world' though it has also grown to challenge the lines separating an 'academic world' as well.) On the one hand, this 'environmental art' was not then what we might expect it to be today. 'Environment', in this context, referred to the nature of the public space of exhibition. It was simply about finding, quite concretely, new environments for art and encouraging real human interaction through which the visitor takes part in the process of creation. However, the decision to search for a new environment does speak of a frustration with the prevailing spatial discourse of exhibitions, and recognition of the need to question its hegemonic hold on the relationship between artist and the public.

This seems to parallel a growing realization at the time of modernism's own waning political antagonism. Alan Sinfield reminds us how easily Greenberg's defence of the autonomous freedom of the abstract expressionist was co-opted into an ideology threading through a number of CIA-funded European exhibitions that served as propaganda in the Cold War (2005: 210–14). There is something of a new social conscience in the attempt to bridge the art world and the real world in Robinson's work of this period. It attempts to connect the gallery with wider, more democratically public environments, and it questions the social and economic implications of setting a work in a metropolitan gallery. Robinson has also noted that there may have even been the beginnings for him of an 'environmental art' in the sense that it is more readily understood today (Smith 2013: 4). In his essay 'Environments' in that same edition of *Studio International* in 1969, the performance artist Stuart Brisley asks: 'To what extent does the artist maintain responsibility for the implications implicit within his artistic processes beyond production?', suggesting that the commodification of art ought *not* to be something of which the artist passively disapproves while continuing to feed (267). For Brisley, as perhaps for Robinson/Drever at that time, 'Environmental work specifies that the artist take a positive position in relation to his own behaviour as it affects other people within the social and physical context' (268).

It was during this same period that Clarrie Wallis recalls the first 'walk-as-art' taken by the young Richard Long and Hamish Fulton, a conscious decision to turn their backs on the city as authoritarian centre of culture. She quotes from Long's diary of 1967:

> We announced we were going to walk (at a normal pace) ..., out of London until sunset. A few didn't start. We went along Oxford Street to the Edgware Road – the Old Roman road of Watling Street – which we followed in a

more-or-less straight line north-west out of London. A few more people dropped out along the way, leaving about six of us at the end. We had no preconceived idea of where we would end up; in fact at sunset we found ourselves in a field, not lost, but also not knowing exactly where we were. The first place we came out to was Radlett, so we caught a train back from Radlett station. (Qtd. in Wallis 2009: 42–3)

Here, the walk-as-art appears an eccentric student experiment influenced no doubt by student marches of the earlier 1960s. But there is a careful spatialization of thought or feeling that encourages us to read this walk as a performance, even a tenuously constituted sculpture. Wallis has gone so far as to describe this moment as representative of a 'shift in consciousness …, the end of Greenbergian modernism and the beginning of a new era. It coincided with a turning point away from technological optimism to preoccupations with ecology, conservation and a crisis of the 1970s as the British were uneasily forced to face their post-industrial and post-colonial future' (2009: 38). In many ways this walk, through the very area where Robinson was living at the time, can be seen to parallel his own departure from London for Aran along a similarly north-westerly axis just a few years later.[3] Both moves offer a performative rejection of the capital at a key time, a rejection of what Raymond Williams has critiqued in modernism as the 'persistent intellectual hegemony of the metropolis' (2007: 38).

It was in this context that Robinson first encountered Flaherty's *Man of Aran* (1934) and began thinking about that dramatic move from the centre to the periphery. The Aran Islands must have seemed the very antithesis to the modernist metropolis he was used to. But if a certain Romanticism fired the initial appeal, it should be noted that Aran became for him not an escape so much as an exploration. This was not a move of retreat from social and cultural politics; Robinson would be drawn to the complex political, international and economic tensions that ran through the life and history of the islands, more so perhaps than even J. M. Synge before him. When Yeats offered that famous

---

[3] Robinson has described himself at the same time taking 'long abstracted country walks', oriented 'by glimpses of the spires of Kilburn, Cricklewood and Neasden' all in fact districts collected around that same ancient trackway of Watling Street (1997: 55). Like Long and Fulton's navigation by an ancient trackway, Robinson's navigation by church spire (and, as he suggests elsewhere, by the sun) speaks of that same search for an older orientation as a foil to the modern urban architecture around him (Dillon 2007: 34).

advice to Synge in the early twentieth century – 'Give up Paris ... Go to the Aran Islands. Live there as if you were one of the people themselves; express a life that has never found expression' (qtd. in Greene 2011: xix) – Synge found a way of life and culture richly alive with the language, history and folklore that had already become so important to a burgeoning sense of Irish national identity. He found, in the cottage of Páidin and Máire MacDonncha, not rural isolation but what had come to be known as *Ollscoil n Gaeilge* (the University of Irish) due to the number of scholars who had stayed there for their research (1992: xvii). Aran might have represented a periphery, for both Robinson and Synge, but it was also a place in which questions of the centre – questions about Ireland as a nation and questions about European modernism – might be addressed.

Patrick Lonergan's account of Synge's Aran writings offers an interesting spatial reading of the idea of 'authenticity' as it is stretched out in a tension between core and periphery. Lonergan draws on Lionel Trilling's quite conservative essay on *Sincerity and Authenticity* in which Trilling argues that for writing to be considered authentic it must 'create a vision of life that is separate from social convention, and which seems different from mass-produced culture' (2013: 71). This separation is read in Aran's peripheral remove from Dublin (in relation to Irish nationalism) and from Paris (in relation to Synge's modernism) and it feeds a 'representation of the regional as authentic' (72). As Lonergan observes, 'The desire for authenticity in art arises from a sense that the real world has become fantastic, and from a related belief that fiction can reveal a truth' (72). However, as he points out, this is plagued by the paradoxical fact that the authentic somehow needs to be verified by the centre and must therefore speak to the prevailing expectations of that centre.

Synge suffered for this tension and found himself often having to defend his work from accusations of inauthenticity. Robinson does not seem to have been criticized in this way but he does nonetheless feel the tension between core and periphery in thinking about where his work is to be recognized. Though Robinson had not read Synge before he left, this sense of the Aran Islands as a centre of culture in their own right, but one nonetheless connected by a long and complicated history to Ireland and to Britain and to European modernism, was something he would very soon come to discover in his own ways. The question of authenticity becomes an interesting one for Robinson too. As he has less and less to do with London and its audience in those early years he has less and less reason to defend his practice as authentic. His concerns, instead, become concerns about a more localized inclusivity. Robinson was not after an authentic Aran but rather an Aran that *included* and reflected the diverse voices, histories, stories, perspectives and so on, something that arose from his making of what would now be called 'deep maps', maps that help to make the invisible visible, maps that work on the outer edge of a place to draw in what is at risk of loss.

In the first few years of living on the islands, Robinson attended an exhibition of Richard Long's in Amsterdam and found on the poster one of Long's sculptures photographed on Árainn in 1975. Long had also spent a summer there but they do not seem to have met at that time. He also describes himself and his wife catching sight of one of Long's sculptures from a plane window when they were returning after a trip away: 'an instantly recognisable mark that told us who had visited the island in our absence' (2008: 44). In fact, he actually gets into a dispute when Long is 'aghast' to find two of his stone-works marked on Robinson's map of the island (2007: 113). 'The essence of his works', Robinson concedes, 'is what he brings home to the artworld: a photographic image in many cases' which serves as 'the entrypoint to a concept, the idea of a journey' (115). Robinson reminds Long that, nonetheless, Long does in fact leave something behind, something that he, as a maker of a very detailed map, could only find it hard to ignore. The tension is here once again between abstraction ('the entrypoint to a concept') and a more tangible real-world social interaction (the stone-work left behind). For Long, the pull back to the metropolitan centre from the periphery was still strong and where the work reached its final realization, but for Robinson, who was by that time beginning to map the islands and recognize them as a centre in their own right, that 'bridge to the real world' was coming to look final.

'Making Amends'

On the south-west coast of Árainn, at the base of its 250-foot limestone cliffs, there is a cave called An Poll Dubh, or 'the black hole', in which a piper is said to have wandered, never to be seen again. The folklore of the islands has it, though, that inland, under the village of Creig an Chéirín, his music can still sometimes be heard. It is a story that occurs across England as well, though sometimes in the guise of a fiddler rather than a piper. Jennifer Westwood and Jacqueline Simpson tell of a group of people in the village of Anstey in Hertfordshire, for example, who were curious about how deep a local cave went so they sent a fiddler below ground, playing his fiddle, while they walked above ground listening as a way of plotting the depth of the cave in the known landscape. In a horrible twist, the music stops suddenly as the fiddler is taken by the Devil and never heard of again while his dog comes running from the cave with its hair burned off (Westwood and Simpson 2005: 332–3). Similar stories are associated with Grantchester in Cambridgeshire, Binham Priory in Norfolk, Peninnis Head in the Isles of Scilly and Richmond Castle in Yorkshire. The story becomes something quite different in Robinson's hands. Though it is not clear whether this is because of its particular inflection in the memory of the islanders or because of a certain licence he takes himself (more than likely it is both), the sense of a community collaborating with the piper is stripped away and he is reported to be exploring the cave alone. The function of his music in the story becomes a little more mysterious too, as in Árainn it shifts from a means of mapping the cave to merely a haunting vestige of a disappeared man. Robinson absorbs this story into a personal mythology in *Stones of Aran: Pilgrimage* and we get a curious glimpse of the lone, questing artist out on the periphery, literally immersed in place, but somehow searching for something more mysterious *within* it as well:

> Thus: the artist finds deep-lying passages, unsuspected correspondences, unrevealed concordances, leading from element to element of reality, and celebrates them in the darkness of the solipsism necessary to his undertaking, but at best it is a weak and intermittent music, confused by its own echoes and muffled by the chattering waters of the earth, that reaches the surface-dweller above; nor does the artist emerge; his way leads on and on, or about and about. (2008: 129)

It is an image in which we can certainly read feelings about his remote and isolated existence in those early years on the islands, perhaps even a certain alienation from the place itself, coupled of course with a fear of being literally swallowed by it. And yet, there is a paradox that emerges in this image as well.

The 'darkness of the solipsism necessary to his undertaking' is, in fact, not a darkness of solipsism at all. It is a darkness that belongs to both the island's geology and its folklore. Robinson's account of a supposed interior, subjective space is contradicted by its origin in the island's own cultural repertoire, the recognition of what was, in fact, a shared cultural space. Though the community who trace the piper's movement from above ground are stripped away from this story, nonetheless, in the 'weak and intermittent music' that does make its way to the 'surface-dweller' we can see the beginnings of a tentative emergence of the artist to his new peripheral social context. For Drever the artist, the withdrawn autonomy of the abstract modernist was beginning to unfold into the manifest reality of the island's cultural landscape as it was encountered by Robinson the hoarder of place lore.

He had begun collecting the place names, stories, and histories like this after Máire Bn. Uí Chonghaile, the postmistress of Cill Mhuirbhigh, suggested that he make a map of the islands. He was surprised to find that no map had been made since the Ordnance Survey's nineteenth-century project which had produced impractical, large-scale maps, copies of which were difficult to get hold of and when studied showed a 'carelessness that reveal[ed] contempt' (1996: 3). He did, nonetheless, acquire copies and began studying them. He learnt Gaelic, still then the first language of the islands, and spent a lot of time visiting his neighbours, walking with farmers and fishermen and talking at length about the topography and its associated history and culture over tea. The maps were full of errors, not just of mistranslation and Anglicization but also of misattribution, and he began to nurture an innocent curiosity as to whether it might be possible 'to make amends' (3). As Robinson began to collect place names and understand the stories and histories associated with them, the rich depths of life and heritage that had been ignored or misunderstood, and that often existed only in the memory of a few ageing individuals, he began to understand that, for the officials planning the survey from Westminster, 'rents and rates came before any other aspect of life', and for many of the soldiers conducting the survey on the ground, the 'language of the peasant was nothing more than a subversive muttering behind the landlord's back' (3). The process of mistranslation was of course memorably dramatized in Brian Friel's play *Translations* (1980) in conversations between the English surveyor Lieutenant Yolland and his Irish translator Owen.

In fact, in 1996, a short essay of Robinson's appeared, appropriately enough, next to an excerpt from *Translations* in a slim volume dedicated to a project of 'parish mapping' carried out by the arts and environmental charity Common Ground that we considered in Chapter 1 (Clifford and King 1996). Both were offered as explorations of the tensions at work in forms of mapping associated with centralized administration. Clifford and King exchanged letters with both Robinson and Friel on the subject of mapping, and both authors were glad to offer their work for republication free of charge. We can imagine the appeal of correcting these errors for Robinson, and of exploring the possibilities of reparation that might be involved with representing, for the first time, the actual geographical complexities he was discovering in getting to know his neighbours. He was, after all, an artist emerging from a movement that Stuart Brisley had described as in search of that 'positive position in relation to his own behaviour as it affects other people within the social and physical context' (1969: 268). The disparities he began to notice and correct were observed on the whole in the recording of place names, their mistranslation, their Anglicization and their misplacement.

Looking at early cartography up to the medieval period, Michel de Certeau reminds us that there was once a much closer relationship between the map and linguistic description than there is today. Early maps were often written on with accounts of tours, histories or itineraries of pilgrimages (1984: 121). Their two dimensions offered up stories of the map-making process; but, he says, these stories were slowly shouldered out to make way for more purely visual-spatial description. The history of the map 'colonizes space; it eliminates little by little the pictural figurations of the practices that produce it' in favour of the top down, precisely surveyed representation of static space dotted with symbols that we have today (121). This erasure of the stories of the landscape from the official representation is nowhere more felt than Ireland. Too small to have developed its own map-making tradition before the English came with theirs, Ireland did nonetheless have its own rich linguistic geography: *dinnseanchas*, the oral tradition of keeping the lore of the land. Charles Bowen describes *dinnseanchas* as 'a science of geography ... in which there is no clear distinction between the general principles of topography or direction-finding and the intimate knowledge of particular places' (1975: 115). He goes on: 'Places would have been known to them as people were: by face, name and history ... the name of every place was assumed to be an expression of its history' (115). Unlike the increasingly spatial mapping practices of the English, this method had a temporal and historical depth to it and existed, not on paper, but in memory and social interaction.

From the 1520s the English government began commissioning maps of Ireland. Begun just before such a trend of recording linguistic description began to die out in the seventeenth and eighteenth centuries, these first maps do in fact contain a few of these examples of the kinds of place lore Bowen refers to actually written onto them in the style of the medieval maps that de Certeau describes. J. H. Andrews tells us that on the Dartmouth Maps of 1598, for example, there is the description: 'O'Donnell camped by this logh where his men did see 2 waterhorses of a huge bigness' (qtd. in Andrews 1997: 202). Or the following curious piece from the same map: 'In this bog there is every whott [hot?] summer strange fighting of battles sometimes at foot sometimes wt horse, sometimes castles seen on a sudden, sometimes great store of cows driving & fighting for them' (202). This was, however, the exception to the rule and such curiosities should be read alongside derisive illustrations of 'wild Irishmen peeping from behind rocks' and in the context of a brutal colonial rule (202). Additionally, as Andrews explains, what there was of this practice soon died out as main roads were introduced and maps of Ireland began to endeavour to be more 'objective' for the purposes of administration, achieving a certain regimented abstraction. A concern for the Irish *dinnseanchas* would not be seen until briefly the Ordnance Survey set up its Topographical Department charged with the collection of heritage information in 1835. Even this, however, was brought to an end in 1842 on the basis that it was 'stimulating national sentiment in a morbid, deplorable and tendentious manner' (Hewitt 2010: 287). In the English mapping of Ireland a certain living history was erased from the map before it ever really found its place on it.

For Robinson, the work that began to present itself was a matter of collecting and identifying the correct place names, representing them on his map in the correct place and then subsequently recording the stories associated with them in supplementary written material. The map and the book together seemed the only logical way of making a record of a place so linguistically alive. Patrick Curry has called this 'a kind of Edenic naming in reverse, a recovery of a world beneath the English language that had imposed itself' (1995: 13). In an interview Robinson describes a typical example of the kind of work he was beginning to undertake:

> A very striking case was a place name that was recorded down at the southeastern corner of the big island. It was something like 'Illaunanaur'. The surveyors had obviously thought that the first part of it was 'oileán', island, when in fact it should have been the Irish 'glean', glen. But apart from making it an island when it was a glen, the rest of the name '-anaur' meant absolutely nothing in English phonetics. But in the Irish the name means 'the glen of tears' – it's exactly the biblical phrase 'this vale of tears', 'Gleann na nDeor'. And the story I heard from the local people, was that, in the days leading up to the famine when there was a lot of emigration from the islands, those emigrating would get a fishing boat to take them over to Connemara and they'd walk 30 miles along the Connemara coast into Galway, where they'd wait for one of the famine ships heading for America. These ships used to sail out past the Aran Islands and very frequently had to wait in the shelter of the islands while a gale blew itself out. So they would be stationary just a few hundred yards off shore from this place, Gleann na nDeor, and people would come down to that little glen where they could wave to their loved ones but not talk to them. So the name had immense resonances and told you an immense amount about the personal griefs behind the statistics of the famine. (Smith 2013: 6)

It is not at all unusual that such a small name as Gleann na nDeor should contain such an elaborate and interesting story. Thinking of this coastal place as a 'vale of tears', a phrase used in Christian theology to describe the world that must be endured before the soul can pass on to Heaven, suggests a poignant sense of hope about the life that might await relatives making their way to America. Yet unmapped, such names were slipping out of memory and there are numerous examples of intriguing names that Robinson is unable to find an explanation for. He describes this work as a kind of 'rescue archaeology', gathering things in from the outer edge before they are lost forever (1996: 13). His achievements have now been celebrated by the people of the places themselves, by a highly commended citation in the British Cartographical Design Awards in 1992 and by a European Conservation Award, recognizing the work of his and his wife Máiréad Robinson's company Folding Landscapes, in 1987 ('Folding Landscapes' 1988: 60).

As for the form of the map itself, he set about exploring something that would be importantly founded on the place. In a sense he was liberated by being able to tailor his map to so specific and small a location. The rules he worked by did not have to conform to so abstract or generalized a standard as those of the Ordnance Survey. For example, on its south-west side Árainn is all cliff and on its north-east all beach, so the angle of vision that looks down on the island in his map is tilted slightly to the south-west – what he calls a 'seagull's-eye perspective' – thereby capturing the shapes of the sea-cliffs (see Figure 4.2) (Dillon 2007: 38). This was important to a fishing culture that navigated by these shapes, and that had their own names for many of the headlands that differed from the inland names that farmers had for the same features. By making his such an isolated study, Robinson was enjoying a freedom of

Figure 4.2 Tim Robinson. Detail, 'Map of Aran', 1996 [1980].

singularity, beholden to no distant, administrative standard, something that of course recalls the surveyors' rods he had created in London in 1972.

While these maps are the work of an individual artist, their collaborative element arising from interactions with a broad range of people and their knowledge and memories of the places meant that Robinson came to view the maps as taking on 'aspects of communal creation' (Dillon 2007: 35). In fact, it was recently discovered that while writing the content for his first book on Connemara, Robinson would publish his findings in the local newspaper, *The Connacht Tribune*, and has described the response:

> I had no idea quite how much attention was being paid to them until quite well into the process I found that everyone was waiting for me to turn up. They were quite indignant if I hadn't turned up to them. And they'd have all their information absolutely on the tip of their tongue ready for me. I'd say in a sort of diffident way: 'O I'm the man from Roundstone who's making the map,' and they'd immediately start 'O himself has a stone he wants to show you,' 'the name of that hill is such and such.' (Smith 2013: 9)

In a range of different ways the 'aspects of communal creation' really did involve the communities themselves then, bringing them closer again to the forms of community mapping that Common Ground were exploring in the UK at this same time. The maps became expressions of collectively informed experience undertaken by an artist breaking out of autonomous modernism and trying to connect with what he called (with a certain wry wit) 'the view from the horizon'. So the idea of the Aran Islands as a periphery begins to break down for Robinson and a more localized sense of place, as an intricate labyrinth of horizons, emerged. Robinson's work was becoming focused on recording, collecting, representing and folding together discrete forms of knowledge and memory. David Harvey has described such intangible forms as 'small heritages', from anything as modest as a field name or a superstition to or pneumonic (2008: 20). The plural form that Harvey articulates here is in contradistinction to the idea of an 'Authorised Heritage Discourse' administered from the top down or from the centre. Small heritages are to be understood as intangible, living and changing forms, often kept alive only by their very articulation, communication and performance (20). Both Robinson's maps and the books together began to constitute a new cultural space that could contain such diverse forms, but crucially they were also offered as unfinished and open-ended, as a horizon always on the move. The openness of this process found itself very eloquently expressed in a recent return of the periphery to the centre when Robinson exhibited his Aran map in London. In 2011 he was invited to take part in Hans-Ulrich Obrist's 'Map Marathon' at the Serpentine Gallery alongside Louise Bourgeoise and Ai Weiwei. Robinson's contribution was a twenty-two-foot vinyl print of his map of the Aran Islands laid on the floor. Come and walk on it, he invited. Come and dance on it. Come and write your name or your message on it. Pens were provided and people did and the map has gathered all kinds of annotations now, recalling the earlier public participation in his work at Kenwood House but also giving a useful visual metaphor for all those different community contributions that his vision of Aran, the Burren and Connemara has accrued over the years ('Map Marathon').

A quest for Space

'Space', as Robinson describes it, is his preoccupation (1996: vi). Aran and Connemara we might more readily and more comfortably describe as *places*, but, as was suggested in the introduction, they have become sites in his work for investigating the wider question of space itself as well. Seamus Deane, in a review of the Aran books, suggested that they represented 'not perhaps a quest for Aran but a quest to which Aran gives shape and meaning' (1989: 9). The quest has perhaps been 'for' space itself: the inward, subjective recesses, the outward, subjective projections, the historical depth, the community feeling, the disciplinary varieties and the imaginative possibilities of space in its fullest understanding. The early geometrical spaces that his artwork explored in London, when he was just beginning to invite public and social interaction, found themselves complicated by the two clearly contested and 'interlocking' spaces that he uncovered in Aran in tensions between the islands' *dinnseanchas* and the Ordnance Survey maps (1996: vi). Space as plural, contested and yet common became an experiential reality for him through the map-making and it was not long before a growing interest in different, more complex, forms of space began to shoulder out his previous interest in Euclidean conventions.

In the book that completes his *Connemara* trilogy, *Connemara: A Little Gaelic Kingdom*, Robinson addresses precisely this interest, taking, 'as a source of metaphor and imagery', the fractal geometry of Benoît Mandelbrot (2011: 252). He is prompted to do so by Mandelbrot's 1967 essay 'How Long Is the Coast of Britain?', which he applies to the intricate folds and convolutions of the Connemara coastline. The answer is surprisingly elusive, dependent as it is on the scale at which one is looking. Increasing the scale unearths greater detail, time and time again, and so the answer grows the closer one looks. The problem is that any measure, at however small a scale, is forced to simplify complex ambiguities which might otherwise reveal further intricacies of their own. When he writes of the intricate and changing coastline of this landscape, it is increasingly with a realization of the inadequacy of Euclidean geometry as a means of representing its complexity. Not only this, but we begin to hear an echo in the language suggesting a parallel with the inadequacy of the Ordnance Survey as a means of representing Irish cultural geographies. The land is described as 'largely composed of such recalcitrant entities, over which the geometry of Euclid, the fairytale of lines, circles, areas and volumes we are told at school, has no authority' (2011: 249). And again, coastlines are 'too complicated to be described in terms of classical geometry, which would indeed regard them as broken, confused, tangled, unworthy of the dignity of measure' (249). The lack of 'authority' chimes with the book's earlier chapters on Connemara's histories of political and cultural rebellion, and the mention of something 'confused, tangled, unworthy of the dignity of measure' could as easily describe the English bafflement and contempt for the Irish *dinnseanchas* as it describes here a mathematical difficulty.

The edge, the periphery and the coast become spatial forms that exemplify the *depth* of place for Robinson, which is always a depth receding from view wherever we are stood. Mandlebrot's mathematical conundrum is intricately complicated by the idea of historical and cultural depth: 'There are more places within a forest, among the galaxies or on a Connemara seashore, than the geometry of common sense allows,' he suggests (2011: 252). For Robinson, this proliferation of places is bound up with the numerous and interlocking human experiences of them, indefinitely troubling our ability to calibrate any final measure (in fact it undermines the very assumptions that the idea of a final measure carries). Questions of history, community, tradition, disciplinary perspective and language – or *languages* – open up and multiply a single place into many and we might understand this as a kind of fractal cultural geography of the periphery. For Robinson though, such a fractal vision only becomes possible through the contours that language opens up.

The spaces of stories and histories are a part of that 'interlocking' of 'all our mental and physical trajectories' that he suggests when he claims that 'ultimately there is no space but Space'. They are a part of the community's or the culture's intersubjectivity, that empathic belief in a common lifeworld shared by others (1996: vi). While few would disagree that our distinctive knowledge, memories and experiences of space are 'interlocking', what Robinson is curious about is the manner in which this 'interlocking' takes place, the manner in which it *might potentially* take place and the role that writing can play in working with the textures of this common but plural 'Space'. It is in this sense that his interest in 'Space' has gone beyond the safeguarding of a body of oral history knowledge balanced on the edge of memory. It is an interest that draws attention to space as a social and artistic medium underlying a place and, at its edges, dynamically alive and in a state of becoming.

In a recent essay he tells us that for a good many years now he has been building a computer database on CD-ROM of all the topographical knowledge he has been collecting, a way of indexing and preserving the research in a more detailed manner than the paper maps allow and in a more systematic manner than the literary books allow. In this essay – called 'The Seanachaí and the Database', where *seanachaí* comes from the same root as *dinnseanchas* – he begins to weigh the strengths and weakness of his database against the strengths and weaknesses of the *dinnseanchaí* (or 'keeper of topographical knowledge and lore of place') (2003: 46). He finds that the database 'transcends' the local memory 'in powers of recall and logical organization'; it is searchable and has no limit to the amount of information it can store (47). However, the database falls far short when it comes to 'ambiguous or doubtful data' and 'as a memorandum of lifelong inhabitation' (47). The *dinnseanchaí* is not simply a vessel containing historical and cultural information but perceives and creates meaningful relationships between the different parts of the retained lore. He or she is capable of ordering or reordering the history and lore according to values related to that lifelong inhabitation. This is echoed in Ian Biggs's claim that deep mapping's preoccupation with bringing the past to light always has an eye on the contemporary as well and on necessary investigations and productions of meaning 'so as to enact constructive reconciliations in the present' (2010: 5).

Though Robinson does not make such a claim himself, it is precisely this lively negotiation of relationships and the capacity to *create* meanings that we see in his writing, and that distinguishes it from the maps and the database.

The capacity of his prose to draw on detailed knowledge of, for example, botany, archaeology, folklore, geology and history, all in the same chapter or essay – his attempt at 'interweaving more than two or three at a time of the millions of modes of relating to a place' – shows something more deliberate and creative than the bringing forth of peripheral and precariously located knowledge that we find in the maps and their accompanying booklets (2008: 363). It shows an attempt to make the discrete layers of space belonging to different disciplinary perspectives known to one another and present to one another for the reader. There is a creative practice in this, reaching into the imagination of the artist at one extent and into the cultures with which a given place is invested at the other. This gives rise to two identifiable traits in his written work. First, as Pippa Marland has shown, there is an extraordinary range of experimental writing styles through which he moves, self-reflexive moments of pastiche and parody, mischief and humour, moments of elaborate construction suddenly undermined by irrepressible self-doubt, all of which engage with the often overwhelming possibilities available to an author seeking to do a kind of literary justice to a place (2015: 19–21). This variety of registers is something that Susan Naramore Maher describes as characteristic of the form of writing associated with deep mapping in the United States, and something that she reads through Mikhail Bakhtin's writings on heteroglossia and the dialogic imagination in the work of William Least Heat-Moon (2001: 7). And it should be noted that his threefold practice of art, maps and writing is in itself to be understood in this range. However, second, there is a more consistent and identifiable formal trait in Robinson's recurrent endeavour to relate and intertwine distinctive perspectives on place, looking for what he calls, after E. O. Wilson, 'consilience' (Wilson 1999: 10). The abiding question that he puts to the test again and again is 'can the act of writing hold such disparate materials in coexistence?' (Robinson 2008: 210).

One such example of this we have in *Connemara: The Last Pool of Darkness* in which he describes the large cleft in the hillside that forms the valley of Little Killary near the coast. Here in the land's unusual geology 'ancient uncouth states of the earth have been broken through and thrust one over the other' (2009a: 2), then gouged and worn away by glaciers. At the head of the valley there is a chapel and well dedicated to the little-known St Roc where people used to bring their dead for funeral rites. Local folklore explains the dramatic landform by suggesting that it was here that St Roc struggled with the Devil: as the Devil tried to pull him away to Hell on a chain, St Roc resisted 'so violently that the chain cut deep into the hillside, creating the pass and funerary way' (2). 'Thus geology reveals itself as mythology,' Robinson claims. However, it was also on the edge of Little Killary that Wittgenstein once stayed during a period of retreat from Cambridge while struggling with the philosophical argument about 'the difference between seeing something, and seeing it as something' (the famous example is of the shape that appears as a duck from one angle and a rabbit from another) (1). This particular branch of Wittgenstein's thought has huge significance for Robinson insofar as different perceptions can give way to different explanations of place residing in the same 'Space'. So Robinson suggests: 'In some future legendary reconstitution of the past it will be Wittgenstein's wrestling with the demons of philosophy that tears the landscape of Connemara' (2–3). Here, mythology, geology and philosophy are all brought into a resonant proximity by geographical and historical association, and intertwined through the narrative of the essay. Wittgenstein's own problem about seeing something as something else is playfully deployed and perhaps even celebrated by revealing a literary form of the duck/rabbit diagram in the form of geological rift/St Roc's struggle/ Wittgenstein's conundrum. The conflicting meanings are resolved in a prose trait that recurs throughout the writing in different forms and that Robinson describes as a form of 'consilience' (Smith 2013: 10).

For E. O. Wilson, consilience is a means of bringing the, predominantly scientific, disciplines together in the joint endeavour of expanding the horizons of human knowledge, but it too has a relationship to the religious past for him:

> We are obliged by the deepest drives of the human spirit to make ourselves more than animated dust, and we must have a story to tell about where we came from, and why we are here. Could Holy Writ be just the first liberal attempt to explain the universe and make ourselves significant within it? Perhaps science is a continuation on new and better-tested ground to attain the same end. ... Preferring a search for objective reality over revelation is another way of satisfying religious hunger. (1999: 5)

There is, however, an important difference here. Wilson's understanding of consilience is fundamentally teleological, with religion fumbling in the dark behind us and the light of scientific explanation on 'better-tested ground' ahead of us (theologians might find themselves irked by the thought that religion is a naïve form of scientific endeavour). However, Robinson's understanding of consilience is not so teleological and is, instead, interested in the thoughts that appear as different layers of knowledge coincide, as different ways of seeing the same thing 'as something' multiply its phenomenological and intersubjective possibilities. Wilson's expanding frontier gives way to Robinson's intricate and fractal periphery. Robinson thinks like an artist, Wilson like a scientist. As Wilson himself suggests, somewhat reductively, 'The love of complexity without reductionism makes art; the love of complexity with reductionism makes science' (1999: 54). Michael Quigley has also suggested that 'no book containing such a vast amount of detail on such a small portion of landscape could possibly be sustained were it not for its intrinsic literary quality' (1998: 117). The artist and the cartographer eventually find a curious fulfilment of their quest for richer and richer forms of space in the contours and possibilities made available through language and the literary imagination. Literary aesthetics and the experimental form of the essay becomes Robinson's final articulation of the shifting horizon of the places he has made his home.

Robinson has described the 'base-triangle' of his philosophy of space as 'that formed by the three church-towers of Proust's Martinville' (1996: 19). The 'base-triangle', in cartography, is the measure from which all other measures are unfolded, one triangle after another. For the Ordnance Survey this first base-triangle was a precise measure taken with extraordinary care over a two-month period with help from members of the Royal Artillery on Hounslow Heath in the summer of 1791 (Hewitt 2010: 124–6). From that measure the survey worked outwards until it had taken in the whole of the British Isles. For Robinson, ever complicating the measures of Euclidean and imperial space, the reference to Proust suggests something much more deeply felt and subjective that is related to the impulse to write. The mysterious intensity of feeling that Proust describes upon watching from a coach window the triangulation of Martinville's two church towers with Vieuxvicq's one ignites in his narrator the need to write a response. The sense 'that something more lay behind that mobility, that luminosity, something which they seemed at once to contain and to conceal' wrenches open an irresistible need to respond creatively which, once fulfilled, produces feelings of extraordinary elation (1922: 184). Robinson's suggestion, then, that this moment in Proust serves as his own 'base-triangle' expresses a very primal and mysterious response to what a place might at once 'contain and conceal' (and we might think back to the image of the piper in the cave again here). Part of what a place contains and conceals for Robinson is, of course, these 'interlocking' spaces both of historical depth and diverse subjective and disciplinary perspectives. It contains these, but it also contains the endlessly deferred promise of a total form of spatial revelation, a revelation implicit in the very idea of concealment itself.

The central philosophy, introduced in the first Aran book, but running through both, is Robinson's idea of 'the good step', an ideal, single footfall that traverses a portion of the Earth while somehow containing an unthinkable awareness of all possible ways of knowing the place it is traversing: what he describes as an 'unsummable totality of human perspectives' (2008: 8). The 'good step' is an aspiration to do a form of cognitive and spatial justice to a given place, to unlock it spatially. It is an ideal realization, if not revelation, of all that is 'contained and concealed'. 'The good step' relates in certain important ways to Synge's own prior struggle with authenticity. What Lonergan calls the 'dynamic between inside and outside, between core and periphery' (2013: 79) that runs through Synge's plays, meant that in the end the 'construction of the authentic was an aesthetic strategy' (69). For Robinson, the aesthetic strategy of consilience similarly arises out of a realization about the impossibility of this authentic 'good step'. The key difference here is that the authenticity aspired to is, by this time, far beyond a regional or national authenticity. The Aran Islands as a geographical periphery have been replaced by Robinson for the Aran Islands as 'ultimate place', the fractal edge at which topography opens onto the labyrinth of intersubjective and interdisciplinary space. 'The good step' is an ideal concept that endeavours to address a disparity between human experience and the Earth in a manner related to the way that the maps endeavoured to address the disparity between imperial and Irish geography. This is Aran as an edge that extends from national and regional scales both up towards a planetary continental shelf, and down towards the intricate horizons of every hyper-localized patch of ground.

It is, of course, he declares, 'inconceivable' in the end but this does not prevent it, as an ideal, from shaping his attitude to the next step (ad infinitum), honouring the impulse to reach for and respond to the contained and the concealed even if the revelation may only ever be partial, the horizons always to some degree receding from view (2008: 363). That what sustains the view for moments is an aesthetic strategy suggests a way in which space comes to take on the qualities of a social and artistic medium, one worked over by language; worked in the sense that it is *produced*, but with an effortlessness that gives it the impression of *revealing* its own nature instead. Through this interesting tension between the production of space and the revelation of space we learn something about the shifting horizon of place itself, and perhaps the methods of deep mapping. A deep map explores a means of place-based social transformation but Robinson's practice shows that this can happen fruitfully through creative and inclusive work at the level of space. But space here is privileged as something with a psychological texture, a social engagement and a cultural value. It is a medium invested with and constituted by multiple perspectives at the intersection of history and community.

Robinson's secular metaphysics of 'Space' are, in the end, a deep complement to his investment in place. They are, first, his route *to* place, out of the isolated abstraction of twentieth-century metropolitan modernism. They were always what place was embedded within cosmically for him, but they became the lifeblood of place too, its interior labyrinth through which contested versions of the same place were found to be 'interlocking'. It is in the latter of these understandings of space that he came to realize the potential for the positive social contribution of his work, producing and developing deep layers of space in socially engaged forms of ad hoc heritage work, ad hoc insofar as they were generated from the ground up, outside of any institutionalized heritage discourse. Research in critical heritage studies has argued for the recognition of the fundamentally creative nature of all heritage work. That even when it appears to be simply preserving the past from the threat of contemporary life, it is nonetheless producing a narrative for the present and into the future (Harrison 2010: 100). From the mid-1980s there have been calls for contemporary artists to be more involved in heritage work because of the way that they 'have continued to struggle with the material of the present' when the heritage industry had turned its back on it (Hewison 1987: 144). Robinson's work in Ireland represents just this kind of relationship between heritage and contemporary art. It relates the work of place writing to the changing horizons of place itself. While his early map-making revealed those 'interlocking' spaces, his later written work began to interweave them in search of that 'consilience' that could produce and reveal space simultaneously. In this sense the space of the writing returns full circle to the abstract and gestural work of the earlier artist, only this time the space being worked is not merely geometrical but bears and embodies place too, in all its fractal minutia. In this sense Robinson writes as he mapped and as he painted, as an artist whose distinctive investigation, practice and aesthetic of space reveals space itself to be a medium approached by various means capable of influencing the life of a place.

Place and social engagement are ideas that might be thought antithetical to modernism, and Robinson's work does show a disruptive tension that emerged in the 1970s. However, there is another way of thinking about this. Recent work on 'regional modernisms' (Alexander and Moran 2013) and 'archipelagic modernism' (Brannigan 2014) suggests that, as much as the equation between modernism and the city is being rethought historically, modernism's legacy might also be traced in artists like Robinson and perhaps even in the wider project of deep mapping itself. As such, Robinson offers a very singular and surprising view on the relationship between modernism and deep mapping, a curious line of inheritance, if not a bridge. As much as deep mapping is about history, community and place on the margins, it too is concerned with the imaginative manipulation of space through innovative and experimental practices in an antagonistic relationship with modernity. Place is increasingly becoming the site of such experimental practices in the twenty-first century, revealing itself to be as fissured and fractured, as protean and volatile, as *deep* in its cavernous passages as the mind ever was for modernism at the beginning of the twentieth century. Robinson's work draws attention to the mechanics of place heritage on its outer edge as an imaginative social and spatial work, encouraging us to think of place itself as a form of art intervening in the tensions between centre and periphery.

5

Archipelago

The written and visual works published over the last decade in the literary journal *Archipelago* (2007–present) have produced a distinctive and enduring landscape vision of Britain and Ireland as a remote cluster of islands perched precariously on the Atlantic edge of Europe. It is a vision of a craggy, sea-swept but inhabited periphery that has found a surprising purchase in the cultural imagination of the twenty-first century (with reviews appearing in *The Guardian* and the *TLS* among other places). However, unlike many other more amenable examples of what Joanne Parker has called the 'countless vying maps' of these Isles, this vision exists at an argumentative tilt to the more conventional orientation of the United Kingdom and the Republic of Ireland (2014: xi). It privileges and celebrates the northern and western margins of what the journal's editor, Andrew McNeillie, has come to refer to as the 'unnameable archipelago', its channels and seas, its firths and bays, its peninsulas and of course its many islands. It celebrates, too, the languages, cultures and place names of these locales and micro-regions, exploring their uncertain relations to the inland world and, in particular, to a partially devolved Britain.

Julian Bell's striking, monochrome illustration, which has appeared on every front cover so far, shows the archipelago as glimpsed all at once looking down through diving gannets from somewhere in the north-west out beyond St Kilda. Most of the south-east is occluded behind the head of a gannet in the foreground or is disappearing under shadow near a dark and slightly curved horizon. In fact, we see more of Normandy's Cotentin peninsular poking up towards the West Country (a reminder of those old connections between the fishing communities of northern France and Cornwall) than we see of Kent, Sussex, Hampshire, any of the 'Home Counties'. 'I would like [a] somewhat tilting, distorted map,' the journal's editor suggested to the artist, 'pushed to the lower right hand frame of the picture, with south-east England chopped off by the frame' (McNeillie 2006a: n.p.). At first glimpse it does take a moment to 'discover' Britain and Ireland upside down in the image. But as you do so there is a mental reorientation that suggests the wider agenda of resisting an Anglocentric, mainland and metropolitan view of the Isles.

There are layers of significance to this reorientation. The argument between centre and periphery – in which the periphery is summoned up in all its linguistic variety and ecological richness – is important in its own right. Many of the journal's launch events over the years have taken place in that most central of English locations, Oxford, in the Bodleian Library no less, and have involved invocations of landscapes and seascapes as remote and coastal as the litany of the shipping forecast. There is a quality of 'speaking back' to the centre about this, and a sense in which the journal is attempting to inculcate a corrective literary culture. This is a familiar trope in the literary history of islands, as we saw in the previous chapter, in which the relationship between island and mainland, or island and continent, is understood as a binary opposition often inflected with colonial or postcolonial history: *Archipelago* continues the argument established through Robinson's 'view from the horizon' and, like Robinson, it can be seen to complicate this binary as well (1997). Recent work published in the field of island studies has called for an exploration of more complex topological formations of space and place that fully embrace the implication of thinking with archipelagos rather than just with islands (Stratford et al. 2011; Stratford 2013; Pugh 2013). Elaine Stratford, Godfrey Baldacchino, Elizabeth MacMahon, Carol Farbotko and Andrew Harwood have argued for a fresh approach to island thinking that goes beyond the 'island/mainland' binary. For this group, such a binary leads to assumptions about 'insularity' and 'singularity' that can be counterproductive. Instead, they have argued that close attention to *archipelagic* island spaces reveals spaces that are 'inter-related, mutually constituted and co-constructed' emerging from processes of 'connection, assemblage, mobility, and multiplicity' (2011: 113–14). If we concentrate on this literary journal's vision of the north-westerly periphery itself, away from its relation to any mainland or state centre, we find that just such an intertwined, topological vision begins to reveal itself, one of diverse and intertwined cultures, histories and geographies. Not only this, but the watery spaces in between the islands become spaces of experiment, collaboration and creative energy. A familiar cartography is revisited and worked over in a manner that complicates the idea of a United Kingdom and in so doing celebrates a devolved account of the busy and fluctuating relations of its constellated, marginal parts.

Understanding Britain as an archipelago of divided and connected islands suggests more than just observing its material constitution as an archipelago. It goes to the heart of understanding its complex network of localities and it draws attention to the intricate relationships between them. As John Kerrigan puts it in that most canonical work of archipelagic criticism, *Archipelagic English* (2008) (a book that has rather strangely been overlooked in these recent theorizations of archipelagic thought associated with island studies), thinking with an archipelago in mind, in a British context, helps to 'strip away modern Anglocentric and Victorian imperial paradigms' and to 'recover the long, braided histories played out across the British-Irish archipelago between three kingdoms, four countries, divided regions, variable ethnicities and religiously determined allegiances' (2). Kerrigan was influenced in this by the historian J. G. A. Pocock who voiced concerns about the suspicious English bias to British history writing as early as the 1970s. The term 'Atlantic archipelago', Kerrigan claims, designates a 'geopolitical unit or zone'; it does so 'neutrally (avoiding the assumptions loaded into 'the British Isles'); and it implies a devolved, interconnected account of what went on around the islands' (vii). It encourages us to think in terms of 'polycentrism', of shifting relations and allegiances and of mobilities that strike dialogues between places, fractious or fruitful as these dialogues might be.

This chapter will explore how such dialogues and such relations have proved a fertile imaginative resource for a number of authors and artists associated with *Archipelago* and how we can read in the journal's editorial vision a self-conscious intervention in modern British place culture that moves from a privileging of the periphery to the promotion and stimulation of a pluralist, archipelagic localism during a period of uncertainty and instability about the union of the British 'sovereigntyscape' itself (Nairn 2000: 125). With over a thousand pages of diverse material published by over one hundred different authors, no account of the journal could be comprehensive, nor should it attempt to be. However, by looking closely at the earlier work of the journal's editor and a handful of its more regular contributors, a sense of decentred space can be seen to emerge; one that is meticulously located but that also remains alert to being '*between* and *among* islands' (Stratford et al. 2011: 124; emphasis in the original). In such a space, allegiances are all the stronger for being both plural and on the move. *Archipelago*'s editor, Andrew McNeillie, is a poet and author himself who was, at the time of the first edition, emerging from a career as a literature publisher and commissioning editor in Oxford (in fact he is thanked in the acknowledgements as an early reader of Kerrigan's *Archipelagic English*). He started the Clutag Press in 2000, hand-setting and printing poetry by new and established poets. Though other publications have included original works by Geoffrey Hill, Tom Paulin and Anne Stevenson among others, *Archipelago* has come to be the most regular and foremost output for Clutag, and McNeillie's editorial work with the journal has helped to direct the historical and literary critical methods of archipelagic criticism into an attempt to shape a contemporary literary movement for the twenty-first century, one that has overlapped in important ways with the New Nature Writing.

Archipelago 1 was launched in 2007 at an event in Cambridge organized by Robert Macfarlane in memory of the late Roger Deakin. In the opening editorial McNeillie made the following, memorable claim:

> Extraordinary will be its preoccupations with landscape, with documentary and remembrance, with wilderness and wet, with natural and cultural histories, with language and languages, with the littoral and the vestigial, the geological, and topographical, with climates, in terms of both meteorology, ecology and environment; and all these things as metaphor, liminal and subliminal, at the margins, in the unnameable constellation of islands on the Eastern Atlantic coast, known variously in other millennia as Britain, Great Britain, Britain and Ireland etc. (2007a: vii)

For Alan Riach, such 'extraordinary ... preoccupations' have led the journal to offer something of a 'corrective' not only to the idea of a United Kingdom but also to modernism's 'forensic detachment'. Riach suggests that *Archipelago* has foregrounded a literary tradition of twentieth-century authors, for twenty-first-century readers, that 'bears the weight of conscious connection with society, family, language and national history' (2010: 48). As such we have figures like Ivor Gurney, Jack Clemo, Ian Niall and Hugh MacDiarmid quoted, revisited and reconsidered in review articles. They are reconsidered not *in spite* of their 'regionalism' but because, through their vivid and felt connections to place, the journal suggests, we discover our understanding of these islands enlarged, their landscapes and their literatures enriched, by being so carefully located. Behind this celebration of geographical and linguistic diversity, Riach goes on, is an insistence on 'the understanding that imperial authority is always being resisted by people in places unconquered by metropolitan centralism, unimagined by its arbiters of canonicity' (48). The recovery of such figures from the century just gone has helped to determine coordinates for what might be called an early-twenty-first-century literary movement that has inherited twentieth-century modernism but has done so filtered through the diverse cultural geographies of the archipelago.

In this sense the journal contributes to a growing interest in what Neal Alexander and James Moran have called 'regional modernisms'. Alexander and Moran have challenged the 'well-rehearsed narrative about modernism' that defines it as 'essentially metropolitan and international in character', a narrative that, they argue, forgets D. H. Lawrence's Nottingham-Derbyshire borderlands, Hugh MacDiarmid and the Scottish renaissance, Yeats's and Pound's winters together in Ashdown Forest between 1913 and 1916, and Joyce's meticulously mapped Dublin (2013: 1–2). Gesturing to the 'transnational turn' in modernist studies, they present an image of modernism that might in fact be described as 'archipelagic' when they argue that 'modernism simultaneously vaults beyond the bounds of national affiliation *and* attests to local differences which threaten to undermine any cultural image of national integrity' (4). It was just such an interest in 'locality and interconnectedness' that fed John Brannigan's account of *Archipelagic Modernism*, which reimagines modernism in the receding shadow of metropolitan supremacy (2014: 17).

An Aran Keening

McNeillie has extended a metaphor through a number of artworks and editorials for *Archipelago* in which the journal itself has figured as a boat setting out to sea with its net spread wide for new writing. Ishmael has been occasionally alluded to (2009: n.p.) but the metaphor of the 'good ship archipelago' (2011: n.p.) eventually settled on a smaller and more ordinary fishing boat (a more modest vessel, but with a nod to the prophetic grandiosity of W. S. Graham's 'The Night Fishing' too, suggesting that fine line between ordinary experience and extraordinary perception).[1] It is a very appealing extended metaphor in which the journal moves vividly '*between* and *among* islands' (Stratford et al. 2011: 124; emphasis in the original). For example, in one such instance, the 'good ship archipelago' is described as once or twice a year making landfall 'to publish … and be damned in the arc-light glare of the dawn fish-market' (McNeillie 2015: n.p.). In this the coast itself takes on a particular meaning too, as the edge of our conventional world, criss-crossed in search of fresh experiences and refreshing perspectives. Crossing it affords a way of looking back at the land. Such experiences and perspectives are often delivered like a prescription to an ailing, inland society, its 'post-Thatcherian mismanagement culture'. 'Growth' is the 'religion' in such a society, 'quantity the be-all, and nothing for quality (of life), unless approved by the Committee for Homogeny and signed off by some hubristic Walter Mitty' (2011a: n.p.). There are precedents for such a critical, sea-borne position on inland life. Jonathan Raban has described a nineteenth-century prose genre of the 'sailing-alone book': John MacGregor, R. T. McMullan, and E. E. Middleton all went to sea in the 1860s 'to teach the land a lesson' in journeys that treated the sea as 'that biblical wilderness in which the true prophet must temporarily dwell' (1992: 25–6). The difference in *Archipelago* is marked though, as McNeillie is never alone in his 'good ship'. The whole process is founded on a sociable advocacy of plural views on the Isles that would have been abhorrent to the disgruntled Tory patriotism of these Victorian men.

The metaphor of this 'good ship' as a fishing vessel is particularly apt when we consider that the vast majority of the literary or artistic contributions either involve travel between islands or tracing a form of coastal geography. Locating on a map of Britain and Ireland whatever poems and essays from these ten editions it is possible to locate reveals the majority to be north-westerly, all but a handful to be marine or coastal, and

---

[1] A watercolour by McNeillie published on the journal's blog shows the 'good ship' at sea at night and written in the sky is 'THE NIGHTFISHING' (McNeillie 2015: n.p.).

almost all of those that are not north-westerly to be nonetheless coastal.[2] Such an overarching attempt to understand a place through a view from its edge or, to borrow Tim Robinson's phrase, again through that 'view from the horizon', suggests a certain fugitive allegiance, an allegiance pledged to the ongoing lived experience, to the instability of place as it is being redreamed at the edges. There is an attempt to celebrate complexity, divergence, difference and local distinctiveness, all in contradistinction to the unified idea of a nation state, certainly in contradistinction to that 'Committee for Homogeny' (1997).

This fugitive sense of criss-crossing coasts and being *between* islands seems appropriate for an editor whose own lineage draws on a Scottish family line, a Welsh childhood, a very formative year on the Aran Islands and a career spent in Oxfordshire. But in this there is also a broad and very modern understanding of *place* itself that emerges. 'Places', writes the philosopher Edward Casey, 'are matters of experience. We make trial of them in culturally specific ways'; being in or from a place is a part of 'an ongoing cultural process with an experimental edge' (1993: 31). This 'edge' that Casey describes here finds a topographical counterpart in the maze of borders and north-westerly coastlines as they appear in the journal. It is an edge being brought into focus and *worked* by the 'good ship archipelago', crossing back and forth bringing images and languages, place names and stories, from one place to another and back again. We might recall Doreen Massey's description of place as an 'event', as 'a constellation of processes rather than a thing' (2005: 140–1). The image of a boat among the islands of an archipelago, gathering in and giving out news, endlessly renewing the relationships between places, seems apt for this dynamic understanding of place.

The sense of space and the rhythm of this trawling and island hopping are underpinned by McNeillie's own 'sea-pastoral adventure' when, in 1968, he spent a period of time living alone on the Aran Islands in the mouth of Galway Bay. Inspired by J. M. Synge's account of Aran as a young man, McNeillie had visited, fallen for the place and returned later to stay for nearly a year with a trunk of books, tinned food, fishing tackle and as much as he

---

[2] Of course, it is not possible to place all contributions on a map but it is also worth noting that the majority of those contributions that are not mappable concern themselves with subjects that may yet be considered marginal in some sense: geology, fishing, Gaelic language, birds, sea life and so on.

had been able to save in wages. The time had a profound effect on him just before he settled down to marriage and working life inland, but it would be thirty years before he published his travel memoir, *An Aran Keening* (2001). The book draws on his journals of the time but is firmly grounded in the voice of the older man looking back ('Almost every plank of my vessel has been replaced since I first crossed Galway Bay') (x). Reviews of the book note the surprising decision of a young writer to set out for the periphery in the year of the general strikes, occupations and protests that had brought Paris to its knees in 1968 (Gillen 2002: 156; Higgins 2001: 135). However, there is an assumption in this that the periphery is an apolitical space. Certainly, it is remote, arrived at by two long boat trips, with no electricity, no telephone but for one in the post office and before television came and 'changed everything' (as one islander tells him when he returns in 2000) (2001: 217). But the decision to live somewhere remote should not be equated with the decision to somehow abandon the world. As we saw in the last chapter, the late 1960s also saw a generation of artists turn their backs on the city as a site of political and cultural authority and explore rising concerns about 'ecology, conservation and a crisis of the 1970s as the British were uneasily forced to face their post-industrial and post-colonial future' (Wallis 2009: 38). And McNeillie's own personal and cultural centre was always pulled north-west anyway. The formative literary coordinates of his youth ('Owen, Kavanagh, MacDiarmid, Thomas, Thomas, and Thomas'), as well as the presiding influence of his father, Ian Niall, map out an important cultural geography (2001: 176).

Less an escape *from* Europe or Wales or London or Britain behind him, the book represents rather an escape *into* a little-known world with a distinctive quality of experience, one that might serve as an educative comparison to later life in Britain. On the one hand, the Aran of 1968 is the cinematic and elemental archipelago of Flaherty's *Man of Aran*, a place in which McNeillie was able to 'learn about time as space', in which the moving constellations, the rhythm of the tides, weather and the repetitive *crex crex* of the corncrake offer coordinates that supersede the clock and the British city's working day (2001: 47). On the other hand, it is also a world vulnerable and susceptible to the pressures of modernity and he has a keen eye for this. When he returns to write the postscript in 2000, the corncrake – such a forceful nocturnal presence in his journals – has become locally extinct to the islands and the local community itself is also described with an unsentimental sharpness of vision:

> Though a community there was, skeletal yet interwoven, stressed with resistances and rivalries, and bound together by affections and loyalties, tragedy and comedy, common necessity no longer held it as intimately together as once it had. It was a symptom of the modern age, the incipient self-help era. And this was striking to observe because the past remained such an immediate neighbour. So intimate was it that some still wore its clothes next to their skin, and occupied its houses, and tuned their mindsets to its fading wavelengths. (66)

McNeillie is, of course, to some degree insulated against much of the hardship involved in staving off the perils of poverty or hunger that attend any idleness for those who take their living from the sea or the land in such a remote place. He is, in his own words, a 'the archetypal uninvited stranger' (91) who will return to time's 'linear tyranny' (47) such as it is in the city. He is under no illusions about becoming part of the community, though he does, of course, make friends. Like Synge before him, he was there to glimpse and connect with a singular way of life 'right at the edge of the western world, in a northern sea, like living in the corner of a scene by Bruegel' (193).

Nonetheless, there is a moment that vividly recalls the Europe that he is supposed to have left behind him at one of the book's most westerly and peripheral locations when he is fishing on the limestone pavements under the southern cliffs:

> I was still using my handline then and catching only pollack, when the mackerel came in a shoal a hundred yards wide and as deep as a three-storey house, deeper than the eye can see in even such clear water, a squad of helmeted militia, inch-perfect in their drill, like Red Square on May Day, or a Nuremberg rally, or riot police on high alert in the Paris streets of '68. Naïvely I raised my arm to throw a line – like a revolutionary with a Molotov cocktail on its sling – thinking I couldn't miss. But in the instant my arm went up, the thoroughbred shysters turned themselves inside out, turned on their tails and sped, like a startled flock of birds, thousands of them, in their phoney tiger stripes and metallic blue-green armour. (187–8)

In a moment of hallucinatory loneliness, the sudden swell of post-war Europe erupts, and disappears as quickly, leaving him stood holding something that he connects to a Molotov cocktail. The 'riot police', seen through the skin of water as if through a glass between worlds, disappear off into the dark again ('phoney' even lends the passage the air of Holden Caulfied's difficult relationship with the social world). The image offers a way of thinking about the spatial orientation of McNeillie's Aran to Europe, and to Britain and to Ireland. It is a world at a remove but not separate from Europe, even though on its edge: he is looking west when we find this echo of Europe's capitals swimming in. The islands afford a critical distance, from which the author is looking, rebellious, resolved and alone. The counter-image to this one is of the older McNeillie in later life 'delaying too long before the fishmonger's slab and fancying I can taste the salt-and-iodine, the mineral sea, and even hear it surge beneath the cloud of harrying herring gulls at the dead centre of England' (xi). In both images there is a sense of elsewhere brought to bear on the meaning of the given place, a plaiting together of disparate experiences and a making sense of them together.

These images of *elsewhere* and *between* that fold together locations in an archipelago come across in McNeillie's poetry as well. In the playful and knotted short poem 'Belonging', a sense of place emerges that is spatially complex. The poem offers a disruption of the sense of the word 'belonging' as we might recognize it as meaning 'rooted in' or 'possessed by', inflecting it with something paradoxically more fluid and mobile:

BELONGING
Who put the longing into it?
The longing to leave so that
We might belong in longing
To return again, and again?

Who put the being into it?
The being that is never the same
So that when we come back to it
All we have is a name?

(2002: 65)

The sense of place and of belonging comes through the repeated process of departure and return as much as through location itself. To answer the rhetorical questions, nobody put either 'longing' or 'being' in the word 'Belonging' – the *OED* directs us to entirely different roots for the word – and so the questions suggest a projection of a modern experience, the shifting emotions of a mobile life, carrying a collection of disparate worlds within and struggling to hold them in relation to one another.

In an early review of *Archipelago*, Fiona Stafford distinguishes between 'the isolation and individualism' of a literary *island* and a very different logic, distinctive to an archipelago, 'of clustering and analogy' (2007: 24). The fugitive allegiance of 'the good ship archipelago', then, is something that began in McNeillie's own experience, an emotional tension that prompts the editor to reimagine the Isles from the point of view of a boat crossing seas, collecting in news from the periphery and building an alternative vision with which to answer back to the centre. In fact the whole spatial organization of centre/periphery begins to come undone. McNeillie might have travelled out in 1968 from the centre to the periphery but by the time he launched *Archipelago* as a journal it was with this sense of clustered places, a sense of moving *among* a network of cultural centres whose own relations were changing.

The good ship

The very first issue of *Archipelago* begins with a short prose poem by Seamus Heaney describing the poet's trip by boat back to the mainland from an island, reflecting on exchanges with a man who is himself 'a mystery to the islanders' (2007: 1). It is a poem of movement between islands and plays out a form of haunting influence as something is carried across the water. The next piece in this first issue is a coastal poem by Derek Mahon which contemplates the clash of modernity and our animal origins at the water's edge. The speaker longs for the sea in a moment's melancholy exasperation at our 'interesting times' (2007: 4), in what Hugh Haughton has called Mahon's 'own brand of romantic materialism, or metaphysical ecology' (6). These poems immediately establish a rhythm of criss-crossing the coast – a rhythm of hauntings and longings – that threads through every issue in different ways, weaving these island spaces together with the sea that divides them. This is compounded in the third piece in this first issue, an essay by Robert Macfarlane which begins aboard another boat, travelling out this time, not quite from the centre to the periphery (though it might seem so at first glance), but from Wales into the

Irish Sea, a body of water described by John Brannigan as 'the geographical centre of the archipelago' (2014: 68).

Macfarlane describes a night spent on the island of Ynys Enlli off the Llŷn Peninsula where he travels in search of what he calls 'a tradition of archipelagic writing' that 'goes as far back as the Celtic *peregrini* of the sixth to tenth centuries AD' (2007a: n.p.). These *peregrini* were monks, solitaries, anchorites and pilgrims who travelled 'in their thousands to the bays, forests, promontories, mountain-tops and islands of the Atlantic littoral' (2007b: 7). For Macfarlane, this is a part of that wider project to pursue the contentious idea of 'wildness' across modern Britain and Ireland and it is an early version of the first chapter of *The Wild Places*. The purpose of this trip in particular though is less an attempt to discover a modern and vestigial version of wildness itself on the island (though that is there too) than an attempt to trace something of the monks' own distinctive apprehension of life in this remote coastal world. We might think back to his earlier book, *Mountains of the Mind*, which was less concerned with mountains than with the fascination that mountains inspire. Likewise, by visiting the places in which these monks lived and wrote, Macfarlane endeavours to glimpse and connect with traces of their particular fascination as much as with the wild place itself.

The tension between the topology of centre/periphery and the topology of an archipelago is also apparent here. The story of these monks and their pilgrimage is initially described as one which explores 'the brinks of Europe and beyond' but as the essay goes on it begins to suggest rather a movement between uncertainly related worlds (8). Like McNeillie's own journey to Aran, it is not an *escape from* the European world of their day, but an *escape into* something worldly, a shift in perspective towards the periphery. The monks' journey is initially described as an effort to 'act out a movement from history to eternity' but the goal does not remain 'eternity' for long as poetic sketches and Gaelic marginalia begin to locate the focus of their attention somewhere *between* history and eternity, a place of carefully differentiated animal noises, lively weather, and a sense of wonder (8).

> Their poems speak eloquently of a passionate and precise relationship with nature, and of the blend of receptivity and detachment which characterised their interactions with it. Some of the poems read like jotted lists, or field notes: 'Swarms of bees, beetles, soft music of the world, a gentle humming;

brent geese, barnacle geese, shortly before All Hallows, music of the dark wild torrent.' Others record single charmed instants: a blackbird calling from a gorse branch near Belfast Loch, foxes at play in a glade. Marban, a ninth-century hermit who lived in a hut in a fir-grove near Drum Rolach, wrote of the 'wind's voice against a branchy wood on a day of grey cloud'. A nameless monk, responsible for dry-stone walling on the island of North Rona in the ninth century, stopped his work to write a poem that spoke of the delight he felt at standing on a 'clear headland', looking over the 'smooth strand' to the 'calm sea', and hearing the calls of 'the wondrous birds'. A tenth-century copyist, working in an island monastery, paused long enough to scribble a note in Gaelic beside his Latin text. 'Pleasant to me is the glittering of the sun today upon these margins.' (12)

Monks who were apparently turning their back on the world become transfixed here by different types of geese, carefully observe weather conditions and are moved to express poetic figures such as 'the wind's voice'. Macfarlane is interested in the compulsion to write about these things, to engage with them in some way and make a record, turning acts of perception into interactive and creative experiences.

'Receptivity and detachment' is the frame of mind he notes here and, beyond connotations of the ascetic life, this also speaks to a distinctly archipelagic mentality which moves '*between* and *among*' places, resisting (or detaching from) the hold of centrism, and managing (or receiving) multiple and fugitive affiliations, experiments in personal reconfigurations of space (Stratford et al. 2011: 124). In the long poem that opens *Archipelago 4*, 'Instructions to a Saintly Poet', Douglas Dunn plays on this same writerly monasticism. To be detached is one thing: to forfeit the conventional social allegiances and sail a little closer to the edge of the known world with all the exposure and vulnerability that this might risk; but here too 'receptivity' also suggests a willingness to take on new coordinates and to positively encourage a reorientation by them, to recognize a constellation of centres where others see an edge. In this sense 'receptivity' suggests an attempt to complicate the horizon and enrich the familiar world; to intensify the level of detail, yielding to the 'small stories' of locality; to enlarge the view of the periphery by revealing its intricacy.

This process finds an intriguing expression later in Macfarlane's *The Wild Places*. Ynys Enlli is the first of many places in which he finds and brings home an object, in this case a 'heart-sized stone of blue basalt, beautifully marked with fossils' (2007d: 34). He gathers many such stones and pieces of wood and keeps them together at home as 'a way both to remember and to join up my wild places' (88). He describes this process in terms of an unusual cartographic form that lends itself to an archipelagic topology that enables something of a mental counter-mapping. 'Fifteenth century mapmakers', he goes on, 'developed the concept of the "isolarion": the type of map that describes specific areas in detail, but does not provide a clarifying overview of how these places are related to one another' (88). This is how he understands these material objects, each a detailed description of a place but not fixed and organized by a central authority. 'The objects seem to hold my landscapes together without binding them too tightly' (88). In the following passage from the final chapter of *The Wild Places* we see him begin to think through the spatial and temporal possibilities at play in the looseness of the isolarion.

> The evening I got back from the Hope Valley, I took down my stones from their storm beach on the shelf, and laid them out on my desk, adding my gritstone lozenge to the pattern. I began to move them around. First I arranged them into a long line of their finding, with the earliest to the left and most recent to the right. Then I moved them into order of their ages, as best I could: Cambrian, Ordovician, Silurian, Devonian, Permian, Jurassic. ... Then I dispersed them into a rough shape of the relative places of their findings, so that they made an approximate mineral map of the archipelago itself, and my journeys within it. (313)

This flexibility that the isolarion offers him prompts an arrangement according to personal and temporal relations as well as conventional spatial relations. But the personal and temporal reconfigurations here are less about representing real-world geography than about simply exhibiting this flexibility as a thought experiment, trying out new relationships across the archipelago.

The experiment speaks to an uncertainty about the changing cultural geographies of the archipelago at a time of upheaval in the union: uncertainty, but also possibility. It recalls John Kerrigan's discussion of the effects of the 1997 referendums on Scottish and Welsh independence that resulted in their partial devolution: 'Devolution matters because it has encouraged the peoples of the islands to imagine different relationships with one another, and with the peoples of Europe ... but also because of the opportunity it gives the

Anglophone world as a whole to reconfigure its understanding of where it comes from' (2008: 2).

A reflection on an archipelagic spatial order reveals and encourages these experimental ways of connecting up disparate parts. Far from becoming divided and isolated, such configurations positively encourage the possibilities of relationship offered by the constellation of plural centres. Macfarlane concludes:

> My journeys had revealed to me new logics of connection between discrete parts of Britain and Ireland, beyond the system of motorway and flight paths. There were geological links: tor answering to tor, flint to flint, sandstone to sandstone, granite giving way to mud. ... The connections made by all these forces – rocks, creatures, weathers, people – had laid new patterns upon the country, as though it had been swilled in a developing fluid, and unexpected images had emerged, ghostly figures showing through the mesh of roads and cities. (2007d: 314)

These 'new logics' are geological, arboreal, fluvial, coastal and archipelagic for Macfarlane, and there is something protective about his summoning them out of the 'mesh of roads and cities'. It is an invocation of sorts that seems to breathe life into the landscape vision. But this is not a geography of places that is reactionary or that seeks to wall-off, guard and retreat but is one that is dedicated instead to the imaginative possibilities of place-to-place connections.

In part through the influence of Macfarlane, *Archipelago* has added this ecological inflection to what has otherwise been a field dominated by political and cultural histories. In a review of the first edition, Macfarlane glosses his own understanding of the adjective 'archipelagic' and proposes it as a description of a broader tendency in contemporary British and Irish art and literature concerned with landscape: 'It can be hard to know what to call this new body of work,' he wonders. '"Landscape art" is blandly tepid. "Nature writing" is sapless and text-specific. "Pastoral" summons swains and greenswards. "Environmental" has become gummed by politics. Perhaps the adjective "archipelagic" might serve, catching as it does at imaginings that are chthonic, marine, elemental and felt' (2007a: 13). *Archipelago*'s treatment of the geology, birdlife, wildflowers and the imaginative significance of the sea itself has also celebrated the richness of this slightly different meaning to the 'archipelagic'. This is a vision of the these islands as an 'elemental' archipelago, that is, a subnational, pre-national and post-national space all at one and the same time. The journal offers a vision of a wild space in the sense of the stripped back 'disidentification' discussed in Chapter 2. However, far from being an idealized version of 'the wild' – a term we have seen to be hotly disputed recently – the ecologies of this elemental archipelago are often revealed to be vulnerable, depleted and polluted. It was in *Archipelago* that Tim Dee published his account of 'Nature Writing' (referred to in Chapter 3) in which he described a version of modern nature as 'under the human heel … pushed, bloodied, shrunken and ruined to the front of the stage [where] even enfeebled, it has called for new descriptions, fresh thoughts' (2011: 22). Writing of Tory Island, Macfarlane himself, in an uneasy and curious coupling of adjectives, suggests of the littered coastline that 'the abject and the sublime are never far apart here' (2009b: 40). *Archipelago* has brought together these two archipelagic landscape visions: the celebration of a rich diversity of intertwined cultures and languages and the 'chthonic' and 'elemental', the wild archipelago in which sea life, coastal flora and birds are foregrounded as the survivors of our modern excesses. 'Littoral and vestigial' as both of these archipelagos may seem at times, the imaginative power of the journal has been to mark their resilience and actively stimulate new work at the intersection of these two senses of 'archipelagic'. It has drawn attention to the intrinsic link between a richly plural constellation of cultures and the diverse ecosystems and topographies from which they have emerged and to which they are indebted.

Art's no-place

Tha mi beag, agus is toil leam na rudan beaga:
an sìol adhlaict' a sgoltas an cabhsair;
an t-sileag uisg' a chaitheas a' chlach;
a' ghainmhein mhìn a thiodhlaiceas am biorramaid;
a' chiad eun a chuireas fàilt' air a' ghréin;
an dùthaich bheag, an cànan beag;
facal na fìrinn as truime na 'n Domhan.

(I am a small thing, and like the small things:
the buried seed that splits the sidewalk;
the water-drop that devours the stone;

the grain of sand that inters the pyramid;
the first bird that welcomes the sun;
the little country, the little language;
the word of truth that is heavier than the world.)

(Qtd. in Williams 2007: 81)

Quite early on Andrew McNeillie published an essay by Mark Williams on contemporary Scottish Gaelic language poetry, and these few lines by Fearghas MacFhionnlaigh were offered in translation from his long poem 'The Midge'. The speaker suggests an alliance between his language and this list of wild and elemental things to describe a marginalized form of cultural resilience. The 'little language' is hanging on to the neglected edges here, 'littoral and vestigial' as our depleted wildlife. And though MacFhionnlaigh's meaning is singular in its protective regard for Scottish identity, nonetheless the imagery that carries it, imagery that comes to threaten city and empire, is surprisingly plural. A 'water-drop' does not devour stone on its own but by centuries of repetition; a 'grain of sand' does not inter the pyramid alone but as a sandstorm; the 'first bird' only begins the many-voiced dawn chorus. These images of marginalization take comfort in the wealth of collective power, a united front of numerous 'little languages' allied to qualities of the earth itself.

The journal has shown a sustained interest in the 'little languages' of the archipelago and their close relationship to geography. But as in other areas, the sense of centre/periphery relations so evident in 'The Midge' also gives way to more intricate, archipelagic relations elsewhere. In a rare instance of published literature making use of the St Kildan dialect, the contemporary poet Peter Mackay gives us 'Exodus from Hiort', a poem in which the speaker prepares to leave the most remote of those islands, one assumes when they were finally evacuated in 1930 ('we will leave our books open/at Exodus, and cast/ourselves onto seas'). But there are three languages and cultures overlapping here, since the poem is first given in Scottish Gaelic, with the St Kildan dialect words glossed below *and* with three italicized words of English in the last stanza. Then, overleaf the poem is translated into English, this time with the three italicized English words given in Scottish Gaelic and glossed below. The glossing of the words in Gaelic in the English translation draws our eye to the original and we notice an important difference. This last stanza describes the tragic fate of the speaker once he has left the island, and the three things that suggest his ruin are the words given in English: *pub, leper* (sickness) and the *desert* (or at least his sense of spiritual desert). In the English translation, upon leaving he will 'kill a man over *uisga-beatha*' (whisky, or *pub*) and then, 'eaten by *caitheamh*' (consumption, or *leper*) he'll 'die in forsaken *fàsaichean*' (deserts/unpopulated places) (2009: 26–7). The implication of publishing the poem in this bilingual way is a form of cultural confusion. For the St Kildan, what seals his fate are English things that he must use new English words to describe, things that he only encounters after arriving in the inland world. But for the English reader, what seals the man's fate are Scottish things, things that (to someone unable to distinguish between St Kildan and Scottish Gaelic) he might even appear to bring ashore with him. The different vocabularies suggest different, and conflicting, attributions of blame. Not only does the intertwining illustrate poignant and tragic misunderstandings, but the very theme of the poem is one of migration between islands. The tension and drama here arise across the difficult relations between the islands and their different languages but also through the real and difficult movements that bring them into contact and conflict. It is a modest but fine example of those 'long braided histories' (here quite uneasily braided) that John Kerrigan describes, suggestive of the complex depths of meaning that emerge from their interconnection, and testament to the energy that exists '*between* and *among*' islands when we think with an archipelagic framework in mind (Stratford et al. 2011: 124).

Robin Robertson also shows the linguistic energies alive in the ocean spaces between St Kilda and the Scottish mainland, in a long poem that returns us to the close connection between language and topography. 'Leaving St Kilda' is a poem from *Archipelago 4* that invokes an itinerary of coastal place names translated into English and spread over ten pages and is interspersed with the artist Norman Ackroyd's monochrome etchings of many of the places called to mind. The poem describes a journey towards the mainland from that outermost of the Hebridean islands, but it becomes at times a long list naming cliffs and islands, sounds and outlying rocks, as it goes. Tim Robinson has described place names as being like 'so many isolated lines from a lost epic of everyday life' and this can be felt very strongly in this poem (2003: 51). Robertson's poem seems to celebrate the way the place names gesture and allude to worlds loaded with memory in which story and history blend together, half-present, half-lost: names such as 'The Well of Many Virtues',

'The Plain of Spells', 'The Stack of Doom', 'Point of the Strangers' and 'Skerry of the Son of the King of Norway' (2009: 19-21). It is a poem which collects its intangible, linguistic geography into the public consciousness, but doing so it leaves the invocation hanging precariously somewhere between celebration and elegy. The inclusion of Ackroyd's etchings on every other page provides a visual topographical reference for the litany and generates a sense of geographical immersion among the places named that no map of the same area could have expressed.

The visual aesthetic that has helped to shape *Archipelago*'s distinctive version of the Isles is indebted to, more than anything, etchings such as these by Ackroyd that have appeared in every edition so far. Ackroyd has described finding his calling as an artist when a fisherman offered to take him out around the 450-foot of red sandstone sea stack, the Old Man of Hoy, off the coast of the Orkney Islands (*What Do Artists Do All Day*). Since then he has spent a lifetime making engravings of the craggy outliers and islands of the north-west, sketching in fishing boats, then transferring to copperplate back home in London. Now, on an easel in his Bermondsey studio, there sits a map of Britain and Ireland with a cluster of pins in an arc around this north-west coast, one in every location at which he has worked. The boat, and the fishermen who have taken him out time and time again, play an important role in Ackroyd's art. They provide him with those recognizable perspectives on the rocky edges. It is an art that exemplifies the sense of being *among* islands that comes across psychologically in so much of the writing of *Archipelago*. Again and again the view is from a point that is hazardous, exposed, engulfed, encompassed and immersed, taking stock of the land from among its towering broken edges, and this is something that is reflected in the technique as well. McNeillie describes how Ackroyd's etching process – an unpredictable technique for which trial-and-error is an important part – is 'as fickle and spectacular in its effects as the weather itself' and how it is unusually subject to 'immediate hazard and serendipity' (2009c: 32). Ackroyd's aesthetic is that of the 'chthonic' and 'elemental' archipelago that Macfarlane describes. It is pared back and wild but it bears witness to the littoral edges, currents and weathers across which these more intangible relations and dialogues take their meaning.

The elemental nature of Ackroyd's coastal etchings, the soft washes that suggest low cloud and curtains of rain – a product of his use of aquatint – might lend the works an almost abstract quality of dark forms receding and protruding on the picture plane, but he rarely shows a desire to abstract entirely. The titles of the etchings are always careful to locate the images as precisely as possible, and he, like Macfarlane, reminds us that these have been 'densely populated' places, in which a culture has been delicately and patiently cultivated in connection to the topography and wildlife, and in connection to the other islands. In the foreword to a book of his Irish etchings, Ackroyd reminds his reader:

> Many of the islands supported self-contained communities most of which are now abandoned. They have left moving reminders in the ruins of their villages and field systems. Nearly every island of any size has associations with early Christian saints, and their churches and oratories. ... High Island off Connemara boasts an extraordinarily sophisticated eighth century watermill system indicating that the monastery, on this almost inaccessible rock, must have supported a population of about fifty monks. On Inishkea, off Co. Mayo, a midden on Bailey Mor indicates a factory for boiling molluscs to extract the blue-purple pigment much used in scriptoria. (2009: 7)

Ackroyd's archipelago, then, is one with cultural and historical depth, connected to Christian Europe, and this comes across too in his love of the place names. At an event celebrating ten years of Clutag Press in Oxford in 2011, in the Bodleian Library, he stood to offer from memory a litany of all the names of those places in which he has worked on the north-west coasts, one for every pin in that map in his studio. He asked the audience to imagine a compass extending an arm from his childhood home in the 'ancient kingdom of Elmet' and reaching out some three hundred odd miles along the outer edge, evoking a peripheral geography from Muckle Flugga and Out Stack due north right round to the Great Famine graveyard at Skibbereen in the South of Ireland. He pointed out the mix of languages (Gaelic, Scots, English, Norse) that makes up this wide arc, calling them to mind as if bringing them to bear on the central and landlocked towns of the southern English counties.[3]

For Ackroyd, the boat has been as much an artistic tool as the sketching paintbrush or the etching acid, a part of the process of searching out and bearing witness. Its venture out through instability and hazard produces a

---

[3] This event was filmed and a DVD distributed with *Archipelago 8*.

geographical vision that can be articulated back on land. His use of the boat is a literal counterpart to McNeillie's metaphor of 'the good ship' gathering in views from beyond the (relatively) landlocked security of the Home Counties. In fact, the intersection between reality and metaphor has yielded some intriguing results from time to time, and in one essay by McNeillie himself, a real boat plays host to a collaboration between Norman Ackroyd and the poet Douglas Dunn (it is worth noting that what we have here is a Welshman writing about a collaboration between an Englishman and Scotsman). The poet and artist travelled by boat together along various coasts to create *A Line in the Water*, a book of poetry and etchings published in 2009 by the Royal Academy of Arts.

> ... we boot our way toward
> Undersea dreamscapes, surreal, eel-fathomed
> Depths in the super-dark, the silent, dumbed,
> Unpainted and unwritten floors
> Of the visionary deep, the great outdoors,
> Geology, botany, sky, sea, birds, fish,
> So commonplace to here it's just outlandish.
>
> (Qtd. in McNeillie 2009c: 40–1)

Together they have cut themselves loose of the inland world. 'Outlandish' carries the pun that doing so permits them a certain imaginative license, brushing up against the wildness of the dream world and the 'surreal'; a bubbling away of the unconscious that might, in time, be instructive to the landlocked, conscious mind.

From time to time Dunn addresses Ackroyd directly and his 'wide night-view's nocturnal aquatint':

> For you are lovers of the East and North,
> The West, and waters, and your art's no-place,
> Invention's home, that better place to be.
>
> (Qtd. in McNeillie 2009c: 42)

The 'no-place' of art here is Ackroyd's distinctive, boat-bound perspective, outside looking in, between and among the islands, a momentary embodiment of what Heaney has called the 'free creative imagination' in all its temporary and struggled-for suspension of allegiances, in all its tension with the 'constraints of religious, political, and domestic obligation' (1992: 87). This is 'Invention's home', a paradoxically stable image for a boat balanced on the swelling waves. The boat becomes 'place' and 'no-place' at the same time, defined and undefined, at the edge on which place itself is being reappraised and renegotiated. This is 'the good ship archipelago' itself, suspended in the connective interstices, home to creative collaborations, and producing a vision of the land in which the identities of, and the relationships between, nations, locations, regions and micro-regions are open-ended questions calling for dynamic and inclusive responses. The achievement of *Archipelago* through these first ten issues has been to offer a view of Britain, Northern Ireland and Ireland that responds to political and cultural instabilities and the uncertainty they have produced by grounding a cultural vision of the archipelago at a local and human scale. It has refused the simplifications and abstractions of the 'Committee for Homogeny' and opted always for something more difficult and more complex, revealing in every locale the presence of a network of cultural and ecological relations and nurturing these relations as a resource. In the end there is something recuperative about this vision that takes its recuperation as much from mobility and social relations as it does from the wild periphery itself. It has helped to conserve, but also to nurture, a cultural vitality on the margins at a time when this is much needed.

6

Geologies

'All is lithogenesis'. The opening phrase from Hugh MacDiarmid's 1934 poem 'On a Raised Beach' sets out a relationship between stone and the written word that will serve as a starting point for this chapter's exploration of a growing interest in geology in British landscape writing.[1] The poem is another work from the periphery of the archipelago, thought to have been written during a three-day stay alone on the uninhabited West Linga in the Shetland Isles, an island composed largely of gneiss and schist with some intrusions of granite, much of which has been dated to around 420 million years (Lyall 2006: 121). The scale of the poem and of the poet's stay on the island seem impossibly insignificant against the scale of geological time, but it is in precisely such incongruity and discord that much of the poem's drama arises. The *OED* defines 'lithogenesis' as 'the production or origin of minerals or rocks' but, as the poem goes on, the word takes on other meanings as well that bring this chthonic force into relation with the writer's work. Alan Bold has described the stones of the poem as 'the embodiment of a creative intensity' for MacDiarmid (1983: 183). On one level this creative intensity broadens out towards the theological, gesturing to the 'Genesis' in 'lithogenesis': 'These stones go through Man, straight to God, if there is one' (MacDiarmid 1993: 179). On another level there is a narrowing in on something more human, gesturing to the poet's own (relatively) inadequate capacity for creation: 'My fingers over you, arris by arris ... / Bringing my aesthesis in vain to bear' ('arris' describes the sharp edge formed by two connected planes) (11–13). The 'All' of 'All is lithogenesis' flattens the boundaries between these meanings and grounds them on the presence of this ancient stone. It humbles the poet and human history shrinks

---

[1] References to the poem are given by line number to the 1934 edition as published in MacDiarmid (1993: 423–33).

under the combined glare of a geological and theological sense of deep time: 'Cold, undistracted, eternal and sublime' (192).

MacDiarmid continues with a passage that addresses the stones' resistance to language, setting a gulf between himself, the poet and writer, and the silence of the stones:

> Deep conviction or preference can seldom
> Find direct terms in which to express itself.
> To-day on this shingle shelf
> I understand this pensive reluctance so well,
> This not discommendable obstinacy,
> These contrivances of an inexpressive critical feeling,
> These stones with their resolve that Creation shall not be
> Injured by iconoclasts and quacks.
>
> (25–32)

This is a poem of the highest reverence for Creation, but for Creation *as Creation*, for stone as stone, beyond the ways in which we have quarried and reconstituted it. In a later line that calls to mind Christ's temptation in the desert, MacDiarmid claims that 'bread from stones is my sole and desperate dearth' (68). The line refers to the Gospel of Luke in which Christ declines to turn stones to bread in the desert at the behest of Satan after fasting for forty days (Lk. 4.3). It is crucial for MacDiarmid (as for Christ) that there remains this negative capability, this 'dearth'. Temptation to make the stones anything else would be dark magic, the work of 'iconoclasts and quacks': 'We must reconcile ourselves to the stones, / Not the stones to us' (MacDiarmid 1993: 219).

Elizabeth Ellsworth and Jamie Kruse, the editors of a recent anthology of writing and artwork about geology published in the United States, have described what they call 'the contemporary geologic turn' in an 'emergent cultural sensibility' (2013: 18–19). It is a turn that draws its inspiration from a modernist tradition, to which MacDiarmid's poem here belongs, as it has been inherited by those concerned with the shifting relations of place and planet in a state of environmental crisis. It is concerned with fracture and discord, uncertainty and instability, a withdrawal of human primacy and a cautious self-reflexivity. Responding to the identification and naming of the Anthropocene among scientists, social scientists, historians and philosophers – in particular to the recognition that we as a species have become 'agents of planetary geologic change' (8) – Ellsworth and Kruse began to gather together work that deployed 'methods, models, ideas, and aesthetic experience ... that seek to recalibrate "the human" in relation to the "the geologic"' (9). Environmentalism of the 1970s, they argue, was concerned with biosystems, our impacts on wildlife, forests and living ecology, whereas more recently attention has also been drawn deeper into the planet and further out into the sky.

The identification of anthropogenic climate change, superstorms like Katrina and Sandy, the earthquake, tsunamis and nuclear fallout of the Fukushima disaster, the Great Pacific Garbage Patch and a new 'sedimentary layer' (24) of space debris floating above our heads have all encouraged us to expand the purview of environmentalism from the bio- to the geo-, to the whole planetary system: 'No longer the inert matter outside of ourselves that is there to support us and our buildings, the geologic is a cascade of events. Humans and what we build participate in their unfolding' (25). Reconciling ourselves to the stones today does not mean quite what it did when MacDiarmid was writing. On the one hand, the urgency of the challenge has increased. On the other, with human beings as 'agents of planetary geological change' now, we may have already bent the stones too far to our own collective will. That flattening totality of 'All is lithogenesis' suddenly takes on a vertiginous and sinister connotation as the level of human agency no longer looks so small and insignificant.

As Timothy Clark has argued, one of the great dilemmas in understanding the human species as a geological force arises from the question of scale. It is *as a species* that we have altered the composition of the planet, not by way of intention, not even by way of any straightforward accident, but as the result of vast, cumulative and chaotic processes of emergence (2015: 8–9). As our individual actions get scaled up towards the complex species agency that puts pressure on earth systems a degree of interiority is lost. As Dipesh Chakrabarty has argued, 'Humans are biological agents, both collectively and as individuals. They have always been so. ... But we can become geological agents only historically and collectively' (2009: 206). The challenge facing us now, as Clark suggests, is to recognize a 'new reflexivity as a species' through which the 'human Leviathan achieves some kind of responsible consciousness' (2015: 16–17). This is, of course, easier said than done. Considerable obstacles stand in the: at the scale of government and administration, we have political short-termism incapable of regional and national planning up to fifty years into the future (Chakrabarty 2009: 212); at the scale of the individual, we have what Clark calls a 'withdrawal of affect' bringing on a kind of paralysis, an instinct for self-preservation in the face of seemingly insurmountable goals (2015: 160).

One contributor to *Making the Geological Now*, the Canadian poet Don McKay, suggests a way forward through an alliance between poetry and geology which chimes with the austere perspective of MacDiarmid's 'On a Raised Beach'. The effect of geology on poetry and the effect of poetry on geology determine a response that he considers instructive. 'Geology inhibits the tendency, most common in romantic poets, to translate the immediate perception into an emotional condition, which is then admired or fetishized in preference to the original phenomenon – fossil, bird, lichen or landform' (2013: 49). At the same time, however, poetry's capacity to slow things down, 'to experience astonishment and to stop in that astonishment for a long moment or two' (he is quoting Adam Zagajewski here) 'counteracts the tendency, perhaps most common in scientists in the grip of triumphalist technology, to reduce objects of contemplation to quanta of knowledge' (49). Together, poetry and geology bring on a hiatus in these patterns, a space for reflection on our conscious relationship, and unconscious entanglement, with the earth. It might not be what Clark ambitiously calls for in a 'new reflexivity as a species' but it does nonetheless stretch these Romantic and scientific sensibilities, enlarging our existing individualist reflexivity through a relationship to geology, and this might be a start. Ellsworth and Kruse conclude their introduction by arguing that the geologic in its vast scale of deep time, and in its dauntingly unpredictable, uncontrollable, seismic force, might be 'capable of instructing not only architecture and design practices, but everyday life as well' (2013: 26).

But what might everyday life look like under the instruction of the geologic? What might be different about a life attempting to reconcile itself to the stones in the twenty-first century? This chapter takes the possibility of this instruction, this hiatus and this elusive reconciliation as a starting point and explores 'lithogenesis', or the creative power of stone, in two ways. First, I discuss the 'geopoetics' of place writing in prose works by Kenneth White and Tim Robinson, suggesting ways in which they have attempted to engage with these kinds of relations to geology; attempts that have not necessarily succeeded.

In fact, I will argue that their failure to conciliate the human and the geologic nonetheless produces complex, plural and self-reflexive modalities of place writing that generate their own dynamic forms. Second, I consider the idea of a 'geopoetics' of place more broadly, insofar as it has inspired a place culture involving people and their environment on the Isle of Harris, with particular reference to the work of Alastair McIntosh, but also Tim Robinson. Here too any conciliation between people and environment is complicated in favour of the recognition that place too is fundamentally a dynamic and self-reflexive act. The sense in which we must 'reconcile ourselves to the stones' becomes, for White, an ongoing imperative for wider 'cultural renewal' that responds in ever more creative ways to the ground beneath our feet. In McIntosh's *Soil and Soul* (2001) we see a practical example of this in a project that revivifies a local community's sense of place and identity, grounding it and opening it up at one and the same time.

Clearings

In thinking about this dynamic and creative relationship between people, geology and writing we might turn to Heidegger's work on aesthetics, which differentiates between the concepts of 'earth' and 'world'. Exploring the spaces generated and produced through the entanglement of, and the tension between, these two concepts, Heidegger developed the idea of a 'clearing' (*Lichtung*). In 'The Origin of the Work of Art' he suggests that the materiality of the work is brought to the fore in all its obstinate presence (unlike e.g. the materiality of a tool, the effectiveness of which is measured by how much it vanishes to us through its use) (2002: 9–10). This intrusive material presence brought forth in the work of art is what he calls 'the earth'. 'The earth', Heidegger suggests, 'is openly illuminated as itself only where it is apprehended and preserved as the essentially undisclosable, as that which withdraws from every disclosure, in other words, keeps itself constantly closed up' (25). In fact, the metaphor he uses for earth is actually one of stone.

> What is the earth, that it reaches the unconcealed in just this manner? The stone presses downwards and manifests its heaviness. But while this heaviness weighs down on us, at the same time, it denies us any penetration

into it. If we attempt such penetration by smashing the rock, then it shows us its pieces but never anything inward, anything that has been opened up. The stone has instantly withdrawn again into the same dull weight and mass of its fragments. If we try to grasp the stone's heaviness in another way, by placing it on a pair of scales, then we bring its heaviness into the calculable form of weight. This perhaps very precise determination of the stone is a number, but the heaviness of the weight has escaped us. (24–5)

'World', however, is quite the opposite and is inextricably bound up with human development: it is 'the self-opening openness of the broad paths of simple and essential decisions in the destiny of historical people' (26): in fact 'world' becomes a verb for Heidegger meaning a human-led opening up: *World worlds* (23). 'World and earth are essentially different,' he suggests, 'and yet never separated from one another. World is grounded on earth, and earth rises up through world' (26). But the relationship between the two in the work of art is always 'intrinsically belligerent' and based on 'strife' (*Streit*), each tangling to pull the other in its opposite direction (31). The space produced by this difficult entanglement, and hence the space of the work of art, he calls a 'clearing' (*Lichtung*). In the idea of the clearing, the physical presence of the work of art is crucial to its effect as it *lets the earth be earth* in a similar manner described by MacDiarmid in 'On a Raised Beach' and that McKay is arguing for in the alliance between poetry and geology (24).

More recently Jane Bennett has argued for what she calls 'a kind of geological affect or material vitality' that acknowledges an agency (or more specifically an 'actancy') to *things* and that explores our own emergence as beings in the middle of complex assemblages, or nature-culture entanglements (2010: 61). To do so is to expand the tensions at work in the idea of 'the clearing' from the realm of art and art alone, in Heidegger, to a broader and more urgent cultural work that responds to the disturbing diagnosis of the Anthropocene. But for such an acknowledgement of the agency of matter, Bennett argues, there must be a 'perceptual style congenial to the possibility of thing power' (2004: 350) which involves a certain 'naiveté', a belief that we might encounter something of the material earth beyond its appearance as a collection of 'mediated' and 'humanized objects' (357). 'Yes,' she concedes, 'there is a sense in which any thing-power discerned is an effect of culture, and this insight is a valuable counter to moralistic appeals to "nature." But concentration on this insight alone also diminishes any potential we might possess to render more *manifest* the world of nonhuman vitality' (357). Rendering manifest in this way, she suggests, is 'both to receive and to participate', to become responsively involved, intellectually and culturally, in the struggle that for Heidegger produced the work of art (2010: 17). We might contrast the difficulty and slowness of 'receiving and participating' that is at work in the opening of a clearing with the ease of *using and consuming* that is at work in the more familiar opening of a world. In Bennett, we can detect the development of the materialism of Heidegger's earth to see it not just as inert matter worked into art but as, in Ellsworth and Kruse's phrase again, 'a cascade of events' with which we are involved in ordinary life and which it endangers us to ignore.

Also central to the recognition of the earth as earth is what Onno Oerlemans has called the 'material sublime'. This is a 'recognition that it is possible to see at once how thought and existence are estranged from a clear awareness of the physical world, and that they are yet inexplicably rooted in it' (2002: 4). The written word, the poem itself, becomes the medium negotiating a relationship between the two, neither thought alone, nor matter, form, but a little of each, composing that very 'perceptual style congenial to the possibility of thing power' (Bennett 2004: 350). This relationship is no easy conciliation though; in fact, no conciliation at all but more like a brokered compromise. Oerlemans continues to suggest that 'although we can know much about the natural world, and can trace our cultural biological roots to natural objects and processes, we nevertheless experience consciousness as distinct' (2002: 11). This leads him to claim that 'thus any desire we may also feel for a reunion, for knowing our connection with the world, must be to some degree suspect' (11). For Oerlemans, this is 'the fundamental paradox that lies at the heart of environmentalist thinking, and forms its central conjunction with Romanticism' (11). Recent literary relations to stone and geology have proved particularly resistant to the kinds of Romantic and environmental 'reunion' with 'Nature' of which Oerlemans is so suspicious, those feelings of interanimation and reciprocal subjectivity that can lead to a sense of 'oneness' rather than to an existentially struggled-for relationship between two states that remain other to one another. The naive realism that brings us closer to Bennett's notion of vibrant matter, and the restraint put on the human tendency to open worlds in the work of art in Heidegger's notion of the clearing, both emerge from the creative potential unlocked when we nurture a sensibility more alive to the intricacy and complexity, the difficulty and opacity, of the earth at our feet.

An encounter with stone or geology, like MacDiarmid's 'On a Raised Beach', and others in prose that I will go on to examine, is an encounter with that quality of the earth that Heidegger describes which is most overtly resistant to us; an encounter with that which maintains the integrity of its otherness most strikingly. The writing occurs in an unbridged and unbridgeable gap but it is all the more interesting for this. It becomes a struggle, at the heart of which is not *mimesis* but *poesis*, an original articulation or presentation ('poesis' as 'creating or producing' (*OED*)) rather than an imitation or *re*presentation of something else. In this sense, the 'clearing', for Heidegger, becomes a matter of announcing and generating an originary truth: 'Art is, then, a becoming and happening of truth' (2002: 44). Such a 'clearing' becomes a space of creative generation, a genesis in its own right, producing the space of a work of art. It may also be possible to think in this way about the creative production of a geographical space of human inhabitation. Such a space suggests an interesting connection between the poetics of place writing and the creativity of place culture. Like place writing, place culture might be a more self-reflexive art than is often popularly assumed and one for which the acknowledgement and revelation of non-human presences and agencies can be a resource helping us to understand place as an ongoing process of discovery, development, consensus and creation perpetually emerging out of dynamic entanglements of the human and the non-human (to which we will return in the final part of this chapter).

Geopoetics

In 1785, after delivering his second lecture 'Concerning the System of the Earth, Its Duration, and Stability' to the Edinburgh Royal Society, the 'famous fossil philosopher' Dr James Hutton set out on a series of field trips (qtd. in Repcheck 2003: 146). He was going in search of evidence to support his claim that the Earth was far more than 6,000 years old, a period arrived at from calculations made through interpreting the Book of Genesis and commonly accepted among natural philosophers at the time. It was a controversial proposition, demanding as it did a Copernican leap of the imagination and, unsurprisingly, it was met with scepticism and misunderstanding. Little did even Hutton know that the planet would later come to be dated at closer to 4.6 billion years old. Just as significant, in its dismantling of a prevalent world view, was Hutton's suggestion that geomorphology was *ongoing*, that the 'fracture, flexure and contortion' of the earth was still at work beneath our very feet (Hutton qtd. in Repcheck 2003: 152).

After the lecture he travelled to Glen Tilt just south of the granite massif of the Cairngorms, to Cairnsmore of Fleet near the west coast, where great veins of granite may be seen intruding into the schist and sandstone from below. He took with him the artist John Clerk of Eldin who made sketches of the rocks that would serve to illustrate Hutton's theory (Furniss 2014: 568–71). He travelled along the coast of the Isle of Arran looking for violent disruptions in coastal strata. In the following passage, Hutton is looking south from Arran towards the smaller island of Pladda, and to Ailsa Crag beyond that, wondering if these diminishing islands were ever connected by land to Arran, Britain and even Europe behind him. A startling vision of the archipelago on the move emerges:

> By thus ascertaining the first step in our cosmological speculation, we advance with some degree of certainty into the annals of a continent which does not now appear; and in tracing these operations which are past, we foresee distant events in the course of things. We see the destruction of a high island in the formation of a low one; and from those portions of the high land or continent which remain as yet upon the coast and in the sea, we may perceive the future destruction, not of so little island only, which has been saved from the wreck of so much land, but also of the continent itself, which is in time to disappear. Thus Pladda is to the Island of Arran what Arran is to the island of Britain, and what Britain is to the continent of Europe. (Hutton qtd. in Furniss 2014: 582)

It is an unsettling idea, a reminder of the tenuous hold such a vast enterprise as Britain (then only eighty years a United Kingdom) might have on the Earth. Extraordinary that a vision founded on stone could suggest so vividly that the archipelago was in dynamic flux, that islands, nations and even continents were in such fluid relationship with one another.

Geology as just such an intrusion of the earth onto a prevailing worldview, as a destabilizing cultural influence that can open its own worlds in us, has been a driving force behind the essayist Kenneth White and the Franco-Scottish literary movement known as 'geopoetics' that he has spear-headed. White established 'L'Institut International de Géopoétique' in France in 1989 and a Scottish Centre for Geopoetics was opened by Tony McManus in 1995. In an echo of Heidegger, White claims that geopoetics is 'concerned, fundamentally, with a relationship to the earth and with the opening of a world' (2004: 243). With geopoetics, White sets out with the intention of opening our limited, human world view onto the scale of the earth in all its depth and instability – just as Hutton did before him – as a source for 'cultural renewal' (2004: 243). It is meant not as a single act of opening, but rather as an initiation of the continuous process of world-opening in relation to the earth. But this is not an opening in the pure sense of 'worlding' as Heidegger might put it. Because it is an opening *onto* the earth, attempting to acknowledge the earth as earth, it is closer to the idea of a 'clearing'. The forgetfulness of a world's opening which, for MacDiarmid, becomes 'iconoclasm', is refused by grounding it on the material presence of earth, consciously involving it in that 'belligerent' wrestling forth. White quotes Hutton: 'We are not to limit Nature with our imbecility' (2006: 18).

White is a Scottish poet, professor and man of letters who has been living and working in France and travelling extensively for several decades in what he calls a 'little transnational atopia' (2004: 45). He does not see this as exile in the tradition of so many displaced modernists but as a certain Scottish 'extension and expansion', a 'wanderlust' that he suggests is 'to do with a continentality that is Unbritish, Unenglish' (2006: 56). But he does not mean this to assert a sense of Scottish national identity, however nomadic. Quite the contrary, White's geopoetics thrives on the fluid uncertainty that comes with a national identity crisis: 'It's when the national culture is broken up', he has written, 'that the individual can emerge, relieved of history's heavy weight, and open new space' (2004: 45). Once again, the archipelago is on the move here. We might imagine him reading Hutton's passage above about the disintegration of the European coastal shelf as a stirring call to creative action, an imaginative emancipation through which the individual is inspired to explore and assert identities beyond any static understanding of community, nation or region.

In 2005, in a lecture given in Inverness, White attacked the word 'region', as a description of the Highlands and Islands, for its connotations of 'administration' and 'Empire', for the way that, he suggests, regionalism as a cultural policy threatens to 'replace a field of creative energy' with 'identity ideology' (2006: 59). Raymond Williams has also gestured to the way 'region' or 'regional' (both stemming from *regere* to direct or to rule) are terms that, politically, 'are within this assumption of dominance and subordination' (1976: 265). In place of 'region', White suggests the term 'territory': 'Every territory, while maintaining its presence and compactness, is open, if one knows how to read it' (2006: 76). Geology, zoology, linguistics, even hydrography, all come into White's argument for the use of the word 'territory', because they all ignore national or regional fixity by straying over borders, thereby contributing to his idea of an 'open world poetics' (76). Fault lines or escarpments, migrating animals, loan words or folktales, or rivers that meander, all ignore the political administration of bordered units.

However, at no point does *place* disintegrate into generalized space for White either. In fact, geopoetics allows him to intensify a particular aspect of place as distinct from the ideas of region and nation. The location of the lecture itself is important here, and White is aware of this. Inverness sits at the top of the Great Glen Fault, the line of lochs terminating in Loch Ness. It is a fault that around 500 million years ago connected to its North American counterpart, the Cabot Fault, which runs just below the St Lawrence River between Newfoundland and Nova Scotia in Canada. As White reminds his audience, all of the land to the north of the Solway Firth was once attached to the North American continent divided by the Iapetus Ocean. This is a transcontinental fault in the heart of Scotland, on which White has chosen to contemplate such terms as region and nation. Again, the earth beneath is summoned up to be read and brought to bear on the world above it, pulling a little at its self-certainty and offering an alternative spatial order. There is something of the geologist's flair for theatrical presentation about White's lecture, given its venue.[2]

Geopoetics is primarily a poetics of the essay, rather than that of a finished poem, story or novel (though it may also be conceived and expressed in other

---

[2] Ralph O'Connor has shown that geology in the nineteenth century was not shy of a little theatre and that as much as the Romantics learnt from geologists so the geologists also learnt a lot from the picturesque essay and the philosophy of the sublime (2007).

forms as well). White explicitly favours the essay in his writing on geopoetics, describing it as a form that is 'creative of new space' and as 'abandoning established genres' (2004: 76). He goes on to remark that 'the essayist is out on his own, working in the open. Knowing very well that the last word will never be pronounced, maintaining a distance both from dogmatic totality and the detailed report, he makes attempts, *essays*, he tries out ways, he takes surroundings' (58). These remarks direct the reader back to Montaigne, who coined the term 'essay' itself (*essai*), which literally means 'an attempt' or 'a try'. It is this 'trying out' with its emphasis on creativity that goes to the heart of the poetics of the essay and the *poesis* of geopoetics: making new, opening a textual and mental world *onto* an underlying, expansive, geological earth, wrestling to arrive at that 'clearing' which Heidegger describes as a form of *poesis*. As we saw in the introduction, this sense of the essay as a form of creative experiment is also a helpful way of understanding the whole variety of collected writings this book has explored as a genre, both proposing possibilities and brokering new relationships. However, although many of White's own essays map out a fascinating canon of marginalized and overlooked non-fiction works, they are typically less effective in their exploration of place and the earth than the work of Tim Robinson, to which I now return as a way of elucidating some of these thoughts on geopoetics.

Robinson begins *Stones of Aran*, his two-volume study of the Aran Islands in the mouth of Galway Bay off the west coast of Ireland, with a vertiginous and unsettling view of their geological foundation. The limestone on which the author stands, so he tells us, was laid down 320 million years ago as the floor of a tropical ocean; 50 million years later it was raised out of the ocean by tectonic plate collisions that created the mountains of southern Europe, from which moment on, its soluble stone began to be eroded, shaped and 'polished' by the elements, and later by the bite of glaciers (2008: 7). 'So the geographies over which we are so suicidally passionate', he reflects, 'are, on this scale of events, fleeting expressions of the earth's face' (7). But the instability of the Aran Islands is not just a matter of projecting back into deep geological time. The much more immediate erosion of, in particular, the largest island's western cliffs is a well-known fact. Fishermen talk of the *aragaint* (the ledges and pavements near the water's edge) and the *strapaí* (or stairways) down to them, and many are used to discovering old ways blocked or new ways suddenly opened by rock falls (113). In one extreme case, a boy from

Oatquarter goes back to retrieve the line he has set overnight only to find that not only the line but a whole section of the clifftop has disappeared (113). Field names, archaeological remains and folktales all allude to projections of land on the southern edge that are no longer there, fallen victim to the ever deeper undermining motions of the Atlantic waves at the foot of the cliffs. In this the islands offer a particularly magnified sense of planetary time, 'disconcertingly open to non-human immensities' (27). Robinson concludes: 'Unless vaster earth-processes intervene Aran will ultimately dwindle to a little reef and disappear' (28). The sense of finitude, precariousness and vulnerability that comes with this realization is the outcome of a careful consideration of, not just geology in the abstract, but the distinctive quality of this local geology on the edge of the European coastal shelf. Intriguingly, these particular qualities also suggest that Robinson's writings might be read productively with the Anthropocene in mind. Not a place that is in itself more damaged or developed than other places by any particular margin, nonetheless there is a powerful sense of the earth intruding on the human world on Aran, an undeniable precariousness that chimes with the environmental precariousness of this modern epoch. Isolated as this island experience is, its concomitant exposure suggests an upwelling and intensified sense of planet, but one that comes through the author's response to the island's local geology. Again, as with MacDiarmid, there is a discord in the senses of scale between the individual author's minute insignificance and the vast sense of deep time and continental geography. But once again the discord, the interesting point of tension and drama, arises precisely through a close attention to local detail.

Robinson's alertness to the instability of Aran draws the eye down. It prevents his own literary work from becoming too lofty, too inattentive to the tenuous grasp that he has on the place. As we saw in Chapter 4, it is one of Robinson's guiding interests – in fact, the whole ambition of the book – to ensure that his writing does not betray its subject. The writing endeavours to be as faithful as possible to the ground underfoot, searching out the possibility of a congruence between the human world of culture and the earth on which it is set, in the form of that 'good step'. It is the qualities that he reads in the stone itself that brings this on but these are also what make him wary of too simple a solution. Robinson has described his aesthetic as driven in part by a 'romantic-materialist' (2003: 51) impulse which begins to sound rather like the desire for that 'reunion' between thought and matter of which Oerlemans suggests we should be suspicious (2002: 11). But Robinson's work comes predicated on an underlying difficulty, uncertainty and, in the end, an important sense of impossibility when it comes to that 'good step'.

In the following passage from a chapter called 'The Difficult Mile', Robinson is walking back home on the north side of the island where the coastline is not cliffs but a sloped beach consisting of heavy rubble. In reading this passage, Heidegger's description of the 'intrinsically belligerent' entanglement of non-human earth and human world can help us to explore Robinson's self-reflexive negotiation between thought, experience and language. The passage describes an existential struggle in consciousness, in the mind of a solitary, introverted author. This is a struggle for a version of the 'material sublime', but one that is candid about its own failure to arrive at any reconciliation between earth and world (he is looking across the sea towards the mainland from this rubble beach):

> Then if a sea mist annuls the beatific vision of Connemara and the waves turn leaden and the sky hangs low, the generalizing monotony of the rock-bank is suddenly replaced by a dreadful multiplicity of individual boulders, each an ugly confusion of angles and edges. With every pace one's mood darkens. These endless ankle-twisting contradictions underfoot, amorphous, resistant, cutting, dull, become the uncountable futilities heaped upon one's own shores by the surrounding ocean of indifference. If then one could elevate gloom into metaphysical despair, see the human race as no taller than that most depressing of life-forms, the lichen that stains so many of these bare stones black, one might, paradoxically, march on with a weightier stride that would soon outwalk the linear desert. Instead, the interminable dump of broken bits and pieces one is toiling along stubbornly remains the merely personal accumulation of petty worries, selfish anxieties, broken promises, discarded aspirations and other chips off a life-worn ego, that constitutes the path to one's own particular version of nowhere. (2008: 168)

What is performed here is a graphic failure to conciliate psychology and geology, and in the same breath a graphic failure to 'elevate' individual consciousness to species consciousness (to 'see the human race as no taller than ... lichen'). Instead, out of the failure emerges a tangle of metaphors in which the mind projects its 'petty worries' out onto the stone, each already undermined by the confession of failure. But this makes it an *interesting* failure, layered, expressive and self-reflexive. All the difficulty and indifference of the stony landscape remains difficult and indifferent, uncompromising in the extreme, and the human energy is directed instead towards adapting itself to such indifference. But he cannot do it, so lapses into a projection of his own emotions onto the landscape in a pathetic moment almost of self-parody, in full knowledge of its futility. There are layers of expressive meaning here that dramatize the self struggling to relate to something much grander in scale.

What Robinson's exploratory essays do achieve in their failure and discord is to articulate a self-reflexive difficulty at the point of our entanglement with the earth, one which seems richer in its linguistic inventiveness, in its toing-and-froing over the impossible point of interface, than the Romantic mode of writing Oerlemans is concerned by. This too is a way of rethinking place in response to the Anthropocene. Ways of knowing and writing and thinking about place begin to proliferate from this point of difficulty. In a chapter on the mysterious limestone ruin of Dún Aonghasa which sits high up on the cliff edge of the main island, he concludes: 'Once again I have failed to *be* in this strange place, this knot of stone from which the sky has broken out. So I promise to come back and try again, to approach it from a different angle, take it by storm or moonlight, bring a measuring tape or a bottle of wine' (2008: 109). The failure to articulate the final word on the place and the refusal to endorse a belief in a reconciliation between self and earth means that a labyrinth of possibilities remains open, each way inadequate but each slowed to what Bennett describes as 'receiving and participating' (in contrast to a lazier use and consumption). There is an echo here too of Samuel Beckett's mantra from *Worstward Ho!*: 'Ever tried. Ever failed. No matter. Try Again. Fail again. *Fail better*' (2009: 81; my emphasis). As John Wylie has argued in his Derridean reading of Robinson, there is 'a displacement of land and life from each other' but this displacement is also, crucially, why 'we have something to say' (2012: 375).

Place-making

In this folding together of failure and creativity in Robinson's *Stones of Aran* there are other stones lurking in the background as well. The book takes its title from Ruskin's *The Stones of Venice* (though note the telling loss of the definite article as architectural features recede and geological features come to the fore). It shows the influence of, in particular, Ruskin's attack on industrial labour and its dehumanizing effects. Ruskin also describes a poetics of difficulty and failure in which something more interesting occurs than it might if a forced and inauthentic perfection is aspired to. Speaking of the stonemason making his individualistic carvings on a medieval cathedral as an alternative to the factory worker following orders and copying a design, Ruskin suggests: 'Out come all his roughness, all his dullness, all his incapability; shame upon shame, *failure upon failure*, pause after pause: but out comes the whole majesty of him also' (1853: 161; my emphasis). For Ruskin, as for Robinson, the honest failure of the individual in all his or her roughness is more valuable for its creative autonomy than machinic perfection produced under a scheme of work in which the human becomes a tool in an authoritarian scheme of design controlled from the outside. We might imagine that for Robinson, such an idea must have struck a chord with his investigation of the islands' postcolonial cartography and heritage. Ruskin continues:

> If you will have that precision out of them, and make their fingers measure degrees like cogwheels, and their arms strike curves like compasses, you must unhumanize them. ... The eye of the soul must be bent upon the finger point, and the soul's force must fill all the invisible nerves that guide it ... and so soul and sight be worn away, and the whole human being be lost at last. (161)

For Robinson though, it is not 'the whole human being' that will be lost, but the wholeness of the place (we might imagine a connection between Ruskin's ideal 'whole human being' and Robinson's own ideal of an 'unsummable totality of perspectives' as discussed in Chapter 4). This is a theme that began for him in his first role on the island as cartographer. In fact, for Robinson, the essay has always been a counterpart to the map. As he says early on in *Stones of Aran*, the maps were really 'preliminary storings and sortings of material' that would always give way to 'the world-hungry art of words' (2008: 19).

In their early years on the island, Robinson and his wife planted a potato field outside their house, orienting it by the lines of the paths and the field walls. These paths and field walls in turn followed the fault lines in the limestone underneath which run parallel along an *almost*, but not quite, north/south line. Fault lines such as these can be seen all over the island, so many of them following the same north-north-east by south-south-west line that they come to represent the islands' own north and south. That 'almost' becomes a token of the islands' distinctive identity, and was so significant that Robinson has preserved and published the original map of the potato field as a limited edition four-colour offset and letterpress print with Coracle Press. The whole island is a grid of walls enclosing over a thousand tiny fields that are, generally speaking, in alignment with the limestone faults underneath. Such an alignment obviously appeals to Robinson in search of that congruence between a culture and the earth that bears it. Highly aware of, and fascinated by, this local orientation, he suggests, 'Nevertheless the unchanging abstractions of official cartography insensibly penetrated the time-bound little domain, and I was always conscious of the angle, the argument, between so-called True North and our Garden North' (n.d.). There is an echo of Ruskin here in that 'insensibly penetrated', a surprisingly violent image of some anonymous system reaching its controlling arm into the human being.

Subtle as the 'argument' might be then, 'True North' here carries the cultural connotations of imperial north and the north of British administration, while geological north, or 'our Garden North', suggests a politically loaded deviation from the standard that is more grounded and locally useful. It is also an aspect of the island's particular heritage, an example of an intriguing intersection of geology and history. 'Our Garden north' *fails* again to find a perfect congruence between the British world and the stones of Aran, but it achieves something nonetheless highly interesting in doing so. As an idea, 'our Garden north' makes its own truth, in that Heideggerean sense of instantiating *poesis* but in this case not with a work of art but with the culture of a place. We might see in this 'argument' a shadow of the difference between 'region' and 'territory' for Kenneth White, where region is a definition that reaches into a place from the outside while territory offers that 'bottom-up' definition based on an engagement with the geology underneath. But we can also see Ruskin's argument for the autonomy of the creative craftsman here too. Awkwardly caught in a tension between the open world of imperial space and the closure of the earth beneath, the orientation here somehow necessarily fails both but at the same time succeeds in realizing a geopoetic 'clearing', a space of inhabitation that instantiates its own truth.

Grounded as such a place culture is locally, and engaged once again in that argumentative, archipelagic relationship with colonial Britain, there is a question left hanging. Does such a grounded sense of place culture and heritage close itself off from the outside world, denying what White argues for in the idea of an 'open world' geopoetics? Do frictions between a desire to protect and celebrate local distinctiveness and an anxiety about extrinsic influence risk closing off the geologically grounded place culture to wider senses of community? Certainly, Robinson's recognition with a European Conservation Award in 1987 suggests otherwise but so too does an essay by the American nature writer John Elder. In 'Catchments', Elder explores what he calls a 'dialogue' between a river catchment near his home in the United States below the Hogback Ridge in the Green Mountains of Vermont and the broad and complex catchment of Roundstone Bog above Robinson's home in Connemara (2016: 43). The dialogue he explores is with Robinson's Connemara writings in this case, rather than his Aran writings, but it is one similarly founded on a curious 'correlation between the bedrocks' of the respective areas (49). 'The intricate mix of rocks in the Dalradian schist Robinson describes is closely replicated in the composition of schists in the mountains of Vermont' (Elder 2016: 49). He goes on describe the deep geological processes that once saw the continental shelves on either side of the Atlantic a part of the same continent and a how his Hogback Ridge is a part of a long line of mountains that then ran from western Ireland down through Newfoundland, New England and south into the Appalachians, explaining these surprising 'geological parallels' (50). Once again, the 'fracture, flexure, and contortion' of geology's movements in deep time seem to open these places up, and even to connect them, through this 'dialogue' with one another. The geological correspondence informs a further reflection on the relationship between what Robinson has done for the place lore of Connemara and the loss of such place lore in the United States. Elder describes the way both those descended from the native tribes and those descended from the European settlers in Vermont have been 'impoverished by a general oblivion to the names and stories woven into the land over many centuries by the Western Abenaki' by the violent history of settlement and colonization (47). He describes how the discovery of this 'geological parallel', for him, 'seems to express a longing for values too often neglected in the modern conversation of nations' (51).

We might think of this as an example of what Ursula Heise calls 'ecocosmopolitanism', a form of outward-looking alliance or exchange based on the 'more-than-human-world' that casts them in the light of 'planetary "imagined communities" of both human and non-human kinds' (2008: 60–1). This is not to argue that the connection between these places is 'natural' if 'natural' is to suggest a static and essentialist form of identity (that which Heise challenges in the 'ethic of proximity'). Instead, it shows that a close attention to the slow unfolding movements of even the earth beneath our feet ought to remind us that places are protean things, and that they are intertwined in all sorts of ways with the wider world. Recognizing this can help to bring on place cultures that are similarly protean and intertwined.

Another example from an island further north in the Atlantic may help to address this question more fully. In a very surprising case of dynamic cultural change on the Scottish Isle of Harris, described by Alastair McIntosh in his *Soil and Soul*, an instance of rethinking the community's relationship with geology encourages a similar very open sense of international transatlantic alliance. And it is one that occurs at the same time as the islanders are resisting the proposals of an extrinsic agent in the form of a global corporation. In June 1991, a Scottish businessman began making inquiries on behalf of the multinational building materials company Lafarge Redland Aggregates about the opening of a 'superquarry' near the southern tip of the Isle of Harris. A large quarry in Britain is thought to extract, on average, around 200,000 tonnes of stone each year, but what was being proposed here would extract between 10 and 20 million tonnes each year once it reached full production (148). It would use around 36 tonnes of explosive per week and leave a hole in the side of a mountain called Roineabhal that would be the largest of its kind in the world, covering several square miles and rising to the height of 'six times the white cliffs of Dover' in order to serve the demand for aggregate in such fields as road-building and the construction of sea defences (148). What ensued was a thirteen-year battle between the islanders, who were supported by various charitable NGOs, and the lawyers of Lafarge Redland. This became the longest land development battle in Scottish history. Author, academic and campaigner Alastair McIntosh documented the struggle in *Soil and Soul* and was himself instrumental in encouraging the islanders (who were at one point 90 per cent behind the development) to fight for the conservation of the island (160).

At the heart of the book is an account of a form of environmental activism, inflected both by McIntosh's Christian faith and his sense of place-based identity as a Hebridean islander. He describes the campaign both as 'liberation theology', looking in particular to the Quaker tradition, and also as a form of pragmatic 'consciousness raising'. The latter he associated with the felt attitude to place and the sense of identity that the islanders drew from it, one that helped to shift the community from that 90 per cent in favour to outright opposition (166). McIntosh tells the story of the fight in parallel to another narrative about the inhabitants of Eigg and their successful attempt to buy the island as a community from an absentee landlord. They were responding to the new Scottish land law, brought in post-referendum in 1997–8, in which local communities are offered first refusal on any sale of land (as discussed in Chapter 2). In both instances the 'consciousness raising' that the communities undergo is a practical and creative sense of place-making as a community-driven, bottom-up form of identity development. This McIntosh links to the *poesis* of 'geopoetics' (he describes Kenneth White as the island's 'absentee bard'): 'the making and fresh upwelling of reality'. 'Sociologists have used the word *autopoesis*', he suggests, 'to describe an ordering of social reality that arises out of itself' (153).

Referring to this process as 'autopoesis', McIntosh is emphasizing its groundedness in place and its emanation from the community itself. However the concept of autopoesis can be called into question, especially when considered from the perspective of recent work on post-human ecologies. Kathryn Yusoff has challenged the idea of discrete, autopoetic subjects in relation to human–non-human interactions such as this crucially place-based assertion of identity. For Yusoff, a more complex understanding of identity emerges through an awareness of the human relationship with the geological and the often overlooked agency of stone. In a study of rock art and the pivotal role its history is thought to play in conceptions of becoming human, becoming the cultural beings that we are today, she reveals a non-human excess within the substance and processes of the rock that is both 'anterior and interior' to the story of cave art (2014: 7). In doing so, she is arguing that, even at such moments when humans set themselves apart from the world, there is a non-human presence, even an agency, at work. Such an excess could also be said to be vital to this 'autopoesis' that McIntosh describes, founded as it is on the relationship to the island's geology (and McIntosh would be the first to concede this). By recognizing this 'anterior and interior' non-human agency, Yusoff draws attention to the possibility of 'an identification with the earth' the likes of which we can see at work on Harris, but it is one that, importantly, 'does not start from a point of alienation *or* whole-ism (Gaia), but recognizes an entirely different mode of production' (17). Here, a third way emerges and Yusoff draws attention to the creativity of this cultural work and the way human agency is involved, in this case literally, with lithogenesis. Bringing the 'auto-' of 'autopoesis' into question, then, serves to emphasize human and non-human entanglements in the generative idea of 'geopoesis'.

Of particular interest here is the way such entanglements relate to the perception of the mountain Roineabhal itself. In a chapter titled 'The Mountain behind the Mountain', a phrase borrowed from the poet and critic Kathleen Raine, McIntosh asks, 'What is a mountain actually for?' Obviously the perception by Redland of its value of a few pounds per tonne is at odds with the value it comes to have to the islanders (2001: 155). 'The Mountain behind the Mountain' is a phrase that suggests the perception of the mountain as a place as well as a material, as 'a place of Presence and a place of presences. Only those who can perceive this in its ordinariness can encounter the mountain behind the mountain' (Noel Dermot O'Donoghue qtd. McIntosh 2001: 154). McIntosh himself describes the epiphany he has that sets him on his campaign when he visits the church of St Clement's at the foot of the southern slope of the mountain and finds, halfway up the stairway of the bell tower a rock coming through the wall, 'bedrock protruding from the hill outside' (2001: 155). The history and culture of the parishes around the mountain is bound up with its silent presence here in a striking example of the mountain's being both 'anterior and interior' to the human community, as Yusoff suggests (2014: 7). This awareness stands in stark contrast to the reduction of what would have been nearly half the mountain to a knowable, quantified and monetized aggregate. The place itself – the church wall built around the stone – was *letting earth be earth*, to borrow Heidegger's phrase again. The idea of the mountain behind the mountain is less concerned with knowing the geology of a place, of putting it to work to serve our ends, than, to paraphrase Bennett, with 'receiving and participating' in its presence (2010: 17).

However, perhaps one of the most surprising aspects of the fight for the mountain is the visit from Nova Scotia in Canada of the Mi'Kmaq Warrior Chief Sulian Stone Eagle Herney in 1994. He was invited by McIntosh and the people of Harris to come and give testimony at the British government's public inquiry into the superquarry. The connections are multiple and quite curious but look back to the same geological shifts that excited John Elder. Stone Eagle had been fighting the Kelly Rock Co. in Canada, who had, since 1989, been attempting to site a large quarry in the side of a mountain in the Gulf of St Lawrence deemed sacred to the Mi'Kmaq people. The mountain is situated in an area very near the coastal edge of that geological fault (the Cabot Fault/the Great Glen Fault) shared by Canada and Scotland. As White mentions in his lecture at Inverness, geologically, these two territories were once part of that same landmass, with the Iapetus Ocean dividing them from the rest of the British archipelago. Such similarities and geological connections encourage the islanders in the campaign to see themselves less as Scottish and more as an indigenous people fighting for their land, which, though much more tentatively, they come to realize might be sacred to them as well. If we are to read such a development in place culture as 'geopoesis' (with an echo of 'autopoesis' haunting the word) then it need not be entirely an insular or local development. In fact, geopoesis may be understood in terms of the more extrinsic and relational constellations of meaning with which geographer Doreen Massey has suggested place is always involved (1994: 2005). What is interesting here is that these connections within and between places emerge by thinking down into the earth beneath us.

Following the public inquiry, at which Stone Eagle gave evidence alongside a Calvinist minister, one of the old men of Harris passed a gift to McIntosh to give to the chief to take back to Nova Scotia. The previous evening this islander had climbed to the top of Mount Roineabhal and chiselled off a six-inch pyramid, the summit stone, and wrapped it in cloth as a way of saying thank you. He offered it fully aware of the significance of the act of damaging the mountain with the words, 'it's better than having a superquarry' (McIntosh 2001: 239). Stone Eagle initially refused to accept this gift, aghast that the islanders could have 'decapitated' the mountain (239). After some discussion, though, he eventually agreed to take the fragment of Roineabhal 'into sanctuary' on behalf of his people (241).

If this old man was a character in a novel or a sculptor engaged in a work of conceptual art, how might we read the giving of this gift? It is, in so many ways, an act full of the dense and expressive meaning of a work of art. The stone is transported a thousand miles away and placed among stones that might well be more like it than the stones of the rest of southern Britain. This act of giving and relocation aligns the two peoples' fights for land with the movements of deep geological time, reaching out beyond the scale of the Anthropocene and discovering something in their relationship that is, again, 'anterior and interior' (Yusoff 2014: 7). It does so in such a way that, by contrast, the quarrying company comes to seem like the 'iconoclasts and quacks' that MacDiarmid describes as 'injuring' stone (1993: 32). A clearing is opened between the world-opening development of corporate interests and the austere refusal of the earth itself. The struggle for Roineabhal that McIntosh describes fails to conform to either such world-opening or such refusal but emerges in the tension between the two. 'Decapitating' the mountain suggests a certain alienation from it; in fact it almost prevents the greater crime by recreating it in miniature. The act takes possession of the mountain, but it does so in order to let the mountain be a mountain and in this there is the 'intrinsically belligerent' but fundamentally creative struggle and the eventual opening of a clearing which, in this case, is the renewal of the meaning of a place and the intertwining of it with another place across the Atlantic. For Heidegger this is a form of *poesis*, 'a becoming and a happening of truth' (2002: 44–6). For McIntosh such place-making is a form of social creativity, one that reflects and tentatively reconstitutes a place and a place culture among the people living there. It does so through an attempt to reconcile the people to a deeper and more dynamic understanding of the mountain, the stone itself. There is an attempt to accommodate its instability, its deep time, and its vast scale, and to recognize its already dynamic presence in their midst. Such an attempt yields the possibility of what Kenneth White would call 'cultural renewal'.

What the authors above show is that a certain scepticism towards Romantic ideas of reunification, wholeness and oneness can lead not only to a more intricate understanding of the earth but also to an opening up of the world view as well. In such an expanded world view, we can detect Heise's 'ecocosmopolitanism' again. Disparate communities are connected through an engagement with the non-human, or more-than-human, aspects of the earth. However, this is an openness that comes *through* the local, not as an alternative to it, when we see these communities thinking about locality in more dynamic terms (Heise 2008: 60–1). Such open thinking and ecocosmopolitan alliances might not quite extend to Timothy Clark's call for a 'new reflexivity as a species' (if we recall, this is a reflexivity in which the 'human Leviathan achieves some kind of responsible consciousness') (2015: 16–17). However, what is clear is that if such a species reflexivity is to emerge, it must emerge grounded on a damaged earth and it must be capable of acknowledging inequality, difference and distinctiveness. In this sense, this is a step in the right direction. It is unlikely that this reflexivity will come as a homogeneous totality, and we should be suspicious of any such claims.

Such a reflexivity will not be easy. It must recognize and struggle with difficulty. Like the reflexivity that these authors have explored in conciliating psychology, language, culture and community to the earth it will no doubt fail, but in its failure there may nonetheless lie the opportunity for productive and thoughtful responses that can move us forward. In this reflexivity, a sense of planet is concomitant with a sense of place. What this geologically minded work shows is that a movement of cultural renewal from below can also be a movement of cultural renewal with the planet in mind. The truth of place, far from being a question of identity and authenticity, becomes a matter of articulation, generation, *poesis*; of 'clearing' in the Heideggerean sense of struggle. The ongoing work of a place, thinking geologically, becomes an ongoing inflection of its relationship to the wider planet and to others undergoing the same process of renewal. Our own self-reflexive meditations on place and the new forms they articulate might never truly reconcile *with creation*, but in struggling to reconcile *themselves to* creation, they might nonetheless begin to emulate it. It is in this sense that something beyond either alienation or oneness appears in our relationship to the earth, something that moves in the spaces between lithogenesis and geopoesis.

Afterword: Lyric Place

We have seen that the form of the New Nature Writing has largely been that of the essay, a form which has its roots in the sixteenth-century writing of Michel de Montaigne. For Montaigne, the essay was founded on digressive and uncertain curiosity about the world: 'If my mind could gain a firm footing, I would not make essays,' he wrote (qtd. in Bakewell 2010: 36). Sarah Bakewell suggests that the germ of Montaigne's essays, as a literary form, lay in his recognition that even the 'apparently solid physical world exists in endless slow turmoil. Looking at the landscape around his house, Montaigne could imagine it heaving and boiling like porridge' (2010: 34). She goes on: 'To try to understand the world is like grasping a cloud of gas, or a liquid, using hands that are themselves made of gas or water, so that they dissolve as you close them' (35). The writer of essays makes these various *attempts* and approaches, offering them in the knowledge that his or her word will not be final, but that it might, nonetheless, contribute to the ongoing life of its protean subject.

In a chapter on Tim Robinson's prose work, Karen Babine draws attention to what Mark Tredinnick describes as 'the essentially lyric work' of the essay: 'Its success depends not upon the tale so much as the telling. The essayist imagines and tries to render what is real – deeply, structurally, poetically, eternally real – in a moment, in a place, in a life' (qtd. in Babine 2016: 128). 'Rendering' the real is a term that has layers of significance here: the verb 'to render' carries overlapping meanings: to express or create; to depict or represent; and to read or translate (*OED*). In these layers of meaning there is an intertwining of the given and the made. The lyric makes its own truth at the same time as it reads and represents the given world. The lyric produces its art in 'the telling' rather than 'the tale': it energizes and remakes the given with contemporary, personal, localized life. There is a parallel here between the essay as a lyric form and the understanding of place as a creative process of inhabitation that this book has presented. For example, we have considered place as described by Doreen Massey as 'the unavoidable challenge of negotiating a here-and-now'.

It is a phrase that draws attention not only to the 'endless slow turmoil' of the 'apparently solid physical world', but crucially to our agency in directing the course of that turmoil (2005: 140).

The 'challenge of negotiating a here-and-now' is a challenge for us all. This is a warning that Common Ground offered when it launched *Second Nature* all those years ago, intent on 're-open[ing] the debate about our relationship with the land and with nature' as a 'practical and philosophical concern for us all' (Common Ground 1983). Thirty years on, this seems to be a lesson of the environmental movement that has gradually been taken on in a variety of ways. Grassroots projects of eco-localism have seen a surge in popularity over the last two decades: there is the Transition Towns Network, the Plunkett Foundation, the Network of Wellbeing, regional Wildlife Trusts and the Ecological Land Co-operative – not to mention a range of local and community energy initiatives and other community land trusts. In Frome, in Somerset, there was something of a political coup in 2015 when all seats on the town council went to independent candidates tired of the traditional party politics and keen to see more progressive policies on the environment (Harris 2015: n.p.). In a context of global ecological crisis, the work of these groups represents a groundswell of activity confronting this 'challenge of negotiating a here-and-now'. They are struggling to build alternative forms of social and political architecture that are small in scale, uncertain in form, but networked and progressive. This too is an attempt to 'render what is real'; to articulate, to bring forth, to translate a possible vision into a geographical reality. These small-scale shifts recall Richard Mabey's description of 'microcosmic' cultures of local distinctiveness, which he suggested might be 'not just powerful metaphors, but actually the nano-bricks for rebuilding things' (qtd. in Douglas 2005: n.p.).

It is no stretch to see these forms of networked localism as 'archipelagic thinking', a devolved, decentred and connective organization of space. Such thinking manages to be both globally aware and keenly attuned to local distinctiveness, to a *fineness of grain*. This thinking is open without capitulating to the more homogenizing effects of a logic of free trade globalization, what Bill Gates described in the 1990s as 'friction-free capitalism' (Gates, Myrvhold and Rinearson 1995: 181). Place, as this fineness of grain, represents a kind of friction that is to be celebrated. However, it is a friction based, not on the obduracy of place alone, but rather on its responsiveness. The refusal of the people of Harris to capitulate to the plans of Redland Aggregates was not immediate and stubborn. It was a slow process of both inward-looking and outward-looking cultural creativity that brought a new version of the same place into being through common consensus. The battle of the islanders was small in scale but progressive, challenging this push towards 'friction-free capitalism' by rethinking and reappraising the meanings of the place in something that could be described as a form of lyric activism. The idea of lyric activism foregrounds a connection between the aesthetics of place writing and the cultural activities of local grassroots projects of conservation and heritage. This connection is something that I have endeavoured to draw attention to throughout this book.

In Chapter 1, I argued that a shift in attitudes towards the local can be registered in works of 'New Nature Writing' from the rise of the environmental movement onwards. This shift is something very different from the insular turn towards domestic affairs that Jed Esty dates to between 1930 and 1960. Informed by a sense of global crisis, work of this period turned to the local as a scale at which to confront this sense of crisis. It was not a mode of escape. A fresh urgency began to fuel the struggle for new ways of thinking about landscape and nature, and new ways of articulating the meanings of place. In Chapter 2, I showed that wildness, in a distinctively British register, has provided a fertile resource for such fresh and inventive articulations. I showed the way in which they can trouble convention and, in doing so, can stray beyond literary aesthetics into challenges to conservation policy. This was a subject picked up again in Chapter 3 when I turned to the ambiguous *terrain vague* of the edgelands, contested spaces in which the binary opposition of the country and the city breaks down, forcing a new reflexivity, both in terms of literary aesthetics *and* conservation and heritage practices. The argument developed across these chapters should be instructive for those curious about the word 'New' in the New Nature Writing, and to those too ready to dismiss the form as 'bourgeois escapism' (Poole 2013). Perhaps more importantly, I hope it might be instructive to authors of nature writing themselves, for whom there is a task set to challenge and to innovate, to search for ways in which their writing can engage with the big, difficult questions facing us today. Richard Mabey, Sue Clifford, Angela King, Tim Robinson and Roger Deakin set the bar high with their work over the last decades of the twentieth century. With an echo of Eliot in the air, the *tradition* of this New Nature Writing has become a tradition of *innovation*, from Mabey's *The Unofficial Countryside* in 1973 through to Robert Macfarlane's *Landmarks* in 2015.

In all three of these chapters, I showed how a subtle indeterminacy slipped into the understanding of place through the search for those 'new descriptions, fresh thoughts' (Dee 2011: 22). This indeterminacy has served as a vital resource for reimagining our relationship with a changing world. Place has come to blur its edges as it has come into relationship with ambiguity, plurality, wildness, reflexivity and with other places. Why call it place at all then? We might recall Timothy Morton's argument for 'a poetics of anywhere' in which place dissolves as it is interrupted by its own 'uncanny' double (2010: 50–2). But the point of interest is the very moment of tension that this doubleness provokes. It is in this tension that a lyric quality 'renders' a place anew. It recreates a place as it unsettles it. Where a place is recomposed from adventurous angles, where it is made strange through close attention to the particular, where it is enlivened by an author's attention to wildness, then that place shines all the more brightly, like phosphorescence, for having been disturbed. Think of the pluriform ways of relating to place embedded within the language of that 'counter-desecration phrasebook' made by the islanders on Lewis. This inspires Macfarlane's glossary for the whole country, *Landmarks* (2015), in which a fresh linguistic map of the archipelago summons a new sense of place alive with vernacular detail and playful poetry. This is an extraordinary work of grassroots heritage available to be used, as the Lewisian's 'phrasebook' was intended to be used, in making arguments for conservation.

The connection between place writing and place activism was something developed in Chapter 4 when I examined Tim Robinson's whole oeuvre as a practical form of 'deep mapping' on the margins. Tracing the route from his abstract visual art in London galleries across that 'bridge to the real world', I argued that Robinson's quest for 'Space' showed a radical inclusivity. His work breaks down the boundaries between art and life as it breaks down the spatial organization of centre to periphery. Chapter 5 continued this spatial reorganization as I examined the essays, poetry and artwork of the contemporary literary journal *Archipelago*, showing a landscape vision of Britain and Ireland at an argumentative tilt to its usual orientation. This opened up the possibility of new, fluid, translocal connections between places across the Isles. Chapter 6 offered another example of translocal alliance that emerged from the most unlikely of fluid sources: stone, what James Hutton once called the 'fracture, flexure and contortion' of geology in deep time. Kenneth White's theory of 'geopoetics' served as another bridge between place writing and a form of local activism that set out to stimulate the gradual shift in consciousness on the Isle of Harris. In these three chapters, I showed the way place, as that 'unavoidable challenge of negotiating a here-and-now', has been made all the more creative and self-reflexive through its relationship to literary aesthetics.

We might think of the idea of lyric place as one that shows both the influence of activism on literary form and the influence of literary form on activism. I offer it here at the end of this book as a way of thinking through the future direction of the New Nature Writing. We have seen, in the essay that Mark Cocker published in *The Spectator* in 2015 (discussed in the Introduction), that there is a need for nature writing to think carefully about its relationship to a damaged landscape and to the conservation practices that seek to intervene. But we have also seen in Macfarlane's response to this essay that a retreat from aesthetics would be counterproductive. As Macfarlane makes clear, the lyric qualities of the best recent nature writing are imbued with important meanings and provoke searching questions. Rather than retreat in fear of the lyrical quality of nature writing, we might be better served to ask what more it might do. In the many examples that this book gives, the relationship between place writing and place activism has been one of mutual enrichment. Remembering this ought to be instructive for the direction of the form in future.

Bibliography

Ackroyd, Norman (2009), *Irish Etchings 1987-2008*, Thirsk: Zillah Bell Gallery.
Alexander, Neal and James Moran (2013), *Regional Modernisms*, Edinburgh: Edinburgh University Press.
Andrews, J. H. (1997), 'Paper Landscapes: Mapping Ireland's Physical Geography', in John Wilson Foster (ed.), *Nature in Ireland*, Dublin: The Lilliput Press, 199–218.
Babine, Karen (2016), 'Tim Robinson and Chris Arthur', in Derek Gladwin and Christine Cusick (eds), *Unfolding Irish Landscapes: Tim Robinson, Culture and Environment*, Manchester: Manchester University Press, 126–43.
Bailey, Liberty Hyde (1911), *The Outlook on Nature*, New York and London: Macmillan and Co.
Baker, J. A. (2005), *The Peregrine*, New York: New York Review Books.
Bate, Jonathan (2000), *Song of the Earth*, London: Picador.
Batty, Elaine, Christina Beatty, Mike Foden, Paul Lawless, Sarah Pearson and Ian Wilson (2010), *The New Deal for Communities: A Final Assessment*', Final Report (7 March), Communities and Local Government. Available online: http://extra.shu.ac.uk/ndc/downloads/general/A%20final%20assessment.pdf (accessed 9 August 2015).
Bauman, Zygmunt (1998), 'Time and Class: New Dimensions of Statification', *Sociologisk Rapportserie*, no.7. Department of Sociology, University of Copenhagen.
Beck, Ulrich (1999), *World Risk Society*, Cambridge: Polity Press.
Beckett, Samuel (2009), *Company/Ill Seen Ill Said/Worstward Ho/Stirrings Still*, London: Faber and Faber.
Bennett, Jane (2001), *The Enchantment of Modern Life: Attachments, Crossings and Ethics*, Princeton and Oxford: Princeton University Press.
Bennett, Jane (2002), *Thoreau's Nature: Ethics, Politics and the Wild*, Oxford: Rowman and Littlefield.
Bennett, Jane (2004), 'The Force of Things', *Political Theory*, 32(3) (June): 347–72.
Bennett, Jane (2010), *Vibrant Matter*, Duke University Press: Durham and London.
Berger, Alan (2007), *Drosscape: Wasting Land in Urban America*, Princeton: Princeton Architectural Press.
Biggs, Ian (2010), 'Deep Mapping: A Brief Introduction', in Karen Till (ed.), *Mapping Spectral Traces*, Blackburg: Virginia Tech College of Architecture and Urban Studies, 5–8.

Biggs, Ian (2011), 'The Spaces of Deep Mapping: A Partial Account', *Journal of Arts and Communities*, 2: 5-25.
Bold, Alan (1983), *MacDiarmid: The Terrible Crystal*, London: Routledge and Keegan Paul.
Bowen, Charles (1975), 'The Historical Inventory of the Dindshenchas', *Studia Celtica*, 10: 113-37.
Brannigan, John (2014), *Archipelagic Modernism: Literature in the Irish and British Isles, 1890-1970*, Edinburgh: Edinburgh University Press.
Brisley, Stuart (1969), 'Environments', *Studio International*, 177 (912): 266-9.
Buchanan, Ian (2000), 'Other People: Ethnography and Social Practice', in Graham Ward (ed.), *The Certeau Reader*, Oxford: Blackwells, 97-101.
Buell, Lawrence (1995), *The Environmental Imagination: Thoreau, Nature Writing, and the Formation of American Culture*, Cambridge, MA: Bellknap Press of the Harvard University Press.
Bunting, Madeleine (2007), 'We Need an Attentiveness to Nature to Understand our own Humanity', *The Guardian* (30 July). Available online: http://www.theguardian.com/commentisfree/2007/jul/30/comment.bookscomment (accessed online 18 September).
Burchardt, Jeremy (2002), *Paradise Lost: Rural Idyll and Social Change since 1800*, London and New York: Tauris.
Carlson, Allen (2009), *Nature and Landscape: An Introduction to Environmental Aesthetics*, New York: Columbia University Press.
Carlson, Allen and Sheila Lintott (eds) (2008), *Nature, Aesthetics, and Environmentalism: from Beauty to Duty*, New York: Columbia University Press.
Case, Christine (1996), 'Uplyme Parish Map', in Sue Clifford and Angela King (eds), *from place to PLACE: maps and Parish Maps*, London: Common Ground, 83-6.
Casey, Edward (1993), *Getting Back into Place*, Bloomington: Indiana University Press.
de Certeau, Michel (1984), *The Practice of Everyday Life*, Steven Rendall (trans.), Los Angeles and London: University of California Press.
Chakrabarty, Dipesh (2009), 'The Climate of History', *Critical Inquiry*, 35 (2) (Winter): 197-222.
Chaloupka, William and R. McGreggor Cawley (1993), 'The Great Wild Hope: Nature, Environmentalism, and the Open Secret', in Jane Bennett and William Chaloupka (eds), *In the Nature of Things: Language, Politics, and the Environment*, Minneapolis: University of Minnesota Press, 3-23.
Clark, Thomas A. (2009), *The Hundred Thousand Places*, Manchester: Carcanet.
Clark, Timothy (2011), *The Cambridge Introduction to Literature and the Environment*, Cambridge: Cambridge University Press.

Clark, Timothy (2015), *Ecocriticism on the Edge: the Anthropocene as a Threshold Concept*, London: Bloomsbury Academic.

Clarke, Nick (2013), 'Locality and localism: a view from British Human Geography', *Policy Studies*, 34 (6): 492–507.

Clifford, Sue (1995), 'Parish Maps', *The Independent* (9 April): 75.

Clifford, Sue (1996), 'Places, People and Parish Maps', in Sue Clifford and Angela King (eds), *from place to PLACE: maps and Parish Maps*, London: Common Ground, 3–8.

Clifford, Sue and Angela King (1984), 'Preface', in Richard Mabey (ed.), *Second Nature*, London: Jonathan Cape, vii–viii.

Clifford, Sue and Angela King (1993), 'Losing Your Place', in Sue Clifford and Angela King (eds), *Local Distinctiveness*, London: Common Ground, 7–21.

Clifford, Sue and Angela King (1996), *from place to PLACE: maps and Parish Maps*, London: Common Ground.

Clifford, Sue and Angela King (1997), *A Manifesto for Fields*, Shaftesbury: Common Ground.

Clifford, Sue and Angela King (1999), *Rivers, Rhynes and Running Brookes*, Shaftesbury: Common Ground.

Clifford, Sue and Angela King (2000), 'Preface', in Sue Clifford and Angela King (eds), *The River's Voice*, Totnes: Green Books.

Coates, Peter, Emily Brady, Andrew Church, Ben Cowell, Stephen Daniels, Caitlin DeSilvey, Rob Fish, Vince Holyoak, David Horrell, Sally Mackey, Ralph Pite, Arran Stibbe and Ruth Waters (2014), 'Arts & Humanities Working Group: Final Report', UK National Ecosystems Assessment. Available online: http://uknea.unep-wcmc.org/LinkClick.aspx?fileticket=t884TkrbVbQ%3D&tabid=82 (accessed 15 January 2016).

Cocker, Mark (2015), 'Death of the Naturalist', *New Statesman*, 12–18 June: 43–5.

Cohen, Stephen (2007), *Shakespeare and Historical Formalism*, Aldershot: Ashgate.

Common Ground (1983), 'Second Nature' (Promotional poster), Common Ground Archive. University of Exeter, Special Collections Archives (GB 0029) EUL MS 416/PRO/1.

Common Ground (December 1998 – August 2000), *Confluence Newsletter*, Editions 1–10. The Common Ground Archive. Exeter Special Collections Archives (GB 0029), EUL MS 416/PRO/13.

Common Ground (2005), 'Online Study'. The Common Ground Archive. Exeter Special Collections Archives (GB 0029), EUL MS 416/PRO/9.

Coverly, Merlin (2010), *Psychogeography*, Harpenden: Pocket Essentials.

Cowley, Jason (ed.), 'The New Nature Writing', *Granta*, 102 (Summer 2008).

Cronon, William (1995), 'The Trouble with Wilderness; or, Getting Back to the Wrong Nature', in Cronon, William (ed.), *Uncommon Ground: Rethinking the Human Place in Nature*, New York: W. W. Norton & Co.: 69–90.

Cronon, William (2003), 'The Riddle of the Apostle Islands', *Orion* (May/June). Available online: http://www.williamcronon.net/writing/Cronon_Riddle_Apostle_Islands.htm (accessed 10 Dec 2011).

Crouch, David and David Matless (1996), 'Refiguring Geography: Parish Maps of Common Ground', *Transcriptions of the Institute of British Geographers*. New Series 21 (1): 236–55.

Crutzen, Paul and Eugene F. Stoermer (2000), 'The "Anthropocene"', *International Geosphere-Biosphere Newsletter*, 41: 17–18.

Curry, Patrick (1995), 'Elegies Unawares', *Times Literary Supplement* (8 December): 13.

Daniels, Stephen, Patrick Keiller, Doreen Massey and Patrick Wright (2012), 'To Dispel a Great Malady: Robinson in Ruins, the Future of Landscape and the Moving Image', *The Tate Gallery*. Available online: http://www.tate.org.uk/research/publications/tate-papers/17/to-dispel-great-malady-robinson-in-ruins-the-future-of-landscape-and-moving-image (accessed 19 October 2013).

Daniels, Stephen and Hayden Lorimer (2012), 'Until the End of Days: Narrating Landscape and Environment', *Cultural Geographies*, 19 (1): 3–9.

Deakin, Roger (1999), *Waterlog: A Swimmer's Journey Through Britain*, London: Vintage.

Deane, Seamus (1989), 'Ultimate Place', *London Review of Books*, 11: 9.

Debord, Guy (1958), 'Definitions', in Ken Knabb (trans.), *Internationale Situationniste*. Available online: http://www.cddc.vt.edu/sionline/si/definitions.html (accessed 5 May 2013).

Dee, Tim (2011), 'Nature Writing', *Archipelago*, 5 (Spring): 21–30.

Defoe, Daniel (1995), *A Tour Through the Whole Island of Great Britain*, London: Penguin.

Derwent, May (1996), 'Flora Britannica – Our Wild British Beauty', *The Times*, 28 September: 49–50.

Dillon, Brian (2007), 'An Interview with Tim Robinson', *Field Day Review*, 3: 32–41.

Dirlik, Arif (1996), 'The Global in the Local', in Rob Wilson and Wimal Dissanayake (eds), *Global Local: Cultural Production and the Transnational Imaginary*, London: Duke University Press, 21–46.

Dirlik, Arif (1999), 'Place-Based Imagination: Globalism and the Politics of Place', *Review (Fernand Braudel Center)*, 22 (2): 151–87.

Douglas, Ed (2005), 'Ground Force', *The Guardian* (10 December). Available online: http://www.theguardian.com/books/2005/dec/10/featuresreviews.guardianreview11 (accessed online 14 December 2015).

Drayton, Michael (1612), *Poly-Olbion. Part 1*, London: Humphrey Lownes.
Drever, Timothy (1969), 'Untitled', *Tate Gallery*. Available online: http://www.tate.org.uk/art/artworks/drever-untitled-p04228 (accessed 1 June 2015).
Drever, Timothy and Peter Joseph (1969), 'Outside the Gallery System: Two Projects for Kenwood', *Studio International*, 177(912) (June): 255. Print.
Drever, Timothy, Ed Herring, Peter Joseph and David Parsons (1969), Survey 69 New Space, Camden: Libraries, Arts and Amenities Committee.
Dubrow, Heather (1999), 'Lyric Forms', *The Cambridge Companion to English Literature, 1500-1600*, Cambridge: Cambridge University Press, 178–99.
Dunn, Douglas (2003), *New Selected Poems: 1964-2000*, London: Faber and Faber.
Dyer, Geoff (2011), 'Edgelands', *The Financial Times* (11 February). Available online: http://www.ft.com/cms/s/2/62883e66-3563-11e0-aa6c-00144feabdc0.html (accessed 8 May 2013).
Dymond, Christian (1996), 'Yes, we're parochial – and proud of it', *The Telegraph* (4 May): 3.
Elder, John (2014), 'Introduction: Unfolding the Map', in Jane Conroy (ed.), *Connemara and Elsewhere*, Dublin: Prism, 1–25.
Elder, John (2016), 'Catchments', in Derek Gladwin and Christine Cusick (eds), *Unfolding Irish Landscapes: Tim Robinson, Culture and Environment*, Manchester: Manchester University Press, 41–52.
Ellsworth, Elizabeth and Jamie Kruse (eds) (2013), *Making the Geologic Now*, New York: Punctum Books.
Esty, Jed (2004), *A Shrinking Island: Modernism and National Culture in England*, Oxford: Princeton University Press.
Farley, Paul and Michael Symmons Roberts (2011), *Edgelands: Journeys into England's True Wilderness*, London: Jonathan Cape.
N.a. (1988), 'Folding Landscapes', *Geographical Magazine*, 61: 60.
Furniss, Tom (2014), 'James Hutton's Geological Tours of Scotland: Romanticism, Literary Strategies, and the Scientific Quest', *Science and Education*, 23 (3): 565–88.
Gates, Bill, N. Myrvhold and P. Rinearson (1995), *The Road Ahead*, Rockaldn: Wheeler.
Gibson, Andrew (2017), '"At the Dying Atlantic's Edge": Norman Nicholson and the Cumbrian Coast', in Nicholas Allen, Nick Groom, and Jos Smith (eds), *Coastal Works: Cultures of the Atlantic Edge*, Oxford: Oxford University Press.
Gibson, James J. (1977), 'The Theory of Affordance', in Robert Shaw and John Bransford (eds), *Perceiving, Acting, and Knowing*, Hillsdale: Lawrence Erlbaum Associates, 67–82.
Gifford, Terry (1995), *Green Voices: Understanding Contemporary Nature Poetry*, Manchester: Manchester University Press.

Gillen, Shawn (2002), 'An Aran Keening: Review', *New Hibernia Review*, 6 (3) (Autumn): 156.

Gilpin, William (1972) [1792], *Three Essays on Picturesque Beauty*, Farnborough: Gregg.

Greenberg, Clement (1999), 'Avant-Garde and Kitsche', in Charles Harrison and Paul Wood (eds), *Art in Theory: 1900–1990*, Oxford: Blackwell, 562–95.

Greeves, Tom (1988), 'Local Initiatives Officer Report' (October), The Common Ground Archive. Exeter Special Collections Archives (GB 0029), EUL MS 416/PRO/5.

Grene, Nicolas (2011), 'Introduction', in J. M. Synge (ed.), *Travelling Ireland: Essays 1898–1908*, Dublin: The Lilliput Press, iv–xxvii.

Grove-White, Robin (1996), 'Parish Maps: Local Knowledge and The Reconstitution of Democracy', in Sue Clifford and Angela King (eds), *from place to PLACE*, London: Common Ground, 9–14.

Halberstam, Jack (2014), 'Wildness, Loss, Death', *Social Text*, 121 (32) (Winter): 137–48.

Harris, Alexandra (2010), *Romantic Moderns: English Writers, Artists, and the Imagination from Virginia Woolf to John Piper*, London: Thames and Hudson.

Harris, John (2015), 'How Flatpack Democracy Beat the Old Parties in the People's Republic of Frome', *The Guardian* (22 May). Available online: http://www.theguardian.com/politics/2015/may/22/flatpack-democracy-peoples-republic-of-frome (accessed 17 July 2015).

Harrison, Rodney (2010), *Understanding the Politics of Heritage*, Manchester: Manchester University Press.

Harvey, David C. (2008), 'The History of Heritage', in Brian Graham and Peter Howard (eds), *The Ashgate Research Companion to Heritage and Identity*, London: Ashgate, 19–36.

Haughton, Hugh (2007), *The Poetry of Derek Mahon*, Oxford: Oxford University Press.

Heaney, Seamus (1992), *Sweeney's Flight*, London: Faber and Faber.

Heaney, Seamus (2007), 'Our Mystery', *Archipelago*, 1 (Summer): 1.

Heidegger, Martin (2002), 'The Origin of the Work of Art', in Young, J. and Haynes, K. (ed. and trans.), *Off the Beaten Track*, London: Cambridge University Press, 13–48.

Heise, Ursula (2008), *Sense of Place and Sense of Planet: The Environmental Imagination of the Global*, Oxford: Oxford University Press.

Helgerson, Richard (1986), 'The Land Speaks: Cartography, Chorography, and Subversion in Renaissance England', *Representations*, 16: 50–85.

Henley, John (2010), 'Nature's Lost Generation', *The Guardian* (17 August): 10–11.

Hewison, Robert (1987), *The Heritage Industry*, London: Methuen.

Hewitt, Rachel (2010), *Map of a Nation: a Biography of the Ordnance Survey*, London: Granta.
H. M. Government, *The Localism Act* 2011 (Cabinet Office: London, 2011). Available online: http://services.parliament.uk/bills/2010-11/localism.html (accessed 9 July 2014).
Howarth, Peter (2005), 'The Battle for the Centre Ground', *PN Review*, 166: 43–4.
Hunt, Stephen E. (2008), 'The Emergence of Psychoecology', *Green Letters*, 10: 70–7.
Hutton, James (1899), *Theory of the Earth with Proofs and Illustrations*, Vol 3, London: Geological Society.
Illich, Ivan (1986), *H2O and the Waters of Forgetfulness*. London and New York: Marion Boyars.
Jamie, Kathleen (2002), *Mr. and Mrs. Scotland are Dead*, Northumberland: Bloodaxe.
Jamie, Kathleen (2004), *The Tree House*, London: Picador.
Jamie, Kathleen (2005a), 'Darnconner', in Ian Jack (ed.), *Granta*, 90 (Summer): 85–98.
Jamie, Kathleen (2005b), *Findings*, London: Sort of Books.
Jamie, Kathleen (2006), 'Interview with Kathleen Jamie', *Woman's Hour*, BBC Radio 4 (11 January).
Jamie, Kathleen (2008a), 'A Lone Enraptured Male', *London Review of Books* (6 March): 25–7.
Jamie, Kathleen (2008b), 'Pathologies', in Jason Cowley (ed.), 'The New Nature Writing', *Granta*, 102: 35–52.
Jamie, Kathleen (2013), 'Four Fields by Tim Dee', *The Guardian* (24 August): 13.
Jamie, Kathleen (2015), 'In Fife', *London Review of Books*, 37 (8) (23 April): 26.
Kavanagh, Patrick (2003), 'Parochialism and Provincialism', in Antoinette Quinn (ed.), *A Poet's Country: Selected Prose*, Dublin: Lilliput Press: 237–8.
Keiller, Patrick (2011), 'The Future of Landscape and the Moving Image', *Landscape and Environment*. Available online: http://www.landscape.ac.uk/landscape/research/largergrants/thefutureoflandscape.aspx (accessed 18 April 2011).
Keith, W. J. (1974), *The Rural Tradition*, Toronto: Univeristy of Toronto Press.
Kerridge, Richard (2001), 'Ecological Hardy', in Karla Armbruster and Kathleen R. Wallace (eds), *Beyond Nature Writing: Expanding the Boundaries of Ecocriticism*, Charlottesville and London: University Press of Virginia, 126–42.
Kerrigan, John (2008), *Archipelagic English*, Oxford: Oxford University Press, 2008. Print.
Kitchen, Rob and Martin Dodge (2007), 'Rethinking Maps', *Progress in Human Geography*, 31 (3): 331–4.
Kolbert, Elizabeth (2006), *Field Notes from a Catastrophe*, London and New York: Bloomsbury.

Leach, Steve (2015), 'Peter Macfadyen, Flatpack Democracy: A DIY Guide to Creating Independent Politics', *Local Government Studies*, 41 (4): 650–3.

Least Heat-Moon, William (1991), *PrairyErth (A Deep Map): An Epic History of the Tallgrass Prarie Country*, New York: Mariner Books.

Lee, Joanne (2015), 'Vague Terrain', *Pam Flett Press*, 4 (February).

Leslie, Kim (2006), *West Sussex Parish Maps: A Sense of Place*, London: Phillimore & Co Ltd.

Levi, Peter (1984), 'Knowing a Place,' in Richard Mabey (ed.), *Second Nature*, London: Jonathan Cape, 36–43.

Lonergan, Patrick (2013), 'J. M. Synge, Authenticity and the Regional', in Neal Alexander and James Moran (ed.), *Regional Modernisms*, Edinburgh: Edinburgh University Press.

Lorimer, Jamie (2015), *Wildlife in the Anthropocene*, Minneapolis: University of Minnesota Press.

Lupfer, Eric (2001), 'Before Nature Writing: Houghton, Mifflin and Company and the Invention of the Outdoor Book, 1800–1900', *Book History*, 4: 177–204. Web.

Lupfer, Eric (2003), 'The Emergence of American Nature Writing, 1860-1909: John Burroughs, Henry David Thoreau, and Houghton, Mifflin and Company', PhD Diss., The University of Texas, Austin.

Lyall, Scott (2006), *Hugh MacDiarmid's Poetry and Politics of Place*. Edinburgh: Edinburgh University Press.

Mabey, Richard (1980), *The Common Ground*, London: Arrow Books.

Mabey, Richard (1984), 'Introduction', in Richard Mabey, Sue Clifford and Angela King (eds), *Second Nature*, London: Jonathan Cape, ix–xix.

Mabey, Richard (1996), *Flora Britannica*, London: Chatto and Windus.

Mabey, Richard (ed.) (1997), *The Oxford Book of Nature Writing*, Oxford: Oxford University Press.

Mabey, Richard (2006a), *Gilbert White*, London: Profile Books.

Mabey, Richard (2006b), *Nature Cure*, London: Pimlico.

Mabey, Richard (2007) [1972], *Food for Free*, London: Harper Collins.

Mabey, Richard (2007) [1973], *The Unofficial Countryside*, Toller Fratrum: Little Toller.

MacDiarmid, Hugh (1993), *Complete Poems: Volume I*, Manchester: Carcanet.

Macfarlane, Robert (2003), 'Call of the Wild', *Guardian.co.uk. The Guardian* (6 December 2003). Web. 14 July 2011.

Macfarlane, Robert (2004), *Mountains of the Mind*, London: Granta Publications, 2004. Print.

Macfarlane, Robert (2005a), 'Common Ground', *The Guardian* (26 March – 30 June). Available online: http://www.theguardian.com/books/series/commonground (accessed 14 July 2011).

Macfarlane, Robert (2005b), 'Introduction', in J. A. Baker (ed.), *The Peregrine*, New York: New York Review Books, 2005. Print.

Macfarlane, Robert (2005c), 'Nightwalking', in Ian Jack (ed.), *Granta*, 90 (Summer): 218-23.

Macfarlane, Robert (2007a), 'Go Wild in the Country', *Guardian.co.uk. The Guardian* (14 July): 13.

Macfarlane, Robert (2007b), 'Island', *Archipelago* 1 (Summer): 5-23.

Macfarlane, Robert (2007c), 'Upwardly Mobile', *Guardian.co.uk. The Guardian* (1 September) 18 October 2010.

Macfarlane, Robert (2007d), *The Wild Places*, London: Granta Publications.

Macfarlane, Robert (2008a), 'Blitzed Beijing', in Jason Cowley (ed.), *Granta*, 101 (Spring 2008): 22-59. Print.

Macfarlane, Robert (2008b), 'Gravity and Grace in Geoffrey Hill', *Essays in Criticism*, 58: 3 (2008): 237-56.

Macfarlane, Robert (2009a), 'Bookclub', Bbc.co.uk. BBC Radio 4 (6 September 2009a. Web. 23 September 2009).

Macfarlane, Robert (2009b), 'Tory Island', *Archipelago* 3 (Spring 2009b): 32-43. Print.

Macfarlane, Robert (2010a), 'A Counter-Desecration Handbook', in Gareth Evans and Di Robson (ed.), *Towards Re-Enchantment: Place and Its Meanings*, London: Artevents. Print.

Macfarlane, Robert (2010b), 'The Wild Places of Essex', *Natural World*. BBC. London, 10 February 2010. Television.

Macfarlane, Robert (2011a), 'Review: Edgelands by Paul Farley and Michael Symmons Roberts', *Guardian.co.uk. The Guardian*, 19 February 2011. Web. 21 May 2012.

Macfarlane, Robert (2011b), 'Walking on the West Bank', 'Aliens'. *Granta*, 114 (Spring 2011): 117-34.

Macfarlane, Robert (2011c), 'Way-rights', *Archipelago*, 6 (Winter): 8-23. Print.

Macfarlane, Robert (2014), *Landmarks*, London: Penguin.

Macfarlane, Robert (2015), 'Why We Need Nature Writing', *www.newstatesman.com*. New Statesman 2 September. Web. 14 December 2015.

Macfarlane, Robert (2016), 'Foreword: Tim Robinson', in Derek Gladwin and Christine Cusick (eds), *Unfolding Irish Landscapes: Tim Robinson, Culture and Environment*. Manchester: Manchester University Press, xvi-xxi.

McIntosh, Alastair (2001), *Soil and Soul*, London: Aurum Press.

McKay, Don (2013), 'Ediacaran and Anthropocene: Poetry as a Reader of Deep Time', in Elizabeth Ellsworth and Jamie Kruse (eds), *Making the Geological Now*, New York: Punctum Books, 46-55.

Mackay, Peter (2009), 'Escodus à Hiort', *Archipelago* 4 (Winter): 26-7.

McKibben, Bill (1990), *The End of Nature*, London: Penguin.
McNeillie, Andrew (2001), *An Aran Keening*, Dublin: The Lilliput Press Ltd.
McNeillie, Andrew (2002), *Now, Then*, Manchester: Carcanet Press.
McNeillie, Andrew (2006a), Oxford, Bodleian Library, Clutag Press archive (uncatalogued). Letter from Andrew McNeillie to Robert Macfarlane, 12 March 2006 (RobMacletter.doc).
McNeillie, Andrew (2007a), 'Editorial', *Archipelago* 1 (Summer).
McNeillie, Andrew (2009a), 'Editorial', *Archipelago* 3 (Spring 2009).
McNeillie, Andrew (2009c), 'Where Art Meets Sea', *Archipelago* 4 (Winter): 31–43.
McNeillie, Andrew (2011a), 'Editorial', *Archipelago* 5 (Spring): n.p.
McNeillie, Andrew (2011b), 'Unchartered Waters', *Clutag Press* (19 November). Accessed online: http://www.clutagpress.com/2011/11/19/uncharted-waters/ (accessed 15 January 2015).
McNeillie, Andrew (2012), 'Memories are Made of Fish', *Clutag Press* (28 March 2012). Accessed online: http://www.clutagpress.com/2012/03/28/memories-are-made-of-fish/ (accessed 15 January 2015).
MacNeillie, Andrew (2015), 'Hope and Anchor', *Clutag Press* (October 2014). Accessed online: http://www.clutagpress.com/2014/10/03/hope-and-anchor/ (accessed 15 January 2015).
McRae, Andrew (2008), 'Fluvial Nation: Rivers Mobility and Poetry in Early Modern England', *English Literary Renaissance*, 38 (3): 506–34.
Mahon, Derek (2007), 'Insomnia', *Archipelago* 1 (Summer): 3–4.
Malpas, Simon (2003), 'Touching Art: Aesthetics, Fragmentation and Community', in John J. Joughlin and Simon Malpas (eds), *The New Aestheticism*, Manchester: Manchester University Press, 83–95.
'Mappa di Comunità' (2008), n.a. *Mappa di Communità*. Available online: http://www.mappadicomunita.it/?cat=5 (accessed 12 January 2016).
'Map Marathon', *The Serpentine Gallery* (2010). Available online: http://www.serpentinegallery.org. 16–17 October 2010 (accessed on 19 October 2012).
Marland, Pippa (2015), 'The "Good Step" and Dwelling in Tim Robinson's Stones of Aran: The Advent of "Psycho-archipelagraphy"', *Ecozon@*, 6: 1–6.
Massey, Doreen (1994), *Space, Place and Gender*, Cambridge: Polity Press.
Massey, Doreen (2005), *For Space*, London: Sage.
Matless, David (2009), 'Nature Voices', *Journal of Historical Geography*, 35: 178–88.
Merleau-Ponty, Maurice (2000), *Nature: Course Notes from the Collège de France*, in Dominique Seglard (ed.) Robert Vallier (trans.), Illinois: Northwestern University Press.
Monbiot, George (2013), *Feral*, London: Penguin.

Monbiot, George (2014), 'No wonder land owners are scared', *The Guardian* (3 December). Available online: http://www.theguardian.com/commentisfree/2014/dec/03/landowners-scotland-britain-feudal-highland-spring (accessed 21 December 2015).

Moran, Joe (2008), 'We do like to be beside', *The Guardian* (19 August). Accessed online: http://www.theguardian.com/commentisfree/2008/aug/19/1 (accessed 21 March 2012).

Morris, David (2004), *The Sense of Space*, New York: State University of New York Press.

Morton, H. V. (1936) [1927], *In Search of England*, London: Methuen & Co. Ltd.

Morton, Timothy (2007), *Ecology Without Nature*, London: Harvard University Press.

Morton, Timothy (2010), *The Ecological Thought*, London: Harvard University Press.

Nairn, Tom (2000), *After Britain: New Labour and the Return of Scotland*, London: Granta.

Naramore Maher, Susan (2001), 'Deep Mapping the Great Plains: Surveying the Literary Cartography of Place', *Western American Literature*, 36: 4–24.

O'Connor, Ralph (2007), *The Earth on Show: Fossils and the Poetics of Popular Science*, Chicago: University of Chicago Press.

Oerlemans, Onno (2002), *Romanticism and the Materiality of Nature*, Toronto: University of Toronto Press.

Orage, Alfred Richard (1922), *Readers and Writers, 1917-21*, London: G. Allen and Unwin Ltd.

Oswald, Alice (1999), 'Oswald Creates a River Dart Community Poem for the Millennium', *The Poetry Society* (May): http://www.poetrysoc.com/content/archives/places/dart/ (accessed 23 November 2011).

Oswald, Alice (2002a), *Dart*. London: Faber and Faber.

Oswald, Alice (2002b), 'Interview with Alice Oswald', Radio, *Woman's Hour*, BBC Radio Four. London, 12 October).

Oswald, Alice (ed.) (2005a), *The Thunder Mutters: 101 Poems for the Planet*, London: Faber and Faber.

Oswald, Alice (2005b), 'Wild Things', *The Guardian* (3 December). Available online: http://www.theguardian.com/books/2005/dec/03/poetry.tedhughes (accessed 9 December 2011).

Oxenhorn, Harvey (1984), *Elemental Things: The Poetry of Hugh MacDiarmid*, Edinburgh: Edinburgh University Press.

Parker, Joanne (2014), *Britannia Obscura*, London: Jonathan Cape.

Pearson, Mike and Michael Shanks (2001), *Theatre/Archaeology*, London: Routledge.

Perrin, Jim (2010), 'The Condry Lecture by Jim Perrin', *The Condry Lecture*. Accessed online: http://www.thecondrylecture.co.uk/archive.html (accessed 18 June 2011).

Phillips, Dana (2003), *The Truth of Ecology: Nature, Culture, and Literature in America*, Oxford: Oxford University Press.

Pocock, J. G. A. (2005), *The Discovery of Islands: Essays in British History*, Cambridge: Cambridge University Press.

Poole, Stephen (2013), 'Is our love of nature writing bourgeois escapism?', *The Guardian* (6 July). Available online: http://www.theguardian.com/books/2013/jul/06/nature-writing-revival (accessed 11 Mar 2014).

Potts, Ruth, Andrew Simms and Petra Kjell (2005), Clone Town Britain. New Economics Foundation. Available online: http://www.neweconomics.org/publications/entry/clone-town-britain (accessed 13 January 2013).

Proust, Marcel (1922), *Remembrance of Things Past, Volume One: Swan's Way*, C. K. Scott Moncrieff (trans.), New York: Henry Holt and Co.

Pugh, Jonathan (2013), 'Island Movements: Thinking with the Archipelago', *Island Studies Journal*, 8 (1): 9–24.

Quigley, Michael (1998), 'Natural History and History of Ireland', *Irish Historical Studies*, 31 (121) (May): 115–123.

Raban, Jonathan (1992), *The Oxford Book of the Sea*, Oxford: Oxford University Press.

Rees-Jones, Deryn (2005), *Consorting with Angels: Essays on Modern Women Poets*, Tarset: Bloodaxe.

Repcheck, Jack (2003), *The Man Who Found Time: James Hutton and the Discovery of the Earth's Antiquity*, Philadelphia: Perseus Publishing.

Rew, Kate and Dominic Tyler (2008). *Wild Swim*, London: Guardian Books.

Riach, Alan (2010), 'Archipelago', *PN Review*, 37 (1) (September/October): 48.

Robertson, Robin (2009), 'Leaving St Kilda', *Archipelago*, 4 (Winter): 17–25.

Robinson, Tim (n.d.), 'Garden North'. Folding Landscapes. Available online: www.foldinglandscapes.com (accessed 21 October 2014).

Robinson, Tim (1996), *Setting Foot on the Shores of Connemara and Other Writings*, Dublin: The Lilliput Press.

Robinson, Tim (1997), *The View from the Horizon*, Roundstone: Folding Landscapes.

Robinson, Tim (2001), *My Time in Space*, Dublin: The Lilliput Press.

Robinson, Tim (2003), 'The Seanchaí and the Database', *Irish Pages*, 2 (1) (Spring/Summer): 43–53.

Robinson, Tim (2005), 'In Praise of Space', *Irish Pages*, 3 (1) 'The Literary World' (Spring/Summer): 18–28.

Robinson, Tim (2007), *Connemara: Listening to the Wind*, London: Penguin.

Robinson, Tim (2008), *Stones of Aran: Pilgrimage*, London: Faber and Faber.

Robinson, Tim (2009a) *Connemara: The Last Pool of Darkness*, London: Penguin.

Robinson, Tim (2009b), *Stones of Aran: Labyrinth*, New York: New York Review of Books.
Robinson, Tim (2011), *Connemara: A Little Gaelic Kingdom*, London: Penguin.
Robinson in Ruins (2010), [Film] Dir. Patrick Keiller, UK: BFI.
Rubio, Ignasi De Solà-Morales (1995), 'Terrain Vague', in *Anyplace*, Cambridge: MIT Press: 118–23.
Rugo, Daniel, 'An Interview with Patrick Keiller', *Mubi.com*. MUBI. 15 July 2011. Web. 18 August 2011.
Ruskin, John, *The Stones of Venice: Volume 2*, London: Smith, Elder, and Co., 1853. Print.
Ryle, Martin (2002), 'After "Organic Community": Ecocriticism, Nature, and Human Nature', in John Parham (ed.), *The Environmental Tradition in English Literature*, Aldershot: Ashgate: 11–24.
Samuel, Raphael (1994), *Theatres of Memory*, London: Verso.
Saunders, Angharad (2010), 'Literary Geography: Reforging the Connections', *Progress in Human Geography*, 34 (4): 436–52.
de Saussure, Ferdinand (2010) [1916], 'Course in General Linguistics', in Vincent B. Leitch (ed.) *The Norton Anthology of Theory and Criticism*, New York: Norton and Company, 850–66.
Schama, Simon (1995), *Landscape and Memory*, London: Harper Perennial.
Schwyzer, Philip (2009), 'John Leland and His Heirs: The Topography of England', in Mike Pincombe and Cathy Shrank (eds), *The Oxford Handbook of Tudor Literature*, Oxford: Oxford University Press, 225–49.
Scott, Charles B. (1900), *Nature Study and the Child*, Boston: D.C. Heath and Co.
Scott, Kirsty, 'In the Nature of Things: An Interview with Kathleen Jamie,' *Guardian.co.uk*. The Guardian 18 June 2005. Web. 22 May 2012.
Searle, John (1995), *The Construction of Social Reality*, London: Allen Lane.
Shoard, Marion (1981), 'Why Landscapes are Harder to Protect than Buildings', in David Lowenthal and Marcus Binney (eds), *Our Past Before Us: Why Do We Save It?*, London: Maurice Temple Smith, 83–101.
Shoard, Marion (1987), *This Land is Our Land*, London: Paladin Grafton Books.
Shoard, Marion (2002), 'Edgelands', in Jennifer Jenkins (ed.), *Remaking the Landscape*, London: Profile Books Ltd, 117–46.
Shoard, Marion (2011), 'Review: *Edgelands: Journeys into England's True Wilderness* by Paul Farley and Michael Symmons Roberts', *The Guardian* (6 March 2011). Available online: http://www.theguardian.com/books/2011/mar/06/edgelands-england-farley-roberts-review (accessed 2 May 2012).
Sinfield, Alan (2005), *Literature, Politics and Culture in Postwar Britain*, London: Continuum.

Smith, Jos (2012), Interview with Sue Clifford (unpublished: 12 September 2011).
Smith, Jos (2013), 'A Step Towards the Earth: Interview with Tim Robinson', *Politics of Place*, 1 (1): 4–11.
Smith, Jos (2014), 'Soft Estate: An Interview with Edward Chell', *The Clearing* (21 March). Available online: http://theclearingonline.org/2014/03/soft-estate-an-interview-with-edward-chell/ (accessed 23 January 2015).
Smith, Laurajane (2006), *Uses of Heritage*, Abingdon: Routledge.
Solnit, Rebecca (2000), *Wanderlust: A History of Walking*, London: Penguin.
Soper, Kate (1995), *What is Nature?: Culture, Politics and the Non-human*, Oxford: Blackwells.
Stafford, Fiona (2007), 'Review of Archipelago 1', *The Times Literary Supplement* (2 November): 24–5.
Stafford, Fiona (2008), 'Local Attachments', *Archipelago*, 2 (Spring): 103–15.
Stafford, Fiona (2010), *Local Attachments*, Oxford: Oxford University Press.
Stanton, John (2014), 'The Big Society and Community Development: Neighbourhood Planning Under the Localism Act', *Environmental Law Review*, 16: 262–76.
Steffen, Will, Wendy Broadgate, Lisa Deutsch, Owen Gaffney and Cornelia Ludwig (2015), 'The Trajectory of the Anthropocene', *The Anthropocene Review* (January): 1–18.
Stratford, Elaine (2013), 'The Idea of the Archipelago: Contemplating Island Relations', *Island Studies Journal*, 8 (1): 3–8.
Stratford, Elaine, Godfrey Baldacchino, Elizabeth McMahon, Carol Farbotko and Andrew Harwood (2011), 'Envisioning the Archipelago', *Island Studies Journal*, 6 (2): 113–30.
Synge, J. M. (1992), *The Aran Islands*, London: Penguin.
Thomas, Keith (1983), *Man and the Natural World*, London: Allen Lane.
Thoreau, Henry David (1972), *The Maine Woods*, in Joseph J. Moldenhauer (ed.), Princeton: Princeton University Press.
Thoreau, Henry David (2004), *Walden*, in J. Lyndon Shanley (ed.), Princeton: Princeton University Press.
Tilley, Christopher (1994), *A Phenomenology of Landscape*, Oxford: Berg Publishers.
Tonkin, Boyd (2008), 'Call of the Wild: Britain's nature writers', *The Independent* (18 July). Available online: http://www.independent.co.uk/arts-entertainment/books/features/call-of-the-wild-britains-nature-writers-870367.html (accessed 20 July 2008).
Walford Davies, Damian (2012), *Cartographies of Culture: New Geographies of Welsh Writing in English*, Cardiff: University of Wales Press.
Walford Davies, Damian (forthcoming 2017), 'Ronald Lockley and the Archipelagic Imagination', in Nicholas Allen, Nick Groom and Jos Smith (eds), *Coastal Works: Cultures of the Atlantic Edge*, Oxford: Oxford University Press.

Wallis, Clarrie (2009), 'Making Tracks', in Clarrie Wallis (ed.), *Richard Long: Heaven and Earth*, London: Tate Publishing, 33–61.
Ward, Colin (1997), *Reflections in the Water: a Crisis of Social Responsibility*, London: Continuum.
Westwood, Jennifer and Jacqueline Simpson (2005), *The Lore of the Land*, London: Penguin.
What Do Artists Do All Day. Part 1, *Norman Ackroyd* (2013), [TV Program] BBC4, 19 March 2013, 19.00.
'What Has Transition Town Totnes Ever Done for Us?' *Transitiontowntotnes.org*. Transition Town Totnes. N.d. Web. 22 March 2012.
Whatmore, Sarah (2002), *Hybrid Geographies*, London: Sage.
White, Gilbert, *The Natural History of Selborne*, in Richard Kearton (ed.), Bristol: Arrowsmith, 1924.
White, Kenneth (2004), *The Wanderer and his Charts*, Edinburgh: Polygon Books.
White, Kenneth (2006), *On the Atlantic Edge*, Dingwall: Sandstone Press.
Williams, Mark (2007), 'The Old Song', *Archipelago* 1 (Summer): 79–96.
Williams, A., P. Cloke and S. Thomas. 'Co-constituting neoliberalism: faith-based organisations, co-option, and resistance in the UK', *Environment and Planning A*, 44 (2012): 1479–1501.
Williams, Raymond (1958), *Culture and Society*, London: Chatto and Windus.
Williams, Raymond (1973), *The Country and the City*, London: Chatto and Windus.
Williams, Raymond (1976), *Keywords: a Vocabulary of Culture and Society*, London: Fontana Press.
Williams, Raymond (1984), 'Between Country and City', in Richard Mabey (ed.), *Second Nature*, London: Jonathan Cape, 209–19.
Williams, Raymond (1989a), 'Culture is Ordinary', in Robin Gable (ed.), *Resources of Hope: Culture, Democracy, Socialism*, London: Verso, 3–14.
Williams, Raymond (1989b), 'Decentralism and the Politics of Place', in Robin Gable (ed.), *Resources of Hope: Culture, Democracy, Socialism*, Gable. London: Verso, 238–44.
Williams, Raymond (2007), *The Politics of Modernism: Against the New Conformists*, London: Verso.
Williamson, Henry (1936), *An Anthology of Modern Nature Writing*, London: Thomas Nelson and Sons.
Wills, Jane (2016), *Locating Localism: Statecraft, Citizenship and Democracy*, Bristol: Policy Press.
Wilson, E. O. (1999), *Consilience*, London: Abacus.
Wilson, A. N. (2003), 'World of Books', *The Daily Telegraph* (3 March). Available online: http://www.telegraph.co.uk/comment/personal-view/3588342/World-of-books.html (accessed 2 June 2011).

Worpole, Ken and Jason Orton (2013), *The New English Landscape*, London: Field Station.

Worpole, Ken and Jason Orton (2014), 'Joseph Wells Fireworks Factory', *The New English Landscape* (24 May). Available online https://thenewenglishlandscape.wordpress.com/2013/05/24/joseph-wells-fireworks-factory/ (accessed 5 June 2014).

Wright, J. S. F., J. Parry, J. Mathers, S. Jones and J. Orford (2006), 'Assessing the Participatory Potential of Britain's New Deal for Communities', *Policy Studies* 27(4): 347–61.

Yusoff, Kathryn (2014), 'Geologic subjects: Nonhuman Origins, Geomorphic Aesthetics and the Art of Becoming Inhuman', *Cultural Geographies*, DOI: 10.1177/1474474014545301.

Yusoff, Kathryn (2016), 'Anthropogenesis: Origins and Endings in the Anthropocene', *Theory, Culture and Society*, 33 (2): 3–28.

Index

Ackroyd, Norman   174–7
Anthropocene, the   12–18, 33, 97, 180, 184, 191, 193, 201
archipelagic criticism   21, 128, 156, 159–61, 172
archipelagic thought   158, 169–71, 172, 174, 204

Baker, J. A.   80–1
Bell, Julian   157–8
Biggs, Ian   132, 150
Bourne, George   9, 24, 40
Brannigan, John   128–9, 132, 156, 161, 168

Chakrabarty, Dipesh   17, 33, 181–2
chorography   47, 50, 53, 57–9, 103
Clark, Thomas A.   80–1
Clark, Timothy   17, 25–6, 34, 181–2, 202
Clifford, Sue   11, 34–7, 45–50, 55, 205
coasts   32, 40, 82, 106, 122, 124, 127, 129, 140–1, 145, 149, 158, 160, 162–3, 167–9, 174–7, 187, 190–1, 192
Cocker, Mark   1, 3, 5, 27–9, 207
conservation   4, 6, 15–17, 28, 35–7, 43–4, 49, 53, 76, 83, 94–8, 99, 145, 198
'critical localism'   44
Cronon, William   75–6, 88

Davies, Damian Walford   6, 131
Deakin, Roger   4, 29, 34, 35–7, 43, 50–3, 55, 61, 69, 72, 78, 85, 111, 160, 205
Dee, Tim   5, 29, 43, 44, 63–70
'deep mapping'   31–2, 132–3, 136, 140, 150–1, 155–6
Drayton, Michael   47, 57–9, 60–1
Dunne, Douglas   169, 177–8

'ecocosmopolitanism'   18, 197, 202
Ecosystem Services   84, 98
environmentalism   135–7, 181
Esty, Jed   10–11, 38

Farley, Paul   114–22, 123
fractals   130, 133, 149–50, 153–4, 156
Frome   204

Halberstam, Jack   74
Harris, Alexandra   10
Harris, Isle of   197–202
Heidegger, Martin   82, 104, 183–6
Heise, Ursula   17–20, 36, 44, 197, 201–2
heritage   2, 5, 13, 35–7, 39, 45–50, 76, 83–4, 98, 107, 122–6, 142, 147–8, 155–6
Herney, Chief Sulian Stone Eagle   200

island spaces   88, 99–100, 127–48, 157–61, 161–7, 168–71, 173–5, 175–6, 179–80, 187, 190–3, 194–6, 197–202

Jamie, Kathleen   14, 30, 65, 76, 84–93, 98–9

Keiller, Patrick   103–5, 109
Kerridge, Richard   11
Kerrigan, John   159, 160, 174
King, Angela   11, 34–7, 45–50, 55, 205

Lewis, Isle of   99–100, 206
Lonergan, Patrick   139–40
Long, Richard   137–8, 140
Lorimer, Jamie   15–18, 52, 73, 76, 95, 97–8, 112

Mabey, Richard   1–3, 4, 6–7, 7, 11–12, 14, 16, 18, 26, 30, 34, 35–6, 55, 100, 107–14, 120, 122, 123, 204, 205
MacDiarmid, Hugh   128, 160, 161, 164, 179–80, 181, 182, 184, 186, 188, 191, 201
Macfarlane, Robert   1, 3, 5, 11, 14, 26, 28, 30, 50, 53–5, 74–5, 77–84, 84–6, 99–101, 160, 167–72, 175–6, 206

MacFhionnlaigh, Fearghas 172–3
McIntosh, Alastair 183, 197–202
McKay, Don 182–3, 184
Mackay, Peter 173–4
McNeillie, Andrew 21, 32, 157–8, 160, 161–7, 172–8
Massey, Doreen 20, 21, 44, 106, 163
Monbiot, George 30, 76, 93–8, 100
Morton, H. V. 11, 38, 39, 41, 50
Morton, Timothy 13, 14, 19–20, 26–7, 44, 62, 112, 206
Muñoz, José Esteban 74, 75, 80, 95, 172

nationalism 10–12, 13, 19, 20, 21, 37–40, 46–8, 50, 58–62, 76, 95, 98, 128, 138, 139, 144, 154, 160, 164, 171–2, 188–9, 196
Nature 12–22, 107–44, 184–5
Nature Writing 3–5, 7–12, 113
'New Nature Writing' 3–5, 11, 35–44, 113
    debates 22–34, 35–44, 84–6
Nicholson, Norman 40–1

Ordnance Survey, the 127, 134, 142, 144, 146, 148, 149, 153
Orton, Jason 107, 122–6
Orwell, George 107–8
Oswald, Alice 4, 29, 43, 50, 53–62, 69, 81

pastoral 9, 21, 27–9, 34, 36, 55, 64, 67, 89, 108, 112, 115, 117, 119, 120, 171
Perrin, Jim 3–4, 22–5

picturesque 13, 21, 31, 53, 103, 110, 115, 116, 117, 120, 121, 122, 189
ponds 50, 117

rewilding 6, 30, 65, 67, 73, 76, 93–101
rivers 45–50, 50–3, 53–62
Roberts, Michael Symmons 114–22, 123
Robinson, Tim 11, 25, 34, 127–56, 158, 163, 174, 182, 190–7

Shoard, Marion 37, 105, 106, 115, 116, 121, 122, 123
Stafford, Fiona 43, 63–4, 167
Synge, J. M. 138–9, 154, 163, 165

Taplin, Kim 41–2
Tilley, Christopher 82
Totnes 47, 59, 60, 61

Ward, Colin 45–6, 48
White, Gilbert 7, 9, 111, 127
White, Kenneth 182, 188–90, 195, 196, 198, 201, 207
Williams, Raymond 4, 7, 20, 24, 27, 28, 37, 39, 40, 54, 59, 108, 109, 138, 189
Williamson, Henry 7–9, 11, 12, 23, 39–40, 42
woods 66, 82–3, 96, 98–9, 119
Worpole, Ken 107, 122–6
Wright, Patrick 20, 39
Wylie, John 193

Yeats, W. B. 138, 161

Lightning Source UK Ltd.
Milton Keynes UK
UKHW021144071218
333616UK00004B/125/P